READINGS ON HUMAN BEHAVIOR

The Best of

SCIENCE '80-'86

READINGS ON HUMAN BEHAVIOR

The Best of
S<small>CIENC</small>E
'80-'86

The Best of

Allen L. Hammond

Philip G. Zimbardo
Stanford University

Scott, Foresman and Company
Glenview, Illinois   Boston   London

Library of Congress Cataloging-in-Publication Data

Hammond, Allen L.
  Readings on human behavior.

  1. Psychology.   2. Psychology, Pathological.
3. Human behavior.   I. Zimbardo, Philip G.
II. Title.
BF149.H26 1988   150   87-23496
ISBN 0-673-18941-4

$\boxed{\text{A}\text{CKNOWLEDGMENT}\text{S}}$

(pp. 1–7) "The Instinct to Learn" by James L. and Carol Grant Gould. Copyright © 1981 American Association for the Advancement of Science. Photographs by Treat Davidson/NAS/PR (1 top), G. C. Kelley/NAS/PR (1 bottom), ANIMALS ANIMALS/Alan G. Nelson (4 top), Martin Rodgers/Woodfin Camp (4 middle, 7), Mary M. Thatcher/Photo Researchers (4 bottom), J. Markham/Bruce Coleman Inc. (5 top), Lincoln S. Brower (5 middle), ANIMALS ANIMALS/Esao Hashimoto (5 bottom). Reprinted by permission.

(pp. 8–15) "Images of the Night" by Edwin Kiester, Jr. Copyright © 1980 American Association for the Advancement of Science. Photographs by Ted Spagna (10, 11, 13). Illustrations by Ron Miller (9), M. E. Challinor (14). Reprinted by permission.

(pp. 16–23) "Newborn Knowledge" by Richard M. Restak. Copyright © 1982 American Association for the Advancement of Science. Photographs © Mickey Pfleger 1982 (16, 17, 18, 19, 20, 21, 22, 23). Reprinted by permission.

(pp. 24–32) Text excerpt (as it appeared in *Science*) from *The Dieter's Dilemma: Eating Less and Weighing More*, by William Bennett, M.D. and Joel Gurin. Copyright © by William Bennett and Joel Gurin. Reprinted by permission of Basic Books, Inc., Publishers. Photographs by Peter Garfield (25, 26, 27, 28, 29). Illustration by Carol Schwartz (31). Reprinted by permission.

(pp. 33–40) From *The Tangled Wing* by Melvin Konner. Copyright © 1982 by Melvin Konner. Reprinted by permission of Henry Holt and Company, Inc. Illustrations by Dean Williams (33, 34, 35, 36, 37, 38, 39, 40). Reprinted by permission.

(pp. 41–47) "The Way We Act" by Yvonne Baskin. Copyright © 1985 American Association for the Advancement of Science. Photographs by Bill Denison (43), Jeanne Strongin (44, 46), Rene Sherit (45, 47). Illustration by Rob Wood/Stansbury, Ronsaville, Wood Inc. (42). Reprinted by permission.

(pp. 48–55) "The Holy Ghost People" by Michael Watterlond. Copyright © 1983 American Association for the Advancement of Science. Photographs by Mike Maple/Woodfin Camp (48, 49, 50, 51, 52, 53, 54, 55). Reprinted by permission.

(pp. 56–61) "Infanticide" by Barbara Burke. Copyright © 1984 American Association for the Advancement of Science. Illustrations by Brad Holland (57, 59, 61). Reprinted by permission.

(pp. 62–70) "Nice Guys Finish First" by William F. Allman. Copyright © 1984 American Association for the Advancement of Science. Illustrations by Matt Mahurin (62, 64, 65, 66, 67, 69). Reprinted by permission.

(pp. 71–77) "The Shrinking of George" by Perry Turner. Copyright © 1986 American Association for the Advancement of Science. Illustrations by Andrea Eberbach (72, 73, 74, 75, 76, 77). Reprinted by permission.

(pp. 78–85) "Testing the Talking Cure" by Nikki Meredith. Copyright © 1986 American Association for the Advancement of Science. Illustrations by Steve Guarnaccia (78, 79, 80, 83, 85). Box, p. 81, by Helene Ross. Box, p. 84, by Perry Turner. Reprinted by permission.

PREFACE

Science is changing our world—sometimes dramatically and often in ways that for a long time are nearly invisible. Many of the most interesting and sometimes most important developments in science emerge so gradually that there is no news event—no startling discovery, no moment of breakthrough. Yet the impact on our society can be profound.

It is these stories about how things come to be, this larger picture of Science, that *Science '80–'86* set out to convey. We wanted to understand science not only as an event but also as a mode of thought, a human endeavor, a process. We wanted to get beneath the headlines to see how scientists really lived, to share their process of discovery, to look at the world through their eyes. Scientists, after all, are people too—and if you really want to know what science is, you have to put scientists themselves under the microscope.

At the same time, most of the readers of *Science '80–'86* were not scientists—they were people just like you. So we needed to translate not just the words that scientists use, sometimes we needed to use a different frame of reference entirely. While scientists are interested in the details of their subject and the details of their methods, readers are more likely to want to know how a new discovery fits in with what they already know, what it means to their world.

Thus we asked our writers to do more than report what their scientist-subjects said. Tell us, we said, or even better, show us what this area of science means in human terms. Help us gain some perspective. Why should we care about this subject? Why is it exciting or scary or fun?

Finally, we believed that, properly told, the pursuit and the substance of new ideas are inherently interesting, that they appeal to the same curiosity and hunger for novelty that led us as a species to ask questions about our universe in the first place. If it's not interesting, we said, then either it's not good science or it's not well written. We tried to insist on both.

New knowledge can be powerful and, particularly in the area of human behavior, provocative—as I think the reprinted articles in this volume demonstrate.

Allen L. Hammond

INTRODUCTION

When asked why he hadn't written home since leaving for college, one of my students replied: "In order to survive here I've learned not to write anything that does not get graded; there's just not enough time to do anything but *required* reading and writing." One of the major contributions of education to enriching our lives is teaching us the joys that come from reading and the pleasures that can attend writing. Thus, it is sad that these benefits get undercut by imposing extrinsic motivation on what should be the natural desires of every literate person. The problem worsens as each level of the educational enterprise tries to squeeze in as much information as possible in its relatively short time; to feed you all those ingredients assumed to be essential for your educational growth.

But what will happen on that magical day when you graduate and no longer are forced to do the required assignments? Will you then read and write all that you want to or will you end up with no intrinsic motivation left to do the job—just like the young toughs who used to bother uncle Nino.

Nino, an immigrant shoemaker, was continually harassed by a bunch of neighborhood teenage "hoods," as he called them. Nothing he did could get them to stop spraying graffiti on his shop or shouting obscenities and taunting him and his customers. One day, in desperation, he offered the members of the gang $5.00 each if they could shout louder, more horrible, more creative taunts at him—no questions asked why he wanted them to do so. Naturally, they did so with wild abandon, applying much imagination to the task. The next day he offered another $2.00 each if they could outdo their previously impressive work. And sure enough, they did. When they returned on the third day, Nino said that he was short of cash but would give them a quarter each for shouting original obscenities and taunting him as before. "What do you think, we're crazy to work for peanuts? No way old man, get yourself some other suckers!" Nino wasn't bothered anymore once the young toughs refused to do their "required assignment" for small change.

Part of the continuing education program of every student in the world beyond college—or Nino's store—is doing things not because you must but because you want to, because you realize in choosing them that they are good for you. You will discover that you become a more interesting person by keeping informed about current events in society and the world around you; by, among other things, listening to National Public Radio and reading newspapers and magazines that provide in-depth coverage of local and world events. For people interested in special subjects there are many magazines that offer current perspectives on new developments in that field; *Psychology Today* is one obvious choice for those with a concern for psychology in their lives.

To acquaint you with the information that awaits you out there in the "real world" of the consumer of not-required-reading, we are reprinting here some of the most interesting articles on psychological topics that have appeared in the past few years in a superb magazine, *Science '80–'86*. These articles, written with a special flair by outstanding science writers and scientists and beautifully illustrated by talented artists, focus on psychological themes of considerable importance. They were selected primarily because we thought they would offer an interesting addition to your knowledge of psychology.

The 17 essays included here expand upon, further illuminate, or present alternative perspectives to information presented in the textbook, *Psychology and Life*, Twelfth Edition. A complete annotated listing of the articles follows.

By making these essays available to you in their original, colorful format, Scott, Foresman and I hope that you will begin to think about ways to extend your education beyond the confines of the classroom in your lifelong adventure of learning about psychology in your life.

Philip G. Zimbardo

CONTENTS

Date	Article Author/Title

May 1981
James L. and Carol Grant Gould
"The Instinct to Learn"

Although the behavioristic psychology of learning replaced earlier instinct doctrines, ethologists and biologists are fighting back with new evidence that animals, and maybe humans, are genetically programmed with instincts to learn certain things about their natural environment.

May 1980
Edwin Kiester, Jr.
"Images of the Night"

Freud's theory of the psychodynamic function of dreaming is challenged by a new view that dreaming is simply the brain's attempt at interpreting in story form the random, confusing physiological signals from activated cells in its sleep center.

Jan. 1982
Dr. Richard Restak
"Newborn Knowledge"

Within the first hours of birth babies display a remarkable talent for responding to and learning from their social environment; researchers are also surprised to discover how much infants know and can do.

March 1982
William Bennett and Joel Gurin
"Do Diets Really Work?"

When the mind says "Diet," but the body says "Let's eat," which wins—when and why?

Sept. 1982
Melvin Konner
"She and He"

Beyond the contributions of culture to gender differences are the effects of sex hormones on brain and behavior, most importantly, on aggression in males and nurturance in females.

Nov. 1985
Yvonne Baskin
"The Way We Act"

The revolution in neuroscience is demanding that psychologists recognize the biochemical bases of behavior, cognitive functioning, and personality; "all power to the synapse!"

May 1983
Michael Watterlond
"The Holy Ghost People"

The biblical justification for taking up poisonous serpents, handling fire, and drinking strychnine is bolstered by psychological and social factors operating among members of this fundamentalist Christian sect.

May 1984
Barbara Burke
"Infanticide"

When babies are battered and killed in animal and human societies is the culprit a selfish gene that reflects biological imperatives to maximize the killer's reproductive success, rational economic calculations, or a male propensity for violence?

Oct. 1984
William Allman
"Nice Guys Finish First"

Unexpected findings show that the best strategy for dealing with one's neighbors, business rivals, or international opponents is to use the cooperative-retaliative technology of tit for tat.

Date	Article Author/Title

June 1986   *Perry Turner*
"The Shrinking of George"

Therapists from four different orientations (behavioral, cognitive, psychodynamic, and family therapy) offer solutions to the problems reported in the case study of George's unhappiness.

June 1986   *Nikki Meredith*
"Testing the Talking Cure"

As millions of Americans spend billions of dollars annually on hundreds of different forms of psychotherapy, it is reasonable to ask not only does it work for the clients, but also what does it do for society.

May 1986   *William F. Allman*
"Mindworks"

The computer has served as a metaphor for how the brain works, but new "connectionist" theories in psychology are trying to understand how the mind works by using the brain's neural circuits as models for the computer to simulate.

March 1985   *Joseph Alper*
"The Roots of Morality"

The controversy over whether young children have the capacity for moral reasoning is fueled by new evidence that by age 2 they are actively trying to help others in distress and showing altruism as part of a complex prosocial response.

Dec. 1985   *Ronnie Wacker*
"The Good Die Younger"

Survival of the elderly institutionalized in homes for the aged is found to depend in large part on their styles of responding to change and adversity; those more docile and accepting die sooner than those who complain and challenge the status quo.

April 1986   *Duncan Maxwell Anderson*
"The Delicate Sex"

Does the evolutionary basis for infanticide found among female animals extend to sexual competitiveness among women—maybe?

July 1986   *Joseph Alper*
"Our Dual Memory"

Memory researchers have gone beyond studying recall of nonsense syllables to uncover the processes of mind and brain that have recast memory as the basis of our personality and intellect, the very foundation of our humanity.

May 1986   *Joseph Alper*
"Depression at an Early Age"

Researchers disagree over the genetic versus environmental basis of the rise in depression, eating disorders, and suicide among teenagers but concur that these problems are reaching epidemic proportions.

READINGS ON HUMAN BEHAVIOR

The Best of
S*cience*
'80-'86

THE INSTINCT TO LEARN

Birds do it, bees do it, perhaps even humans are programmed to acquire critical information at specific times.

by James L. and Carol Grant Gould

When a month-old human infant begins to smile, its world lights up. People reward these particular facial muscle movements with the things a baby prizes—kisses, hugs, eye contact, and more smiles. That first smile appears to be a powerful ingredient in the emotional glue that bonds parent to child. But scientists wonder whether that smile is merely a chance occurrence, which subsequently gets reinforced by tangible rewards, or an inexorable and predetermined process by which infants ingratiate themselves with their parents.

If this sounds like another chapter in the old nature/nurture controversy, it is—but a chapter with a difference. Ethologists, specialists in the mechanisms behind animal behavior, are taking a new look at old—and some new—evidence and are finding that even while skirmishing on a bloody battleground, the two camps of instinctive and learned behavior seem to be heading with stunning rapidity and inevitability toward an honorable truce.

Fortunately for the discord that keeps disciplines alive and fit, animal behavior may be approached from two vantage points. One of these sees instinct as the moving force behind behavior: Animals resemble automatons preordained by their genetic makeup to behave in prescribed ways. The other views animals as basically naive, passive creatures whose behavior is shaped, through the agency of punishment and reinforcement, by chance, experience, and environmental forces.

In the last few years, however, these two views have edged towards

Critical periods determine exactly when the honey bee learns the color of the pollen-rich dahlia and the white-crowned sparrow the song of his species.

1

reconciliation and, perhaps, eventual union. Case after case has come to light of environmentally influenced learning which is nonetheless rigidly controlled by genetic programming. Many animals, ethologists are convinced, survive through learning—but learning that is an integral part of their programming, learning as immutable and as stereotyped as the most instinctive of behavioral responses. Furthermore, neurobiologists are beginning to discover the nerve circuits responsible for the effects.

Plenty of scientists are still opposed to this new synthesis. The most vociferous are those who view the idea of programmed learning as a threat to humanity's treasured ideas of free will. However, it now appears that much of what we learn is forced upon us by innate drives and that even much of our "culture" is deeply rooted in biology.

As though this were not enough of a shock to our ingrained ideas of man's place in the universe, it looks as though the reverse is true, too: Man is not the sole, lofty proprietor of culture; "lower" animals—notably monkeys and birds—also have evolved various complicated ways of transferring environmentally learned information to others of their own kind.

The honey bee provides entrancing insights into the lengths to which nature goes in its effort to program learning. These little animals must learn a great many things about their world: what flowers yield nectar at what specific times of day, what their home hives look like under the changes of season and circumstance, where water is to be found.

But new work reveals that all this learning, though marvelous in its variety and complexity, is at the same time curiously constrained and machinelike. Certain things that bees learn well and easily, they can learn only at certain specific

"critical periods." For example, they must relearn the appearance and location of their hives on their first flight out every morning; at no other time will this information register in the bee's brain. Beekeepers have known for centuries that if they move a hive at night the bees come and go effortlessly the next day. But if they move the hive even a few meters at any time after the foraging bees' first flight of the day, the animals are disoriented and confused. Only at this one time is the home-learning program turned on: Evidently this is nature's way of compensating for changing seasons and circumstances in an animal whose vision is so poor that its only means of locating the hive is by identifying the landmarks around it.

Since bees generally harvest nectar from one species of flower at a time, it seems clear that they must learn to recognize flower species individually. Karl von Frisch, the noted Austrian zoologist, found that bees can distinguish any color, from yellow to green and blue and into the ultraviolet. However, they learn the color of a flower only in the two seconds before they land on it. Von Frisch also discovered that bees can discriminate a single odor out of several hundred. Experimentation reveals that this remarkable ability is similarly constrained: Bees can learn odor only while they are actually standing on the flower. And finally, only as they are flying away can they memorize any notable landmarks there might be around the flower.

Learning then, at least for bees, has thus become specialized to the extent that specific cues can be learned only at specific times, and then only in specific contexts.

The bees' learning programs turn out to be restricted even further. Once the bits of knowledge that make up a behavior have been acquired, such as the location,

color, odor, shape, and surrounding landmarks of a food source, together with the time it is likely to yield the most nectar, they form a coherent, holistic set. If a single component of the set is changed, the bee must learn the whole set over again.

In a very real sense, then, honey bees are carefully tuned learning machines. They learn just what they are programmed to learn, exactly when and under exactly the circumstances they are programmed to learn it. Though this seems fundamentally different from the sort of learning we are used to seeing in higher animals such as birds and mammals—and, of course, ourselves—careful research is uncovering more and more humbling similarities. Programmed memorization in vertebrates, though deceptively subtle, is widespread. The process by which many species of birds learn their often complex and highly species-specific songs is a compelling case in point.

Long before the birds begin to vocalize, their species' song is being learned, meticulously "taped" and stored somewhere in their memory banks. As the bird grows, the lengthening days of spring trigger the release of specific hormones in the males which in turn spur them to reproduce first the individual elements of syllables and later the sequence of the stored song. By a trial and error process the birds slowly learn to manipulate their vocal musculature to produce a match between their output and the recording in their brains. Once learned, the sequence becomes a hardwired motor program, so fixed and independent of feedback that if the bird is deafened his song production remains unaffected.

This prodigious feat of learning, even down to the regional dialects which some species have developed, can be looked at as the gradual un-

The parents will incubate even large black eggs instead of small speckled ones.

folding of automatic processes. Peter Marler of the Rockefeller University and his students, for instance, have determined that there are rigorous time constraints on the song learning. They have discovered that in the white-crowned sparrow the "taping" of the parental song can be done only between the chicks' 10th and 50th days. No amount of coaching either before or after this critical period will affect the young birds. If they hear the correct song during this time, they will be able to produce it themselves later (or, if females, to respond to it); if not, they will produce only crude, vaguely patterned vocalizations.

In addition, the white-crowned sparrow, though reared in nature in an auditory environment filled with the songs of other sparrows and songbirds with rich vocal repertoires, learns *only* the white-crowned sparrow song. Marler has recently been able to confirm that the parental song in another species—the swamp sparrow—contains key sounds that serve as auditory releasers, the cues that order the chicks' internal tape recorders to switch on. Ethologists refer to any simple signal from the outside world that triggers a complex series of actions in an animal as a releaser.

Here again, amazing feats of learning, particularly the sorts of learning that are crucial to the perpetuation of an animal's genes, are rigidly controlled by biology.

The kind of programmed learning that ethologists have studied most is imprinting, which calls to mind a picture of Konrad Lorenz leading a line of adoring goslings across a Bavarian meadow. Newborn animals that must be able to keep up with ever-moving parents —antelope and sheep, for example, as well as chicks and geese—must rapidly learn to recognize those parents if they are to survive.

To achieve this noble aim evolution has built into these creatures an elegant learning routine. Young birds are driven to follow the parent out of the nest by an exodus call. Though the key element in the call varies from species to species—a particular repetition rate for one, a specific downward frequency sweep for another—it is always strikingly simple, and it invariably triggers the chicks' characteristic following response.

As the chicks follow the sound they begin memorizing the distinguishing characteristics of the parent, with two curious but powerful constraints. First, the physical act of following is essential: Chicks passively transported behind a calling model do not learn; in fact, barriers in a chick's path that force it to work harder speed and strengthen the imprinting. Second, the cues that the chick memorizes are also species-specific: One species will concentrate on the inflections and tone of the parent's voice but fail to recall physical appearance, while a closely related species memorizes minute details of physical appearance to the exclusion of sounds. In some species of mammals, the learning focuses almost entirely on individual odor. In each case, the critical period for imprinting lasts only a day or two. In this short but crucial period an ineradicable picture of the only individual who will feed and protect them is inscribed in the young animals' memories.

By contrast, when there is no advantage to the animal in learning specific details, the genes don't waste their efforts in programming them in. In that case, blindness to detail is equally curious and constrained. For instance, species of gulls that nest cheek by jowl are programmed to memorize the most minute details of their eggs' size and speckling and to spot at a glance any eggs which a careless neighbor might have added to their nest—eggs which to a human observer look identical in every respect. Herring gulls, on the other hand, nest far enough apart that they are unlikely ever to get their eggs confused with those of other pairs. As a result, they are unconscious of the appearance of their eggs. The parents will complacently continue to incubate even large black eggs that an experimenter substitutes for their small speckled ones. The herring gulls' insouciance, however, ends there: They recognize their chicks as individuals soon after hatching. By that time, their neighbors' youngsters are capable of wandering in. Rather than feed the genes of their neighbors, the parents recognize foreign chicks and often eat *them*.

The kittiwake gull, on the other hand, nests in narrow pockets on cliff faces, and so the possibility that a neighbor's chick will wander down the cliff into its nest is remote. As a result kittiwakes are not programmed to learn the appearance of either eggs or young, and even large black cormorant chicks may be substituted for the small, white, infant kittiwakes.

Simply from observing animals in action, ethologists have learned a great deal about the innate bases of behavior. Now, however, neurobiologists are even tracing the circuitry of many of the mechanisms that control some of these elements. The circuits responsible for simple motor programs, for example, have been located and mapped out on a cell-by-cell basis in some cases and isolated to a single ganglion in others.

A recent and crucial discovery is that the releasers imagined by ethologists are actually the so-called feature detectors that neurobiologists have been turning up in the auditory and visual systems. In recent years, neurobiologists have discovered that there are certain combinations of nerve cells,

3

built into the eyes and brains of all creatures, that respond only to highly specific features: spots of a certain size, horizontal or vertical lines, and movement, for example. In case after case, the basic stimulus required to elicit an innate response in animals corresponds to one or a very simple combination of discrete features systematically sought out by these specialized cells in the visual system.

The parent herring gull, for instance, wears a single red spot near the tip of its lower bill, which it waves back and forth in front of its chicks when it has food for them. The baby gulls for their part peck at the waving spot which, in turn, causes the parent to release the food. First, Niko Tinbergen, the Dutch Nobel Prize winner and co-founder of the science of ethology with Lorenz and von Frisch, and later the American ethologist Jack Hailman have been able to show that the chicks are driven to peck not by the sight of their parent but at that swinging vertical bill with its red spot. The moving vertical line and the spot are the essential features that guide the chicks, which actually prefer a schematic, disembodied stimulus—a knitting needle with a spot, for example.

Though the use of two releasers to direct their pecking must greatly sharpen the specificity of the baby gulls' behavior, chicks do quickly learn to recognize their parents, and the mental pictures thus formed soon replace the crude releasers. Genes apparently build in releasers not only to trigger innate behavior but, more important, to direct the attention of animals to things they must learn flawlessly and immediately to survive.

Even some of what we know as culture has been shown to be partially rooted in programmed learning, or instinct. Many birds, for instance, mob or attack potential nest predators in force, and they do

ANIMALS ANIMALS/Alan G. Nelson

The oystercatcher employs a crafty technique to feed on underwater mussels: It stabs its bill through a mussel's open siphon and snips the muscle that clamps the shell tight. Other oystercatchers use two distinctly different techniques to get at the mussel meat.

Martin Rogers/Woodfin Camp (2)

Poles were mere playthings for chimps, above, until one chimp braced his pole to use it for climbing. Then other chimps followed suit. In order to get its parent to feed it, the herring gull's chick, below, will instinctively peck at the red spot on the adult's bill.

Mary M. Thacher/Photo Researchers

In a celebrated case of innovative behavior, blue tits in Britain learned to pierce the aluminum foil caps on milk bottles; the skill spread rapidly through the country.

One experience with a poisonous monarch teaches the blue jay, above, to avoid both monarch butterflies and mimics that look like monarchs. A Japanese macaque, below, finds food tastier when washed, inspiring other monkeys to copy its behavior.

this generation after generation. But how could these birds innately know their enemies? In 1978 the German ethologist Eberhard Curio placed two cages of blackbirds on opposite sides of a hallway, so that they could see and hear each other. Between the two cages he installed a compartmented box, which allowed the occupants of one cage to see an object on their side but not the object on the other. Curio presented a stuffed owl, a familiar predator, on one side, and an innocuous foreign bird, the Australian honey guide, on the other. The birds that saw the owl went berserk with rage and tried to mob it through the bars of the cage. The birds on the other side, seeing only an unfamiliar animal and the enraged birds, began to mob the stuffed honey guide. Astonishingly, these birds then passed on this prejudice against honey guides through a chain of six blackbirds, all of which mobbed honey guides whenever they encountered one. Using the same technique, Curio has raised generations of birds whose great-great-grandparents were tricked into mobbing milk bottles and who consequently teach their young to do the same.

What instigates the birds—even birds raised in total isolation—to pay so much attention to one instance of mobbing that they pass the information on to their offspring as a sort of taboo, something so crucial to their survival that they never question if or why these predators must be attacked? The mobbing call, it turns out, serves as yet another releaser that switches on a learning routine.

Certain sounds in the mobbing calls are so similar among different species that they all profit from each other's experience. This is why we often see crows or other large birds being mobbed by many species of small birds at once. So deeply ingrained in the birds is this

After macaques learned that sweet potatoes are tastier when washed, the troop followed suit.

call that birds raised alone in the laboratory are able to recognize it, and the calls of one species serve to direct and release enemy-learning in others. Something as critical to an animal's survival as the recognition of enemies, then, even though its finer points must be learned and transmitted culturally, rests on a fail-safe basis of innately guided, programmed learning.

The striking food-avoidance phenomenon is also a good place to look for the kind of innately directed learning that is critical to survival. Many animals, including humans, will refuse to eat a novel substance which has previously made them ill. Once a blue jay has tasted one monarch butterfly, which as a caterpillar fills itself with milkweed's poisonous glycosides, it will sedulously avoid not only monarchs but also viceroys—monarch look-alikes that flaunt the monarchs' colors to cash in on their protective toxicity. This programmed avoidance is based on the sickness which must appear within a species-specific interval after an animal eats, and the subsequent food avoidance is equally strong even if the subject knows from experience that the effect has been artificially induced.

But what is the innate mechanism when one blue tit discovers how to pierce the foil caps of milk bottles left on doorsteps to reach the cream, and shortly afterwards blue tits all over England are doing the same thing? How are theories of genetic programming to be invoked when one young Japanese macaque monkey discovers that sweet potatoes and handfuls of grain gleaned from a sandy shore are tastier when washed off in the ocean, and the whole troop (except for an entrenched party of old dominant males) slowly follows suit? Surely these are examples pure and simple of the cultural transmission of knowledge that has

The cells that bring you the world

There was a time when the visual system was thought of as little more than a pair of cameras (the eyes), cables (the optic nerves), and television screens (the visual cortex of the brain). Nothing could be farther from the truth. We now know that the visual system is no mere passive network of wires but an elaborately organized and highly refined processing system that actively analyzes what we see, systematically exaggerating one aspect of the visual world, ignoring or discarding another.

The processing begins right in the retina. There the information from 130 million rods and cones is sifted, distorted, and combined to fit into the four or so million fibers that go to the brain. The retinas of higher vertebrates employ one layer of cells to sum up the outputs of the rod-and-cone receptors. The next layer of retinal cells compares the outputs of adjacent cells in the preceding tier. The result is what is known as a spot detector: One type of cell in the second layer signals the brain when its compare/contrast strategy discovers a bright field surrounded by darkness (corresponding to a bright spot in the world). Another class of cell in the same layer has the opposite preference and fires off when it encounters dark spots.

The next processing step takes this spot information and, operating on precisely the same comparison strategy, wires cells that are sensitive only to spots moving in particular directions at specific speeds. The output of these spot detector cells also provides the raw material from which an array of more sophisticated feature detectors sort for

lines of each particular orientation. These feature detectors derive their name from their ability to register the presence or absence of one particular sort of stimulus in the environment. Building on these cells, the next layer of processing sorts for the speed and direction of moving lines, each cell with its own special preference. Other layers judge distance by comparing what the two eyes see.

The specific information that cells sort for in other retinal layers and visual areas of the brain is not yet understood. Research will probably reveal that these extremely complex feature detectors provide us with what we know as conscious visual experience. Our awareness of all this subconscious processing, along with the willful distortions and tricks it plays on us, comes from the phenomenon of optical illusions. When we experience an optical illusion, it is the result of a particular (and, in the world to which we evolved, useful) quirk in the visual mechanism.

Feature detectors are by no means restricted to the visual system. In birds and bats, for instance, specialized cells have been found that recognize many nuances in sound—locations, repetition rates, time intervals, and precise changes in pitch— that allow the creatures to form an auditory picture of the world.

There is every reason to suppose that our experience of the world is based on the results of this massive editing. Since neural circuits differ dramatically from species to species according to the needs of each, the world must look and sound different to bees, birds, cats, and people.
—J.L.G. and C.G.G.

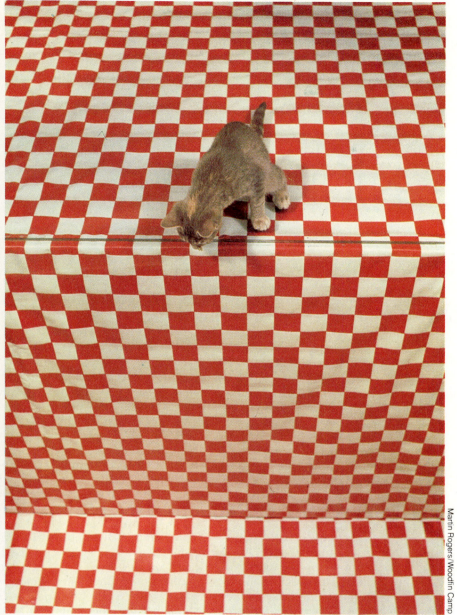

A kitten shies away from the edge of an apparent drop, which is actually covered with glass that the kitten can feel with its paw. Because the kitten has never been exposed to height, however, its caution must not be learned and can only be instinctual.

Martin Rogers/Woodfin Camp

been environmentally gained.

Perhaps not. What the blue tits and the monkeys pass on to their colleagues may have an innate basis as well. The reason for this precocious behavior—and we say this guardedly—may be in a strong instinctive drive on the part of all animals to copy mindlessly certain special aspects of what they see going on around them. Chicks, for instance, peck at seeds their mother has been trained to select, apparently by watching her choices and copying them. In the case of many mammals, this drive is probably combined with an innate urge to

experiment. The proclivity of young animals, particularly human children, to play with food, along with their distressing eagerness to put virtually anything into their mouths, lends support to the experimentation theory. Perhaps it is the young, too naive to know any better, who are destined by nature to be the primary source of cultural innovation. The more mature become the equally indispensable defenders of the faith, the vehicles of cultural transmission.

Patterns, then, however subtle, are beginning to emerge that unify the previously unrelated studies of

instinct and learning. Virtually every case of learning in animals that has been analyzed so far depends in at least some rudimentary way on releasers that turn on the learning routine. And that routine is generally crucial to the perpetuation of the animal's genes.

Even the malleable learning we as humans pride ourselves on, then, may have ineradicable roots in genetic programming, although we may have difficulty identifying the programs, blind as we are to our own blindness. For example, you cannot keep a normal, healthy child from learning to talk. Even a child born deaf goes through the same babbling practice phase the hearing child does. Chimpanzees, by contrast, can be inveigled into mastering some sort of linguistic communications skills, but they really could not care less about language: The drive just is not there.

This view of human insight and creativity may be unromantic, minimizing as it does the revered role of self-awareness in our everyday lives, but the pursuit of this line of thinking could yield rich rewards, providing us with invaluable insights into our own intellectual development. The times we are most susceptible to particular sorts of input, for instance, may be more constrained than we like to think. The discovery of the sorts of cues or releasers that might turn on a drive to learn specific things could open up new ways of teaching and better methods for helping those who are culturally deprived. Best of all, analyzing and understanding those cues could greatly enrich our understanding of ourselves and of our place in the natural order. Ⓢ

James L. Gould, professor of biology at Princeton University, studies the navigation and communication of the honey bee. Carol Grant Gould is a writer and research associate in Princeton's biology department.

IMAGES OF THE NIGHT

The physiological roots of dreaming.

by Edwin Kiester jr.

She walked down the steps of the public library, wearing her nightgown and cradling a bowl of raspberry Jell-O in her arms. At the foot of the long staircase she could distinguish the dim figure of her high school algebra teacher. His right arm was upraised and he seemed to be shouting at her, but she could not make out the words. She hurried toward him, straining to hear . . .

Suddenly the scene shifted. Now she found herself traveling through a dense forest. The sun was setting ahead of her and the forest deepened in darkness. She felt afraid. An unseen menace seemed to be following her, dodging from tree to tree, but when she glanced back in fear she saw no one. She tried to run faster, but her legs would not respond. The pursuer drew nearer, gaining on her, but she was powerless to escape and . . .

Most of us will recognize this intriguing combination of strange behavior, outlandish dress, abrupt scene shift, and inability to run away as the stuff of which dreams are made. We all dream, every night of our lives, and the feelings of flying or falling, the kaleidoscope of colors, and the jumbled memories and prophecies are a source of endless fascination and discussion. What importance we place on dreams, and how we interpret them, of course, is a strictly individual matter. An orthodox Freudian, for example, might see the above dream as supercharged with sexual symbolism. The rhythmic descent of the staircase represents the sex act, the container the female sex organ, the scene shift an avoidance of unpleasant material, the inability to run a suppressed desire to be chased and caught.

But, is it possible that dreams have been overinterpreted? That these mini-dramas of the night do *not* represent the unconscious mind trying to smuggle a message to the conscious one? That dreams are nothing more than the thinking brain's valiant efforts to weave a coherent plot out of disparate and contradictory signals from the lower brain centers during sleep?

That is the new—and controversial—view of this most universal experience. In a number of centers around the world, researchers have put together a neurophysiological picture of dreaming sleep that two Harvard scientists think may change many of our notions about the meaning and origin of the images of the night. J. Allan Hobson and Robert W. McCarley, professors of psychiatry at Harvard and co-directors of the Neurophysiology Laboratory at the Massachusetts Mental Health Center, are careful not to say that dreams are

meaningless and state specifically that everyone's dreams reveal elements of personal experience. Nevertheless, Hobson and McCarley think of dreaming as the psychological concomitant of an essentially biological process. In other words, dreams are the sideshow, not the main event.

The "activation-synthesis" theory of dreaming advanced by Hobson and McCarley is simplicity itself. Based on new knowledge of brain anatomy and chemistry, it states that certain cells of the brain's "sleep center" become activated during Rapid Eye Movement, or dreaming sleep. Like a husband jostling his wife when they share a bed, the cells transmit their activation to nearby cells that control other body functions. These cells in turn signal the higher brain centers that they have been activated. Drawing on previous experience and memory, the brain areas concerned with processing and interpreting information try to assemble these uncoordinated and often contradictory messages into a sensible pattern. The result is the bizarre, disconnected playlet we call a dream.

The world was not exactly lacking for a theory of dreams when the neurophysiological one came along. As the Bible, Shakespeare, and Ab-

raham Lincoln tell us, man always has struggled to understand and explain his dreams but has been handicapped by having little more to guide him than introspection. Freud was one of the first to try to put dreaming on a scientific footing. After his training in the then new science of neurology, he wrote in *The Interpretation of Dreams* that the nighttime images represented repressed taboo wishes pushed out of the conscious mind during the day. They bubbled up in the night in disguised form to be assimilated into the dreamer's psyche.

Freud's theory of dreams held sway for half a century and still influences psychoanalysts' thinking. But in 1953 an important discovery sent researchers off in a new direction. Eugene Aserinsky and Nathaniel Kleitman found in their sleep laboratory at the University of Chicago that there are actually two kinds of mammalian sleep—REM (for Rapid Eye Movement) and non-REM, or NREM, when eye movement is lacking. Most REM coincided with vivid dreaming and produced a distinct set of physical phenomena. The eyes darted rapidly back and forth behind the closed eyelids; brain waves changed in amplitude and frequency; the body lost muscle tone; heartbeat and respiration increased; males had erections and females vaginal engorgement. NREM, on the other hand, was the deepest kind of sleep, divided into four progressively deeper stages,

To sleep, perchance to dream—

Ted Spagna

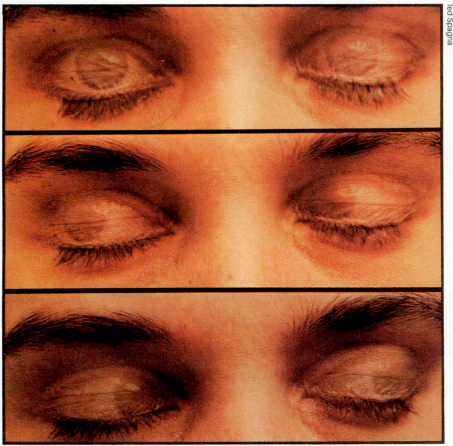

During dreaming sleep the eyes shift rapidly back and forth beneath closed eyelids. Recent research suggests their movement stimulates dreams rather than vice versa.

and its mental activity was strictly humdrum. If you waked a sleeper during NREM and asked what she was dreaming about, she was likely to say, "I was dreaming about what I had to do at the office tomorrow."

Further investigation showed that REM and NREM alternated through the night with approximately 90-minute intervals between REM periods. The REM periods started out lasting five to ten minutes and gradually lengthened until the final one lasted about 50 minutes. In a normal night's sleep, REM totaled 90 to 120 minutes, so that total dreaming time equaled the length of a feature movie. The researchers also found that REM was somehow essential to the body process. Deprived of REM, it becomes increasingly difficult to keep a person from launching into that phase of sleep.

Once they learned to identify the onset of REM sleep, researchers relentlessly began waking sleep lab subjects to inquire what they were dreaming about. They quickly discovered that dreams fell into a pattern. After listening to hundreds of dream reports, Milton Kramer of the Veterans Administration Hospital in Cincinnati, who was con-

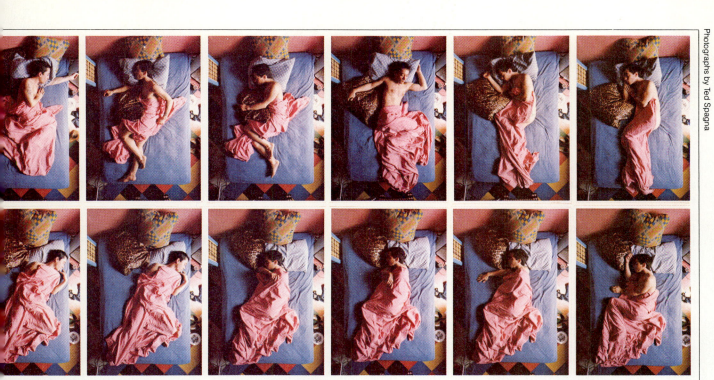

Photographs by Ted Spagna

External restlessness during sleep, documented here by photographs shot at 30-minute intervals over a single night, corresponds to various internal stages of sleep as monitored by instruments including Electroencephalograph (EEG), which records the brain's electrical transmissions, and Electromyograph (EMG), which records changes in muscle tone. During REM sleep, almost total muscle paralysis takes place, except those controlling eye movement.

firming and extending the work of Calvin Hall in California, described a typical dream. It features two characters in addition to the dreamer, takes place indoors, is more passive than active, more hostile than friendly, and is more likely to be unpleasant than pleasant. More strange males than females appear, and most of the hostility centers on these male strangers.

Like fingerprints, Kramer found, dreams are individual and identifiable. But men and women dream differently. Men's dreams are more active and friendly—but also more likely to include fighting. Men also dream more often of appearing naked in public places. Men are the most common characters in the dreams of both men and women—but in men's dreams, they are more likely to be antagonists. In recalling their dreams, men are more likely to use words like "vehicle," "travel," "automobile," "hit"; women use words of feeling and emotion. Women are more often pursued or endangered; men are more likely to find money.

Rosalind Dymond Cartwright of Rush-Presbyterian-St. Luke's Medical Center in Chicago, found that dreams often follow a ritualized format, like a sonnet or an opera. The first "scene" states the night's theme—usually a quick review of a concern left over from the day. The next two review scenes of the past in which a similar problem was confronted and dealt with. Scene Four is a future, wish-fulfillment dream: "What would life be like if I did not have this problem?" The final dream wraps all these elements into one stirring present tense extravaganza. Unfortunately, since most of us only remember the final dream, we are just as baffled on waking as if we had walked into the finale of *Don Giovanni* without witnessing the previous acts.

The research also casts doubt on Freud's theories about dream symbolism and repressed wishes. Far from avoiding delicate material, many dreams are frankly sexual and some are direct representations. "A dream about a banana may quite literally be a dream about a banana," Cartwright once said, suggesting an alternative to the view that any long, cylindrical object represents a disguised penis. In fact, Cartwright said, many dreams are transparent in meaning and often funny. "I often wonder that people don't wake themselves up laughing," she says.

But like the details of dreams themselves, certain elements of dreaming continued to elude the most zealous research. They revolved around two central questions: What do dreams mean? And what function do they serve? The problem was compounded by the fact that dream language was highly individual. "Suppose people go to sleep very thirsty," said Cartwright. "Some may dream of the ocean; some may dream of the desert; some may dream of drinking; some may dream with an emotional quality associated with thirst neither they nor we can understand; and some may have dreams that may not be related to thirst at all. We need a more refined measure of dream content before we can understand meanings."

When Allan Hobson began his research, these questions were still unanswered, and he decided that they were not likely to yield to a direct approach. A Harvard Medical School graduate, the lean, blond, intense psychiatrist had studied sleep phenomena with Michel Jouvet in France. Jouvet is a noted neurophysiologist who has deduced that REM sleep is regulat-

A dream about a banana
may quite literally be a dream
about a banana.

ed in that area of the brain known as the brainstem. This rudimentary cluster of neurons, or nerve cells, just above the spinal cord controls many of the body's automatic functions, not only sleep and waking but respiration and heartbeat. It is so central to REM, Jouvet found, that when the higher brain centers were destroyed in a laboratory cat, the animal went into regular REM sleep despite the deprivation.

Hobson decided to apply Jouvet's observations to dream research. "Previously," Hobson says, "most investigators had been following what I call a 'top-down' approach to dream theory. They took the dream reports and tried to relate it to the physiology. But because the human head is hard to gain access to, it was very difficult to learn precisely what was occurring at the cellular level. We decided that this psychophysiological approach had been very valuable, but that it had reached its limit and that it was time to move on to Stage Two, what we call the 'bottoms-up' approach. We wanted to find out what was actually happening in the brain during REM sleep and compare that with formal aspects of dreaming. In other words, we didn't ask, 'Why does the dreamer see his mother?' but 'How does he see anything? Why are dreams predominantly visual? Why is there no sensation of smell and very little of the auditory?'"

In collaboration with McCarley, Hobson began the investigation of the neuronal mechanisms of sleep. The cat was chosen as the model for REM sleep study. It had long been established that the REM process is similar in all mammals, differing in intensity and length of cycle. The differences seem to be related to body size: the cat's REM-NREM cycle is 30 minutes, the rat's 12, compared to the human's 90. Cats, of course, could not report what they dreamed about, if they

dreamed at all. But presumably, a neurophysiological understanding of cat REM could illuminate human REM and its associated dreaming.

The researchers also benefited from advances in technology. By using a microelectrode, a tiny probe that could be directly inserted into the cat's head, they could tap the activity of a single neuron and even influence it. By injecting microscopic quantities of pharmacological agents resembling the brain's own neurotransmitters, they could actually alter the neuron's normal activity.

For the past 12 years, Hobson and McCarley have been pursuing this line of investigation in their laboratory in the Massachusetts Mental Health Center. The lab, housed in the basement of a fortress-like red brick building in Boston's Back Bay, provides a fascinating glimpse into how modern science approaches an age-old question. A tiger-striped cat lies restrained in a glass box. Leads from its head extend to a polygraph where brain waves, heartbeat, muscle tone, and eye muscle movement are recorded. An audio output snaps and pops— the sound of the neuronal discharge. From time to time, the beat changes as the cat moves from NREM to REM sleep.

"Our cats are kept awake at night so that they will sleep in the daytime," Hobson says, sweeping papers off a chair so a visitor can sit to watch the show. "It can sleep perfectly normally, except that its head is restrained. The small cylinder-like arrangement you see was implanted a month ago. The microelectrode, used to record from nerve cells, can be positioned inside it by remote control so that the cat's normal activities are unaffected."

The activation-synthesis hypothesis of dreaming is based on observations of the behavior of the giant

cells of the pontine ("bridge") section of the brainstem during REM sleep. These cells, as their name implies, are unusually large neurons with lengthy fibers that extend into other parts of the brainstem, including those concerned with eye movement, balance, and such patterned repetitive body and limb actions as walking and running. During immobile waking and NREM sleep, the giant cells are relatively quiet, apparently inhibited by the activities of another group of cells in the nearby locus ceruleus (LC). Just prior to a REM episode, LC inhibition diminishes and the giant cells become excited. This continues at peak level throughout the REM period. Then the excitation gradually dies away, LC inhibition returns, and the giant cells remain quiet until the next REM interlude. Based on these studied observations, Hobson and McCarley developed the reciprocal interaction model of sleep-cycle control.

The mirror sequence of excitation and inhibition is based on the delicate interaction of brain chemistry. In order for a nerve impulse to be carried from one nerve cell to another, a chemical called a neurotransmitter is required to help bridge the gap, or synapse. In the case of the giant pontine cell, this substance appears to be the common transmitter, acetylcholine. At other synapses, an inhibitory transmitter prevents bridging the gap. In the LC neurons, that chemical appears to be norepinephrine.

"The on-off switch for dreaming sleep is quite simple," Hobson says of the apparent relationship between the giant cells and the LC neurons. The LC neurons are off when the giant cells are firing, and we have dreaming. When the LC neurons are on, the giant cells are off and we have waking. This model not only can explain REM sleep and waking, but NREM as

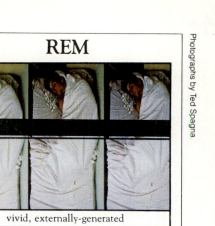

	Awake	NREM	REM
EEG stages Awake S Stage II Stage III Stage IV			
Perception	vivid, internally-generated	dull or absent	vivid, externally-generated
Thought	logical, rational	repetitious or absent	illogical, delusional
Movement	voluntary	infrequent but possible	impossible

The cycle above shows typical sequence of sleep stages. Over a night, the periods of REM sleep increase in duration. Dreams that occur close to time of awakening generally are easiest to recall.

well. NREM is an intermediate stage between waking and dreaming when the balance between excitation and inhibition is changing.

"Furthermore," he continues, "if the model is correct, it should be possible to turn the switch on and off chemically. First we tried activating the on switch for REM sleep by injecting the drug carbachol, which mimics the action of acetylcholine. We were able to produce a very dramatic enhancement of REM sleep. We activated the off switch for REM by using propranolol to block the norepinephrine."

The excitation, of course, extends beyond the giant cells. Among other cell groupings that may be affected are those governing eye movement, those related to the vestibular system which gauges balance and the position of the head and neck, and those of the "motor-pattern generator" that regulates walking, stepping, and running. As they do in waking, these cells "inform" the higher brain centers of the cerebral cortex of their activities; and the cortex interprets them in light of what similar messages have meant in the past. To the sleeper, it all adds up to a dream.

Hobson was intrigued by the pattern of eye movements during episodes of REM. The conventional explanation of the rapid eye movements, which are clearly visible to an observer, even though the lids are closed, is that the dreamer is busily scanning dream images as they pass before him. Hobson holds that the reverse is true. The dream represents the brain's efforts to explain why the eyes are "jiggling around." "Of course," he adds, "the mechanisms are not mutually exclusive and both could be operative. But it may be the non-voluntary movements of brainstem origin that give dreaming its unique visual characteristics.

"Suppose in a dream you are watching a man standing at an intersection," Hobson says. "Suddenly the man turns to the left and runs across the street. The explanation for this event in the dream would be that the REM-generating pontine cells activated nearby eye-movement neurons, specifically those that move the eyes to the left. The cerebral cortex registered this activity and attempted to make sense out of it in light of what had previously occurred in the dream. The logical solution, based on the speed and direction of the eye movements, was to move the man across the street.

"Look here," he says, going to the polygraph and pointing to a distinctive spike in one of the wavy lines. "This represents an abrupt shift of the animal's eyes during REM. Here (pointing to another line) we find that certain activities in the cerebral cortex followed the eye movements by many milliseconds. This may be the substrate of visual imagery and strongly favors the idea that at least some visual cortical events are determined by activities in the brainstem." In fact McCarley has found cells in the brainstem that transmit information about the direction of eye movement to the visual system in REM sleep.

Another intriguing aspect of dreaming is that, although the visual aspects of dreams are highly active, the dreamer is actually immobilized, prevented from moving during REM sleep. Sequential photos clearly show that he does not budge a muscle during REM. Yet motor commands are obviously being generated during REM sleep. Hobson explains this apparent discrepancy by declaring that the motor neurons are inhibited during REM sleep. The Italian physiologist Ottavio Pompeiano was the first to show that there is a blockade against motor output, just as there is a blockade against the reception of outside stimuli during REM sleep.

The explanation that motor commands are given but not obeyed during REM has also been confirmed in an oblique but convincing way. Following up an earlier observation by Jouvet, Adrian Morrison of the University of Pennsylvania has removed parts of the pontine area in cats, then allowed them to go into REM sleep. With the inhibitory areas destroyed, the cats literally act out their dreams. They run, walk, knead their claws, and toy with imaginary mice. Some arch their backs and assume the classic feline attack-and-defense posture. Watching them, one would suppose they were fully awake, but they are generally unresponsive to external stimuli.

"The inhibition of motor activity

13

Illustration by M. E. Challinor

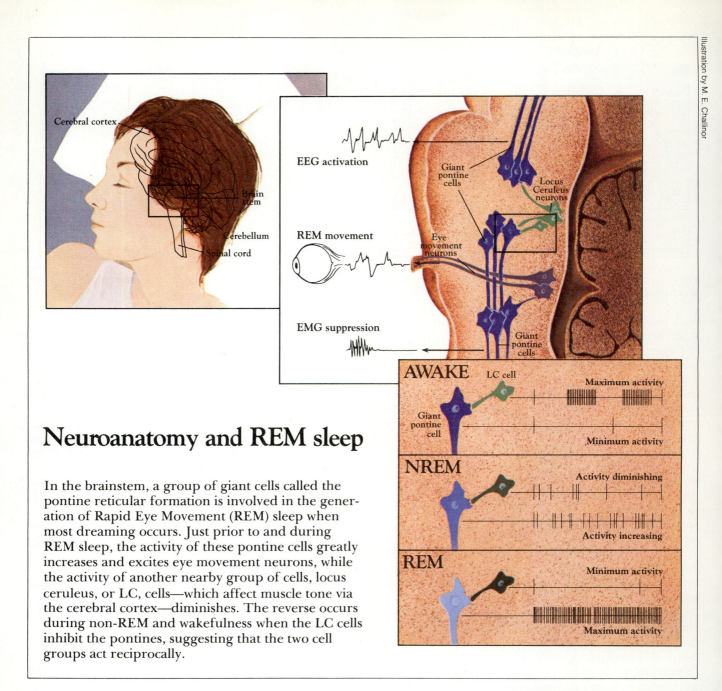

Cerebral cortex

Brain stem

Cerebellum

Spinal cord

EEG activation

Giant pontine cells

Locus Ceruleus neurons

REM movement

Eye movement neurons

EMG suppression

Giant pontine cells

AWAKE — LC cell — Maximum activity — Giant pontine cell — Minimum activity

NREM — Activity diminishing — Activity increasing

REM — Minimum activity — Maximum activity

Neuroanatomy and REM sleep

In the brainstem, a group of giant cells called the pontine reticular formation is involved in the generation of Rapid Eye Movement (REM) sleep when most dreaming occurs. Just prior to and during REM sleep, the activity of these pontine cells greatly increases and excites eye movement neurons, while the activity of another nearby group of cells, locus ceruleus, or LC, cells—which affect muscle tone via the cerebral cortex—diminishes. The reverse occurs during non-REM and wakefulness when the LC cells inhibit the pontines, suggesting that the two cell groups act reciprocally.

may help us explain the classic chase dream," Hobson says. "We do not need an elaborate theory about the wish to be pursued and caught. We feel that we are paralyzed or running in slow motion because the brain is being told we are running but is not receiving feedback from the periphery to confirm it. We are unable to move our feet and that fact is readily communicated."

The "top-down" dream investigators analyzed dreams and tried to fit them together with the physiological facts. But how does the "bottom-up" approach square neurophysiological data from cats with the detailed narratives of dreamers? Over the past two years McCarley, the more subdued member of the team, has been studying dream reports provided by Cincinnati's Kramer, and he finds that the fit is very good.

"If you analyze the dream reports in terms of verbs used in description," he says, "80 percent talk about motion. Thirty-eight percent describe movement of the lower extremities—running, walking, stepping, the kind of activities governed by the motor pattern generator.

"Eight percent of dream reports describe vestibular disturbances. The subject feels that he is floating, flying, or spinning—or that his environment is doing so. This is the kind of experience that almost never occurs in waking life. The frequency in dreams may be due to the fact that the world *does* seem to move when there are sudden, uncoordinated eye movements. Or it may be the influence of the pontine cells on the neurons regulating the position and balance of the head and neck.

"One of the most common expressions in dream reports is, 'And then the dream changed.' Thirty-eight percent of dream reports mention sudden scene shifts. The classic psychoanalytic explanation

Sleep research reminds us once again that body and mind are one.

is that the dreamer is trying to avoid unpleasant material. Our explanation is that a shift occurs when different runs of neuronal activation complete their course and are followed by another sequence with other neuronal activity.

"When you look at dream reports, you also find some sense modalities missing. Visual sensations are heavily represented and sounds are often reported, but almost no one mentions sensations of taste or smell. Pain is seldom mentioned. We are still not sure of the brain mechanisms involving pain, but the absence of the others may result from the fact that they are not integrally connected to the generator cells of the brainstem.

"Seventy percent of dreams could be classified as bizarre. They violate the dreamer's normal behavior and disregard physical laws as well. One explanation may be that the brain must knit together a vast amount of contradictory information, and the only way to do so is by fantastic images like the woman walking down the steps with a bowl of Jell-O."

Perhaps the outstanding example of the interrelationship between the physical phenomena of REM and the psychological aspects of dreams may be the male erection, McCarley says. Erection occurs in every REM period regardless of dream content. When a sexually explicit dream does coincide with erection, it may represent the brain interpreting the information it receives in terms of previous experience, rather than the body reacting to the stimulating images of the brain.

When Hobson and McCarley first published their hypothesis in *The American Journal of Psychiatry* in 1977, a great hue and cry was raised. The initial article analyzed Freud's theories about dreaming as discussed in his unpublished (and disowned) *Project for a Scientific Psychology*. It concluded that Freud's ideas had been based on a misreading of the then fledgling neuron theory and that it had been perpetuated by his disciples even though it was clearly outdated by more recent neurophysiological knowledge. A second report outlined the activation-synthesis theory. The articles brought forth a blizzard of letters, most of them critical.

"Many of our critics said it was unfair to hold Freud responsible for unpublished material. Others read us as saying that dreams mean nothing, that they can tell us nothing about the dreamer," Hobson says, "even though we stated—and believe—the content of dreams is certainly influenced by the individual's motivational state, by his memories, drives, and personality. The memories and experiences on which the brain draws to interpret the messages it is receiving are unique to that individual. How the brain elaborates these details certainly tells us about the individual. We dream about what we're concerned about. Dreaming is a physiological Rorschach test if you will.

"But our hypothesis does raise important questions about accepted dream theory. Most importantly, this view damages the notion that psychological purposes are the primary explanation for dreaming. We reject the disguise-censorship notion of dreaming which ascribes the bizarre features to the mind's need to conceal meaning. Instead, we view bizarreness as the natural consequence of the operating properties of the brain in dreaming sleep. The brain is making the best of a bad job. A dream is a psychological concomitant of an essentially biological process. I certainly don't think a complex decoding system is any longer necessary or justified. Intuitively, I also consider it improbable that nature would invent an important self-communica-

tion system and then make it so inaccessible as to require interpretation. A corollary hypothesis is how dreaming sleep serves a fundamental purpose: brain development and maintenance. Dreams may be the signals made by the system as it steps through a built-in test pattern—a kind of brain tune-up crucial to prepare the organism for behavioral competence."

Because dream theory is the cornerstone of the whole psychoanalytic edifice, shock waves continue to ripple through the psychiatric community. Psychiatrists, like the rest of us, cherish the notion that dreams are especially meaningful and can tell us something about ourselves in a way that nothing else can. According to Cincinnati's Kramer, the Hobson-McCarley hypothesis is "not central to the functional problems of dreaming. When it comes to dreams, two things are important—meaning and function. Do dreams enlighten us about ourselves? Will they make us smarter, change our personality, change our mood, solve our problems, have any application to our daily lives?

"I think the essence of dreams is psychological. It's all very well to find in dreams that a person is walking. The important questions are, 'Where is he walking? Why is he walking there?' Those are the continuing mysteries of dreams, and that is what we want to know."

To which Hobson, reached by telephone, gives an almost audible shrug. "The formal approach *is* relevant to content analysis because it helps us decide at what level to seek meaning in dreams," he says. "But the most important thing is that sleep research reminds us once again that mind and body are one. Even in sleep and dreaming, they cannot be divorced." ⑤

Edwin Kiester jr. is a free-lance writer who specializes in medical subjects.

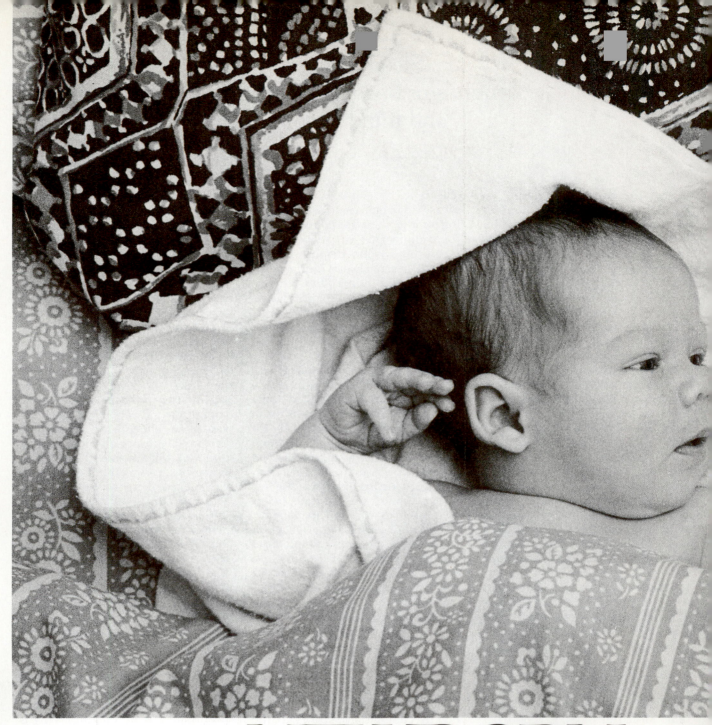

NEWBORN KNOWLEDGE

Infants arrive less wet behind the ears than we thought.

by Richard M. Restak • *Photographs by Mickey Pfleger*

Infant researcher Louis W. Sander has a favorite home movie. It depicts a young married couple standing on the lawn outside their home. The woman is holding their eight-day-old baby who, as the film opens, turns fussy and restless. She hands the baby to her husband, who casually takes the child and places it in the crook of his arm while continuing an animated conversation with the cameraman. As the film unfolds, the father appears to ignore his newborn baby. The baby too seems to be unaware of the father. Nevertheless, after just a few sec-

onds the infant stops crying, grows quiet, and finally, drops off to sleep.

A slow motion, frame-by-frame analysis of the movie reveals a different story. The father looks down several times at his baby, who returns the gaze. Infant and father begin to reach for each other. The baby clasps the little finger of the father's hand and, at that moment, falls asleep.

What delights Sander is the sensibility of the infant, a quality not generally associated with newborns. In light of a host of similar observations, partly made possible by innovative use of videotape,

Surprisingly, a newborn is more playful and bright-faced toward its father than its mother.

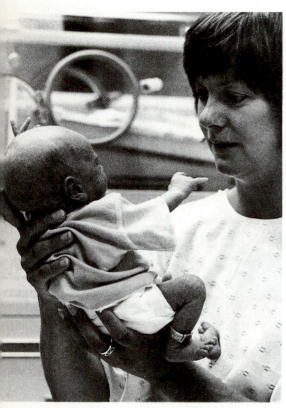

A mother and her premature baby gaze intently at each other at St. Luke's Hospital in Denver. They are part of a clinical research program run by the Denver Children's Hospital called "How to Read Your Baby." The program helps parents interact with their preemies, who are often less communicative than full-term babies. This combined with prolonged hospitalization and the emotional environment surrounding a premature birth often makes it difficult for parents to interpret their babies' signals and respond to them.

scientists are revising a long-held belief that newborns are passive creatures waiting for the world to imprint its wisdom on them. From at least the moment of birth, infants are enormously responsive.

This new knowledge is bringing about a quiet revolution that will affect everything from when and how a baby is delivered to the kind of advice obstetricians and pediatricians offer to new parents.

According to T. Berry Brazelton, Chief of the Child Development Unit of the Children's Hospital Medical Center in Boston, only moments out of the womb, infants are capable of a wide variety of behavior. Eyes alert, they turn their heads in the direction of a voice (they prefer a female pitch), inquisitively searching for the source of the sound that attracted them. Sander, professor of psychiatry at the University of Colorado Medical Center, and William Condon, a professor of psychiatry at Boston University Medical Center, have observed that the infant moves its arms and legs in synchrony to the rhythms of human speech. Disconnected vowel sounds, random noise, or tapping do not suffice; only the natural rhythms of speech will do. And it does not matter what language the infant initially hears: Infants in Sander and Condon's study responded to Chinese in the same way they responded to English. Such behavior provides support for theorists such as Massachusetts Institute of Technology linguist Noam Chomsky, who believes the human capacity for language is inborn and requires only appropriate exposure for normal speech development.

Newborns are particularly attracted to faces. A baby will turn its head and eyes while following a moving drawing of a face, but if pieces of the drawing are scrambled, it loses interest. Soon after birth it recognizes its parents and begins to fasten a special kind of attention on them.

At the Children's Hospital Medical Center in Boston, films of four-week-old infants demonstrate that babies behave differently with their parents than they do with other people and, not surprisingly, with objects. When a bright toy is brought within reach, the infant's attention is hooked, and its fingers and toes point toward the toy with gleeful expectation, but the baby quickly loses interest and gazes elsewhere. A few seconds later a second round of attention begins. The pattern of attention and loss of interest is jagged and irregular. With the mother, in contrast, the baby's movements are smooth and cyclic, and its attention pattern is more sustained.

Babies pay special attention to their fathers as well. "Amazingly enough," says Brazelton, "when several weeks old, an infant displays an entirely different attitude —more wide-eyed, playful, and bright-faced—towards its father than towards its mother." Brazelton describes these cycles with the father as "higher, deeper, and more jagged," corresponding to the father's "more playful, jazzed-up approach." One explanation for the infant's behavior, Brazelton says, is that fathers, on the whole, behave as if they expect more heightened, playful responses from their babies.

Researchers also are beginning to recognize something most relaxed parents have always known: Playing with one's infant is a very important element in its normal, healthy development. This marks a refreshing change from the rather grim, tight-lipped preoccupation with feeding and elimination that has been fashionable in some circles in recent years.

"I think there are several assumptions about infants that we now have to question very seriously," says Daniel Stern, author of

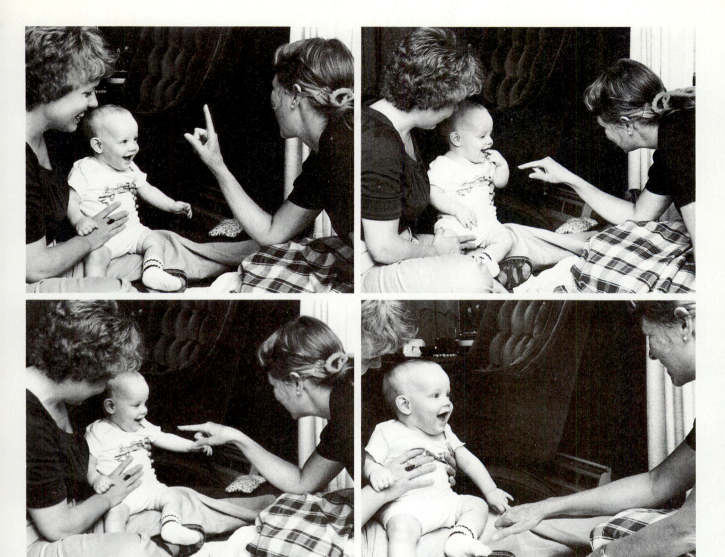

The First Relationship: Infant and Mother. In his laboratory at New York Hospital's Payne Whitney Clinic, Stern has captured on film delicate and evanescent exchanges between mother and infant. Often their responses occur within microseconds, suggesting, according to Stern, an inborn mutual readiness of both mother and infant to respond to each other.

Infant researcher Charles A. Ferguson, a linguist at Stanford University, agrees. In a whimsically entitled study, "Baby Talk in Six Languages," he finds that mothers of six different nationalities speaking their native languages all use a special version of baby talk with their infants. Sometimes the baby elicits from its mother behavior she has never practiced nor seen. Her speech is marked by short sentences, simplified syntax, and non-sense sounds, transforming phrases such as "pretty rabbit" into "pwitty

wabbit." When talking to their babies, mothers invariably raise the pitch of their voices, with long stretches of speech in the falsetto range. They prolong eye contact with the infant well beyond what is normal between adults. Two grown-ups will stare at each other with the same intensity only when they are extremely aroused emotionally—enraptured lovers or fierce enemies.

There are other ways in which infants and parents establish their special relationships. Through trial and error, they establish routines that are mutually gratifying. For example, most parents do not enjoy waking at 3:00 A.M. to feed their babies, so they attempt to persuade the infants to sleep through the night. When the baby learns this routine, a sense of harmony is created not only between infant and parents but with the rest of the household as well. At this point the

The preemie program, which incorporates the ideas of infant researchers Louis Sander, Berry Brazelton, and Daniel Stern, among others, lasts one year and initially involves visits to the home followed by sessions at the hospital lab. During a home visit, psychologist Perry Butterfield, right, the director of the program, shows a mother a game that she can play with her six-month-old. The baby is beginning to socialize, and it is important for parents to respond to the games it initiates.

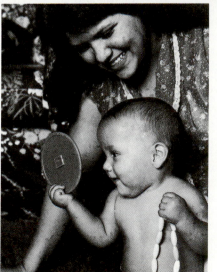

Eight-month-old Sebastian Esquibel, above, one of a pair of premature twins, plays with a mirror. By his age babies begin to recognize their individuality, and they like to share their discoveries with their parents, as Sebastian, right, demonstrates.

baby has finally become an authentic family member.

Gradually and painstakingly, parent and infant establish other routines: mealtime, playtime, even time when it's all right to be cranky. As each mutual adjustment is negotiated, the bond between the two is strengthened. But when these routines are interrupted or, worse, never established, family life can become an unpleasant series of interrupted meals, hurt feelings, and short tempers. Anyone who has ever experienced jet lag knows what it's like to be out of phase with other people's biological rhythms—nodding asleep in a chair, for example, while others are

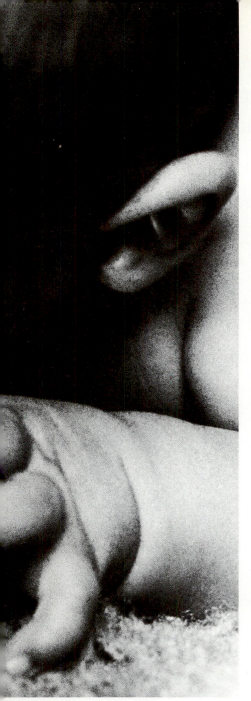

background, will stare selectively at the movie that corresponds to the sound track. The infant's skill at matching sound with picture can be carried even further by superimposing the two movies on top of one another and then slowly separating them. The infant's attention turns to the film that matches the sound track.

In dealing with people the infant exhibits even more astonishing acumen. By one week of age a baby can pick out its mother's voice from a group of female voices and at two weeks can recognize that the mother's voice and face are part of a unit. British researcher Genevieve Carpenter tested two-week-old babies by exposing them to four different situations: 1) the mother speaking to her infant in her own voice, 2) a strange woman speaking to the infant in her own voice, 3) the mother speaking in the female stranger's voice, and 4) the stranger speaking in mother's voice. The babies responded most favorably to the first situation, illustrating that as young as two weeks a baby can tell mother from stranger. More interesting, however, were the infants' responses to the third and fourth situations. They cried and turned away from this bizarre and frightening combination of the familiar and the strange.

Another fascinating study showed that infants and mothers respond to each other when the mother appears on closed-circuit TV screens nearly as effectively as when they are together. But if a baby watches a videotaped recording of its mother, it quickly loses interest, its eyes begin to wander, and it begins to fret. Infants evidently recognize that they get no personal response from their videotaped mothers, while in the live exchanges on closed-circuit TV, baby and mother can make eye contact.

One area of research that is particularly intriguing—and contro-

ready for dinner. So, too, parents and baby all want to have something to say about when food is served, diapers changed, and games played.

Early on the infant learns a wide variety of useful skills; for instance, it combines sight, sound, and touch into meaningful patterns. A three-week-old, blindfolded and allowed to rub its tongue along a toy block, will later gaze at a picture of a block in preference to other objects, a neat demonstration that the infant already integrates sight and touch.

A three-month-old shown two cartoons simultaneously, with the sound track of one played in the

At the end of the first year, Robert Harmon, a psychiatrist at the University of Colorado Medical School, evaluates infant skills and maternal confidence. Above, one-year-old Ian shows his ability to follow through with a play task while his mother looks on.

21

During the first hour, infants may spend 85 percent of the time wide-eyed and inquisitive.

Top, Linda Miller, a neonatal nurse, plays with an 11-month-old during a lab visit while his mother fills out a questionnaire. Below, Perry Butterfield discusses a videotape of the play session with the mother. All the sessions are videotaped so parents can see changes and growth in the reactions between themselves and their babies.

versial—is whether it is essential for mothers and newborns to spend time together immediately after birth. Marshall Klaus and John Kennell of Case Western Reserve School of Medicine in Cleveland have demonstrated that mothers who are allowed an hour with their infants immediately following birth in addition to five hours in the next three days behave differently from other mothers denied the same amount of time with their newborns. During their first hour, infants may spend an astonishing 85 percent of the time in an alert, wakeful state, eyes wide open and inquisitive, a situation that may promote a bond between mother and child. When filmed during the infant's first exam at one month, for example, the mothers who were allowed more time with their infants (so-called extended contact mothers) were more reluctant to leave their babies with strangers and preferred to stay and watch the exam. When the babies were fussy, these mothers were more soothing. Feeding, too, was different: The extended contact mothers all held their babies so that they could look at them face to face.

When filmed during the infants' first-year checkups, the extended contact mothers continued to demonstrate active interest and participation, often helping the pediatrician if their babies were fearful or restless. At two years, these mothers tended to ask questions of their children rather than issue commands. The vocabulary the mothers used was richer and more stimulating, which according to some studies may result in higher infant IQs.

Intrigued with Klaus and Kennell's findings, other researchers extended their studies and found that increased contact between a mother and her healthy, full-term infant in the first few days and weeks after birth is associated with fewer instances of later child abuse. Increased contact also correlates with less infant crying, more rapid infant growth, increased affection, and more self-confidence on the part of the mother.

In fact, many infant researchers now believe that increased contact between mother and infant in the first few days of life affects maternal behavior and infant development for periods of from one month to five years. Some believe the beneficial effects that stem from increased alertness and responsiveness last a lifetime. No one knows for sure. "We strongly believe that there is a sensitive period in the first few minutes and hours after the infant's birth which is optimal for infant-parent attachment," says Klaus.

Critics of the Klaus-Kennell theory feel there are other factors that contribute to optimal bonding. They argue that adopted children, premature babies, and infants born to mothers too sick to respond to them in their first few days still develop normal, affectionate relationships with their mothers. Nonetheless, even critics agree that

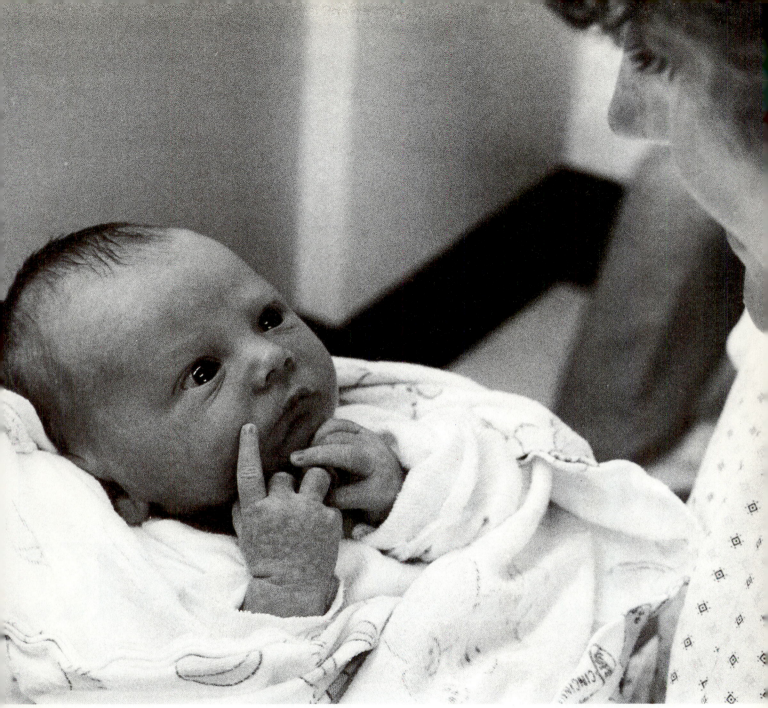

allowing mother and infant to be together during the first few hours is humane and natural. As a result, even though all the evidence is not in, hospitals throughout the world are beginning to allow mother and baby time together in the first hours after birth.

Doctors and hospital administrators are also beginning to realize that intensive care units and rigid hospital routines are potential disrupters of the natural interaction between mother and child. Robert N. Emde, professor of psychiatry at the University of Colorado Medical School, believes it is extremely important for parents and children to be together as much as possible. "For years, theories described how mothers shaped babies, but we are now beginning to appreciate how much babies shape mothers"—and fathers as well.

"No longer can we look upon a newborn as a lump of clay ready to be molded by the environment," says Brazelton. "We've come a long way in our understanding of just how marvelous a creature a human infant really is." [S]

Richard M. Restak is a Washington, D.C., neurologist whose next book, The Self Seekers, *will be published in June 1982.*

A newborn infant gives a nurse his complete attention. All babies are ready to communicate, if their parents just know how to read the messages.

DO DIETS REALLY WORK?

by William Bennett and Joel Gurin

You can read *Vogue.* You can count calories. You can stop eating. But your body knows better.

Photographs by Peter Garfield

If the millions of pounds lost on diets stayed lost, Americans wouldn't be spending billions of dollars each year on diet books, low-calorie foods, and weight loss drugs. Even those dedicated dieters who turn to weight loss clinics for help find their fat hard to part with. For example studies show that only about five percent can expect to lose 20 pounds and keep them off.

Diets may not work, but people want to believe they do. Like any ritual, dieting has found a myth to give it meaning. The central tenet of the diet mythology is that thin people are *better* than fat ones—more beautiful, healthier, stronger of will. The only way to make this invidious attitude palatable has been to argue that virtually anybody can, with a reasonable amount of conscious effort, control how fat he or she becomes. But with rare exceptions, dieters lose weight temporarily and then gradually regain it.

Common ideas about weight control are based on three assumptions. First, that overeating is the key behavior; fat people must eat more than normal. Second, that the body doesn't really "care" how much fat it has; it merely stores the energy leftovers from each meal. Third, that the conscious mind can be used to balance intake and expenditure of energy and thus achieve any desired weight.

These familiar and apparently obvious assumptions are now proving false. It is not true, for example, that a fat body must belong to a big eater. To find out just how much people of different sizes eat, psychiatrist Albert Stunkard and his colleagues observed patrons of fast-food restaurants, snack bars, and ice-cream parlors, places where portions are so standardized that it is relatively easy to calculate the

Adapted from The Dieter's Dilemma. *Copyright © 1982 by William Bennett and Joel Gurin, published by Basic Books, May 1982.*

Fat people eat normal quantities of food and, in some cases, slightly less.

number of calories on any tray that is served. The observers were, to be sure, watching people eat only one of their day's meals and that one in public, where obviously piggy behavior might be embarrassing. But the anonymity of the setting should have been sufficient protection for anyone who wanted two or three hamburgers instead of one. When the observers' sheets were tallied, Stunkard found that the fat customers (those judged to be 30 percent overweight) had eaten no more than the thinner ones. Stunkard's finding is the rule rather than the exception; other studies have also shown that fat people eat normal quantities of food and, in some cases, even slightly less.

Other common notions of fatness are that laziness or a sluggish metabolism is responsible. Such popular theories of weight control have one crucial feature in common: They asssume that getting fat is an accident. If appetite, physical activity, and metabolic needs are all "normal" (whatever that is), then by a stroke of divine good fortune, the person is spared from obesity. But if one of these variables is slightly out of line, the difference accumulates in fat. As an explanation of fatness, any one of these theories leaves much to be desired. Saying of someone, "He's fat because his metabolic rate is low," doesn't answer the question, "Why isn't he eating less to compensate?" And saying, "He's fat because he eats too much," merely restates the problem.

An alternative theory holds that fatnesss is not an accident, that the body does "care" about its fat stores. According to this view, now popular among psychologists, there is a control system built into every person dictating how much fat he or she should carry—a kind of thermostat for body fat. And like a thermostat set to maintain a certain temperature, the body's control system has its own *setpoint* for

fat. Some individuals have a high setting; others have a low one. The difference is not between the weak and the strong, or between the impulsive and the abstemious. According to this theory, it is a matter of internal controls that are set differently in different people.

Going on a weight loss diet is thus an attempt to overpower the setpoint. The skinny person who attempts to overeat and gain weight is fighting a similar battle.

But the setpoint is a tireless opponent. The dieter's only allies are willpower and whatever incentives make chronic physical discomfort worthwhile. But willpower is subject to fatigue, and incentives often lose their value after a time.

The ideal approach to weight control would be a safe method that lowers or raises the setting rather than simply resists it. So far, no one knows how to change the setpoint, but some leads exist. Of these, exercise is the most promising: A sustained increase in phys-

ical activity seems to lower the setting. Most people fatten with age, probably because they exercise less and their metabolism decreases.

To date, there is no easy way to measure what your setpoint might be. It is simply the weight that you normally maintain, give or take a few pounds, when you don't think about it. Of course, many people go through a spontaneous change of weight at one time or another—a gain or loss of five to 10 pounds that occurs within a few months and often after a change in lifestyle that affects daily activity levels. But some variation is to be expected from the setpoint; its tolerance, for example, can be seen in people who repeatedly gain and lose the same 10 pounds.

A few very unhappy individuals seem not to have a functioning setpoint at all. One such person was Robert Earl Hughes of Monticello, Missouri, who died in July 1958 at the age of 32. According to the *Guinness Book of World Records*, Hughes weighed 1,041 pounds when he was buried.

If we all depended on conscious management of our food intake instead of an internal control system, it would be incredibly easy to suffer Hughes's fate. Innumerable diet manuals have presented weight control as simply a matter of measuring calories in against calories out. Fat has been described as the bottom line on a caloric balance sheet. *Credit*: breakfast, lunch, dinner, snacks. *Debit*: the energy used in breathing, running up and down the back steps, having sex, playing tennis. *Net*: an ounce of adipose tissue, one way or the other. It looks easy enough on paper, but consider what it takes, theoretically, to gain 10 pounds in one year. This gain requires no more than a hundred "extra" calories a day. This excess amounts to one tablespoon of butter or a plain muffin without butter or a pear or a cup of minestrone or

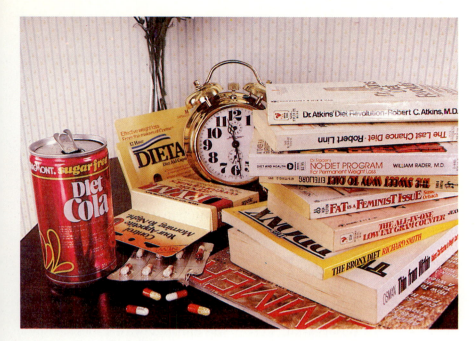

a biscuit of shredded wheat. And the caloric mistake need not be made at a single meal. It can be spread out over an entire day in which 2,000 to 3,000 calories are being eaten and burned away. Just a few extra flakes of cereal at breakfast, three more bites of cheese at lunch, a couple of Life Savers in the afternoon, a chicken breast instead of a drumstick at dinner, and the jig is up.

Even Hughes, according to the standard charts, needed to make only a small daily error to become the "heaviest medically weighed human" on record: 265 calories, about the equivalent of an apple, a tablespoon of butter, and a small glass of orange juice. At this rate he could, theoretically, gain the 523 pounds that he added in the 19 years before his death.

Measuring caloric intake is only half the task. You also have to know how much energy you are expending in the course of a day. For example, a 170-pound man scrubbing the floor for approximately 12 minutes will use up a biscuit of shredded wheat. As he will by spending 30 minutes cooking dinner, or swimming a fast crawl for about eight minutes. But these estimates are even less accurate than the assessment of intake. When you add it all up, the chance of coming out within 500 calories of the real balance between what you have eaten and what you have burned off is ridiculously small.

The alternative is to let your body do the subtraction, and measure the difference on your bathroom scale. But someone who gains 10 pounds a year does so at the rate of three ounces a week, an amount that defies the precision of even the best scales in common use. Hughes himself needed to gain little more than an ounce a day.

According to the setpoint theory, the setpoint itself keeps weight fairly constant, presumably because it has more accurate information about the body's fat stores than the conscious mind can obtain. Critics of the setpoint concept have joked that we would all have to have scales in the soles of our feet to make it work. More likely, at least one chemical substance is released by the cells that store fat. The blood level of this material, which is proportional to the amount of fat being stored, is monitored by the brain. If it falls too low, a complex control system within the brain somehow begins to compensate. This setpoint mechanism may slow the metabolic rate through hormonal and neural signals, so that energy is used more sparingly. At the same time, it pressures the conscious mind—at first almost imperceptibly—to change behavior. This pressure may be experienced as a kind of agitation—a "noshy" feeling, a restless inclination to eat between meals and to eat a little more at each meal. Later, the feeling may harden into voracious hunger, and

restlessness gives way to energy-conserving lethargy. This succession of events was vividly observed during an artificial famine staged nearly 40 years ago.

In the rainy November of 1944, 36 conscientious objectors to military service took up residence in dormitories at the University of Minnesota. They came with the intention of dieting very strictly for 24 weeks. The investigation was led by epidemiologist Ancel Keys, who hoped that information from this experimental starvation would be useful in rehabilitating the starved populations in World War II war zones.

The volunteers were in their mid-20s, of normal height (5′5″ to 6′3″) and weight (136 to 184 pounds) for their age. In the first three months of their stay at the university, the volunteers ate normally—about 3,500 calories a day. They were required to walk about three miles a day, engage in other physical activity several times a week, and carry out various maintenance jobs around their living quarters.

On February 12, 1945, the experiment began. The men were put on half their usual caloric intake while they continued to work and exercise as before. The new diet was principally whole wheat bread, potatoes, grains, turnips, and cabbage—foods intended to resemble those available in European famine areas. Adequate amounts of vitamins and minerals and token amounts of meat and dairy products supplemented their rations.

In the early phases of their diet, the men were cheerful, if uncomfortable, and they sometimes even experienced euphoria. But hunger never went away, and their highs were always followed by depression. They began losing weight rapidly, most of it from their fat stores and a much smaller proportion as protein. After a couple of

The overriding hunger that these men felt was not appeased even by a large daily excess of food.

months, they had lost about half their total body fat. Virtually all of the fat stored under their skin and in their abdomens was gone.

By now the men were irritable and quarrelsome. They also began to conserve energy. Though they continued their required walks and exercise, lethargy led them to avoid as much work, study, or play as they could. Small chores around the dormitory were neglected; their hair went uncombed, their teeth unbrushed. By the end of their sixth month of semistarvation, virtually all the men were deeply apathetic. They were indifferent to their visitors. Mealtimes, which came at half past eight in the morning and five in the evening, became the focus of their lives. The men were impatient to receive each meal but then would toy with it for as long as two hours. They were far from indifferent to flavor, however, and many of them experimented with unorthodox combinations or covered their food with salt and spices to intensify its taste.

At the end of the starvation period, three months of gradual refeeding began. The men had all lost a quarter of their starting weight, and on their new, but still restricted, diets they all began to gain. Even so, they remained miserable. This suggests that daily energy balance was not the secret to the men's discontent since they were now eating more calories than they were burning each day.

At a farewell banquet marking the end of dietary restriction in October 1945, the men were still ravenous; many of them became ill from overeating. Thereafter the 12 who stayed on ate steadily, consuming a daily average of 5,000 calories. Still they reported that they were hungry, even at the end of a very large meal. The overriding sense of hunger that these men felt was not appeased even by a large daily excess of food.

By the time they sat down for the Thanksgiving meal, a year after they had convened for their experiment, about half the men felt that their interest in food had returned to normal. At the same time, something else had returned to normal: their weights. Other measurements made at that time revealed that the men were just recovering all their original amount of fat, though muscle tissue was still significantly depleted. This observation sug-

gests that the missing fat was what made them feel deprived, that their bodies had some means of recognizing the deficiency and strove to restore it as fast as possible. Once that occurred, they no longer felt a caloric monkey on their backs.

People who diet successfully and lose weight only to succumb guiltily to a binge of eating may recognize their experience in this story. They will recall the ceaseless hunger that is not relieved by a single indulgence and the internal pressure to go on eating until all the pounds so triumphantly shed have returned.

Keys' experiment provides some of the clearest evidence that the human body itself demands a certain amount of adipose tissue. Severe disruption can alter this balance, but it is restored with adequate time and food.

If everyone's body really decides on its own how fat to be—if there is a setpoint—then gaining appreciable amounts of weight should be as difficult as losing. Such a project was initiated two decades later by a wiry, soft-spoken New Englander named Ethan Allen Sims. Sims was interested in the metabolic factors connecting obesity and diabetes. In the mid-1960s, after experimenting with hamsters, he realized that nobody really knew whether the metabolic differences between fat and thin people resulted from their different quantities of fat or were instead the cause. So he resolved to find a group of thin people he could make temporarily fat.

In 1964 Sims began an experiment in overeating at Vermont State Prison. A small research area, including a recreation room, dining room, and kitchen, was set aside in the prison's hospital area. Prisoner-volunteers entered the project committed to gaining up to 25 percent of their weight. For 200 days they ate heroically. In the early weeks of the experiment they continued with their usual prison regimen, but near the end they also cultivated sloth as part of the attempt to gain even more weight. To reach their goals, the prisoners virtually doubled the amount of food they normally ate. Only two of the men (later discovered to have a family history of obesity or diabetes) found it easy to gain; the others had to struggle. And once they had successfully added 25 percent to their starting weights, the prisoners could keep it on only by overeating an average of 2,000 extra calories a day, not just the couple of hundred that might seem theoreti-

What sets the setpoint?

According to setpoint theory, when fat stores fall below a certain level, the body reacts by "desiring" more fat. This yearning for body fat is orchestrated by an unconscious portion of the brain, which coordinates behavior and biochemistry to keep the stores relatively constant. The amount of fat that is called for depends, in part, on the number of fat cells in the body.

The cells that store fat are located mostly under the skin, where they are arranged in clusters, like microscopic soap bubbles. Once acquired, the number of fat-storing cells appears not to diminish during a lifetime, and each cell resists shrinking below a minimum fat content. A few years ago, the notion was popular that overfed infants would sprout extra cells, which then would cry "feed me" for the rest of their lives. It now seems unlikely that eating patterns in early childhood have much to do with the way fat cells are acquired. Rather, heredity exerts the major influence.

The brain learns about the state of the body's fat stores through chemical messages, some of them presumably sent by the fat cells. Glycerol may be one of the most important of these molecular signals. When fatty acids (the circulating form of fat) are stored in the fat cell, they are bound to glycerol. Fat cells continually bind and release an amount of glycerol proportional to the fat content of the cell.

By itself, the blood level of glycerol cannot be interpreted, but in conjunction with other information—for example, the blood level of insulin—glycerol may accurately inform the brain about the body's fat reserves. This role of glycerol as a signal for fat control has been highlighted by experiments performed at the University of Illinois. Glycerol injected into a rat's brain suppresses the animal's appetite, presumably by lowering its setpoint.

Fat cells do not, however, run the whole show. An elaborate brain mechanism, which includes regions of the hypothalamus, synthesizes information about the state of the body and the environment and then "decides" what the setpoint should be. External influences, such as the taste and smell of especially rich food, appear to raise the setpoint—probably as a way of allowing the body to take advantage of scarce resources. For example, rats fed on cookies, peanut butter, salami, and other sweet or fatty foods seem to raise their setpoints in response to their new diet and eat more to maintain a higher level of fat.

Certain drugs have the opposite effect; they act in the brain to lower the setpoint. When these drugs, such as amphetamines and other diet pills, are discontinued, the setpoint returns to normal, and weight rebounds. Nicotine often acts in the same way. Physical conditioning also appears to lower the setpoint—most dramatically in fat people—and inactivity causes otherwise normal individuals to get fatter. How exercise works to lower the setpoint is not known, but for now it seems to be a healthier and more effective approach to weight loss than pills or cigarettes.

---

cally necessary. One of the prisoners who gained relatively easily went from 110 pounds to 143, but he had to consume 7,000 calories a day during the last two months of the experiment to acquire and keep his adipose baggage.

The prisoners evidently did not suffer from their experience in quite the same way that Keys' conscientious objectors did. But they all found it trying, and everyone considered dropping out at one time or another. At the peak of their obesity, the men were lethargic, disinclined to take initiative, and neglectful of their prison tasks—an observation suggesting that the weight at setpoint is optimal for activity and mood. Much above or below, apathy sets in.

When the experiment was over, weight loss came readily to all the men, except for the two who had gained most easily. The prisoner who gained 33 pounds by eating 7,000 calories a day began to lose weight the day he stopped force-feeding himself. In this phase of the study he was required to exercise vigorously but allowed to eat whatever he felt like. Of his own accord, he consumed about half his normal daily diet and in 75 days was almost back to his starting weight, though he remained about four pounds heavier.

Sims' experiments demonstrated a remarkable tenacity in human physiology. Even in the face of extreme overload, the prisoners fattened very slowly. Exactly how their bodies kept from getting fat remains unclear, although it seems probable that they had some biochemical means for burning off their surfeit of food.

Most of the time no such sleight of hand is needed. From week to week, though not day to day, appetite spontaneously balances the amount we eat against the amount of energy we burn in activity. In 1953, a dozen British military cadets were followed by physiologist O. G. Edholm at the National Institute for Medical Research. Edholm and his colleagues attempted to record everything the cadets ate and everything they did, compare the two, and see how the books balanced. All of what the cadets ate was weighed when it was served to them, as were leavings on their plates, and careful estimates were made of the calorie content in anything else they ate, such as "chocolate and biscuits" and other foods purchased at the canteen. The energy expended by the cadets in various activities—resting, standing, sitting, drilling—was measured in a series of brief tests. The cadets then kept a record of everything they did all day. The upshot of the study was that, although these normal-weight (137 to 184 pounds), 19-year-old men gave no conscious thought to balancing their energy budgets and were not restricted in how much they ate, during the whole fortnight they managed to eat just what they needed to account for the energy they used.

The lean look has been in vogue for only about 60 of the past 600 years. Since 1400, three types of female figures have been idealized. Like the woman in Botticelli's Primavera *(1477), the first, with her large, swelling belly, carried the promise of childbearing. By 1700 tastes changed and the new ideal was all bosom and bottom. Like the women in an 1888 advertisement, middle, fashionable ladies donned enormous bustles after being forced into rigid corsets. Between 1910 and 1920 fat lost favor in Anglo-American culture. The perfect woman was now lean and angular —nice for the designers, but tough on a lot of the customers.*

Edholm's group was curious to see whether it could find a pattern in the cadets' eating habits: Did they eat a lot on the days when they were most active? They did not; rather it appeared they were consistently eating to compensate for energy they had used two days earlier. A lag between exertion and intake would be expected if increased appetite is a response to depleted fat stores. Although Edholm could not confirm his first finding, the same two-day lag has appeared in other experiments.

At the University of Pennsylvania, another group proved that they could do their caloric arithmetic without referring to a calorie chart, without seeing what they were eating, and without weighing themselves. These men and women agreed to subsist entirely on Metrecal, a milkshake-like diet drink, dispensed to them from a contraption belonging to Henry Jordan, a psychiatrist at the university. A volunteer would enter Jordan's laboratory and sit down at a desk from which a wooden arm jutted up to mouth level. Emerging from this support was a stainless steel nipple connected with tubing to reservoirs of Dutch chocolate, vanilla, strawberry, or coffee flavored liquid in a nearby refrigerator. The volunteer would attach himself to button, start a pump to deliver his meal. He stopped drinking when he felt full.

From a series of experiments with this device, Jordan concluded that people who came in to take a single meal from it were not much influenced by the number of calories in the liquid. Feeling full was mainly a reaction to tasting the fluid and perceiving its volume in their stomachs. Theresa Spiegel, a psychologist working with Jordan, then set out to learn whether the same would hold true if the subjects were to spend several weeks depending on the machine for all their nourishment.

Spiegel's volunteers were instructed to consume nothing but black coffee, tea, or water outside the laboratory and not to weigh themselves. They would come to the laboratory at any time to take as much or as little Metrecal as they wanted. Their only cue to start eating was hunger, their only cue to stop was feeling full.

Most of her nine subjects took a few days to adapt to their new way of life. At first they ate too little, but two to four days later they were back up to their normal intake (about 3,000 calories a day). A week after the experiment began, without telling the volunteers, Spiegel cut the concentration of calories in the Metrecal in half. The fluid was doctored to keep about the same taste and texture, and few of the subjects guessed that it had changed. Again, for a couple of days they took in too little but then, by roughly doubling the amount of fluid they swallowed, brought themselves back up to the number of calories they needed to hold a reasonably steady weight.

What happened to the Metrecal volunteers and the people in the three other experiments tells us a lot about everyday experience, about such things as appetite, hunger and satiety, and the substance—fat—that seems to bind these states of mind together in a working system. One group was starved. One was stuffed. One lived a more-or-less normal life but kept meticulous records. And one was reduced to eating everything from a metal teat. But though these groups were widely separated in time and place, they all showed that certain kinds of behavior—the quest for food, the choice of how much to eat, and so forth—are directed by forces outside of conscious awareness. These forces are not the familiar denizens of a Freudian unconscious—repressed conflict, displaced anger, infantile deprivation. They are, instead, real physiological pressures that are always working to keep a foreordained amount of fat on the body. In this

The truth is, there is nothing terribly scientific about height-weight charts.

Thin may be in, but fashion isn't health.

Go into a typical doctor's office, and you will find posted on the wall, near the scales, the venerable "height-weight chart." It says that, for example, a six-foot man with a light frame should weigh between 152 and 162 pounds. Anything above that "desirable weight" is *overweight*, and, as generations of people have been led to believe, overweight is bad for you.

The truth is, there is nothing terribly scientific about the charts. They are not based on any real medical evidence, and there is no good reason to believe that most people who are heavier than the charts' "desirable" range are any less healthy for it. The key phrase here is "most people."

This does not include truly obese people, a category comprising those who are more than 25 percent over their chart weight. Such people *are* at greater risk of developing high blood pressure, diabetes, and heart disease. Also at greater risk are those who have a family history of these diseases. Medical research shows that such people, as well as those who already have these diseases, can and should improve their health by losing excess weight. However, many of the millions of Americans trying to lose weight do not fall in any of these categories and, therefore, have no medical reason to slim down. These people may not look as trim as a fashion model, but that's fashion, not health.

The height-weight charts grew out of the life insurance industry's desire to find a convenient way of identifying high risk customers. It began in 1901 when Oscar H. Rogers of the New York Life Insurance Company refined the practice of looking for risk factors that would predict a higher death rate in applicants. He found that fat policyholders died younger than those of average weight. The insurance industry didn't care whether fatness *caused* disease and death. It was enough for them to see an association.

It was not long, however, before insurance companies began to think of this marker as a cause of early death. They reasoned that if they could get overweight people to reduce, customers might live longer (and pay more premiums). A pioneer in this effort was Louis I. Dublin, a young biologist who went to work in 1909 for the Metropolitan Life Insurance Company. For the next 43 years Dublin, who was passionately committed to public health education, served Metropolitan not only as chief statistician but as house intellectual and publicist. Dublin coined the phrase "America's No. 1 Health Problem" and applied it to obesity in a campaign to get so-called overweight people to slim down.

In the 1940s, Dublin produced his table of "Ideal Weights," as it was first called. In addition to actuarial figures, it used three somewhat faulty premises. One was Dublin's belief that people should not gain weight after the age of 25. The second assumption was that people could be assigned to one of three "frame" sizes. To this day there is no objective way to measure frames. The third and most critical assumption was that buyers of life insurance were representative of the population at large. It is known now that they are not.

While Dublin's tables were gaining acceptance, medical researchers were beginning one of the most far-reaching studies of health ever undertaken, a study that would prove Dublin wrong.

In 1948 about half the population of Framingham, Massachusetts, between the ages of 30 and 62, some 5,200 men and women, were enrolled in a study that continues to this day. They were examined every two years, and when they died, the cause of death was carefully determined. Although the sample was smaller than Dublin's, it was more representative of Americans at large.

In 1980 the Framingham doctors concluded that, among men, life expectancy was worst for the lightest weight group. Above this lowest level, weight did not have much effect on life expectancy unless it was more than 25 percent above average. Among women, death rates were highest for the lightest and the heaviest, but between the extremes, weight had little correlation with mortality. If the data hint at a "best" weight, it is at or somewhat above the national average for men and women.

The fashion for leanness has become more oppressive than liberating.

case, anatomy is indeed destiny.

The setpoint, it would appear, is very good at what it does best: supervising fat storage. On the other hand, it has some serious blind spots. It cannot tell the difference between a reducing diet and starvation. The dieter who enters the battle with a high setpoint experiences constant hunger, presumably as part of his body's attempt to restore the status quo.

Hunger does accumulate. Dieters demonstrate it; Keys' volunteers demonstrated it. Any laboratory rat will demonstrate it: Take away its rations until the animal loses an ounce or so, then give it free access to food, and it will eat very earnestly until it has restored the missing fat. Satiety also accumulates. Force feed a rat with rich eggnog through a stomach tube, and if you give it more calories than it needs, it will fatten. When you stop, the rat will eat less than normal until the excess is lost. Sims' overfed volunteers showed the same effect.

Rare individuals manage to diet and stay relatively thin, despite permanent hunger. But even dedicated dieters may find, to their dismay, that they cannot lose as much weight as they would like. After an initial, relatively quick loss of 10 or 20 pounds, for example, dieters often become stuck at a plateau and begin losing weight at a much slower rate, though they remain as hungry as ever.

As this experience demonstrates, the body has more than one way to defend its fat stores. Long-term caloric deprivation acts, in ways that are not clear, as a signal to turn down the metabolic rate. Calories are burned more slowly, so that even a paltry diet almost suffices to maintain weight. The metabolic rate, in short, can evidently adjust up or down to correct for deviations from the setpoint. This phenomenon was identified at the

turn of the century by a German nutritionist, R. O. Neumann.

Neumann's idea that the body adjusts its metabolic rate in response to under- and overfeeding has been debated, in one form or another, for decades. Accumulating evidence shows that some excess calories can be burned simply to prevent them from being stored. This type of metabolic heat production is critical to the body's energy equation. It now appears that Neumann's *Luxuskonsumption,* which translates roughly as "extra burning," begins after about two weeks of overfeeding, and a cumulative excess of about 20,000 calories is required to trigger it.

Ethan Sims' work with overfed prisoners provided some of the first modern confirmation of the phenomenon. "I remember" he says, "we used to be really embarrassed to say anything about *Luxuskonsumption.* Dieticians have assumed that people simply burn with an even flame; stoke it a little and they'll gain weight. But we now know that it's a very dynamic situation."

The *Luxuskonsumption* hypothesis, by itself, begs a crucial question. People may burn excess calories when they eat too much—but how much is "too much"? How does the body "know" when it has been overfed? *Luxuskonsumption* does not seem to be triggered by a single eating bout—say a Thanksgiving dinner—but by some cumulative change in the body. The simplest explanation, though it is by no means proven, is that the body only increases metabolism when it begins to move significantly above the setpoint. Deviations in the other direction have the opposite effect: The metabolic rate drops to conserve calories and maintain a stable amount of fat.

The body reacts to stringent dieting as though famine had set in. Within a day or two after semistarvation begins, the metabolic ma-

chinery shifts to a cautious regimen designed to conserve the calories it already has on board. The willing spirit is opposed by flesh that is not at all weak; it is perfectly determined to hoard the remaining supply of energy pending nutritional relief. Because of this innate biological response, dieting becomes progressively less effective and, as generations of dieters have observed, a plateau is reached at which further weight loss seems all but impossible.

If it turns out to be true, the setpoint theory may be disappointing news to people who want to get thinner by eating less. But it may help to counteract the mania for thinness that has become so pervasive, especially among women. In 1979, Bloomingdale's department store advertised its summer line of women's clothing: "bean lean, slender as the night, narrow as an arrow, pencil thin, get the point?" The fashions, and the bodies they enclosed, were illustrated with sketches, perhaps because not even a model could achieve the designer's ectoplasmic ideal.

The vogue for thinness which began around World War I was initially a sign of emancipation. The slender, almost tubular, form came to symbolize athleticism, nonreproductive sexuality, and a kind of androgynous independence. But in a culture that decrees everyone should be thin, the fashion for leanness has become more oppressive than liberating.

Of course, there will always be those select few who can starve themselves by an act of will to overcome their setpoints. But such examples have little to teach the majority of people, who have other things to do with their lives. §

William Bennett is director of the writing program at M.I.T. Joel Gurin is the managing editor of American Health *magazine.*

SHE & HE

The differences start in the genes, trigger the hormones, shape the brain, and direct behavior.

by Melvin Konner

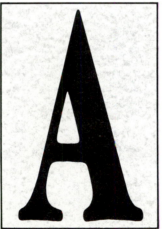

nke Ehrhardt, Patricia Goldman, Sarah Blaffer Hrdy, Corinne Hutt, Julianne Imperato-McGinley, Carol Nagy Jacklin, Annelise Korner, Eleanor Emmons Maccoby, Alice Rossi, Beatrice Blyth Whiting. These are the names of some distinguished women scientists who devote their lives to the study of brain, hormones, or behavior, human and animal. They range from the world famous to the merely well known. Each, within her discipline, has a reputation for tough-mindedness. All have in common that they have given considerable attention (most of them many years) to the question of

After sexism is stripped away, there will still be something different— something grounded in biology.

whether the sex differences in behavior each has observed—in the field, in the clinic, and in the laboratory—have a basis that is in part biological.

Without exception, they have answered this question in the affirmative. One cannot imagine that they did so without difficulty. Each has suffered, personally and professionally, from the ubiquitous discrimination against women that is common outside the academy and within it. Each has worked with some man who envisioned her—in his heart of hearts—barefoot, meek, pregnant, and in the kitchen. Each has sacrificed more than the average brilliant man to get in a position to work on a problem that troubles her intellectually, and the payment of that sort of price makes the truth more compelling. Nevertheless, each is wise enough to know that over the long course of time, the very sorts of oppression she has experienced are bulwarked and bastioned by theories of "natural" gender differences.

These women are doing a balancing act of formidable proportions. They continue to struggle, in private and in public, for equal rights and equal treatment for people of both sexes; at the same time, they uncover and report evidence that the sexes are irremediably different—that after sexism is wholly stripped away, after differences in training have gone the way of the whalebone corset, there will still be *something* different, something that is grounded in biology.

Like many stories in modern behavioral science, this one begins with Margaret Mead. She was one of the greatest of all social scientists. In a world in which all odds were against it, she established a concept of human differences as more flexible, more malleable, more buffeted by the winds of life experience—as delivered by our very different cultures—than anybody had then thought possible. And this concept has stood the test of time.

No question so engaged her interest as that of the role of gender in behavior. In trip after stubborn trip to the South Seas, she gathered information impossible to come by otherwise. Among headhunters and fishermen, medicine men and exotic dancers, in steamy jungles, on mountaintops, on vivid white beaches, in bamboo huts, in meeting houses on stilts high above water, in shaky-looking seagoing bark canoes, she took out her ubiquitous notebook and recorded the behavior and beliefs of men and women who had never heard of American sex roles. By 1949, when *Male and Female* was published, she had done so in seven remote societies.

In all her cultures there was homicidal violence, and in all, that violence occurred at the hands of men. Tchambuli men may have been effeminate in relation to certain American conventions, but they were still very devoted to taking victims—and, more traditionally, hunting heads. Mundugumor men were unthreatened by having their women provide for them. But that was because it freed them to plot and fight.

This may be traced in a like manner through all the world's thousands of different cultures. In every culture there is at least some homicide, in the context of war or ritual or in the context of daily life, and in every culture men are mainly responsible for it. There are, of course, individual exceptions, but there is no society in the ethnographic or historical record in which men do nearly as much baby and child care as women. This is not to say anything, yet, about capacity; it is merely a statement of plain, observable fact. Men are more violent than women, and women are more nurturant, at least toward infants and children, than men.

Even in dreams the distinction holds. In a study of dreams in 75 tribal societies around the world, men were more likely to dream of coitus, wife, weapon, animal, red, while women were more likely to dream of husband, mother, father, child, cry.

Of course, this is ethnographic fact, and that raises some eyebrows. Although cross-cultural surveys are quantitative in nature, they are based on individual studies consisting mainly of mere description. As such, they are the victims of "hard science" snobbery. That snobbery is most ill-founded. Ethnology is in its earliest phase as a science. Just as "mere" description of the look of a newly delineated brain region or a type of liver cancer as they appear under the microscope is a first step on a new path in science, so, equally, is the description of a society—description using the human eye, ear, and mind without computers.

evertheless, we recognize quantification as necessary, and, at least until recently, such quantification was more usual in the work of psychologists than of anthropologists. For many years now, psychologists in the Western world have studied gender differences, and they have done so with an exactitude very difficult to match in the tropical jungle. Eleanor Maccoby, an elder states-woman of American psychology, and Carol Jacklin, a young scientist trained in part by Maccoby, have, after years of work on the problem, written a major book, *The Psychology of Sex Differences*. It not only summarizes their own work but, more important, systematically reviews and tabulates hundreds of carefully described and annotated studies by other investigators. They review studies of sex differences on scores of different dimensions—tactile sensitivity, vision, discrimination learning, social memory, general intellectual abilities, achievement striving, self-esteem, crying, fear and timidity, helping behavior, competition, conformity and imitation, to name only a few.

For most of these dimensions it may be emphatically stated that there is no consistent pattern of gender difference. For almost all there are at least some studies that find a gender difference in either direction—usually both—and many studies that find no difference. Indeed, the main thrust of the book is to demolish cliché after cliché about the difference between boys and girls, men and women. There is no evidence that girls and women are more social, more suggestible, have lower self-esteem or less achievement motivation than boys and men, or that boys and men are more analytic. In the realms of tactile sensitivity and fear and timidity there is weak evidence of a gender difference —girls show more of these. There is also weak evidence that girls are more compliant than boys and less involved in assertions of dominance. In the realm of cognitive abilities, there is good evidence for superiority of girls and women in verbal ability and of boys and men in spatial and quantitative ability.

But the strongest case for gender difference is made in the realm of aggressive behavior. Out of 94 comparisons in 67 different quantitative studies, 57 comparisons showed statistically significant sex differences. Fifty-two of the 57 studies that showed differences showed boys to be more aggressive than girls.

Maccoby and Jacklin do not report on studies of nurturance per se, but in an earlier book, published in 1966, Maccoby summarized 52 studies in a category called "nurturance and affiliation"; in 45 studies, girls and women showed more of it than boys and men, while in only two did males score higher, with five showing no difference.

hile it is difficult to get accurate information in nonindustrial cultures on such measures as verbal and spatial ability, a number of excellent studies have been done on child behavior, using techniques of measurement and analysis that live up to a high standard of rigor. Beatrice Whiting has been a leader in this field, originating techniques of study and sending students out to remote corners of the Earth (as well as making field trips herself) to bring back accurate knowledge about behavior. She is one of the most quantitatively oriented of anthropologists and may be said to have built an edifice of exactitude on the foundation that was laid by Margaret Mead. She has been at it for about 40 years.

In a series of investigations that came to be known as the Six Cultures study, Whiting, together with John Whiting and other colleagues, studied children's behavior through direct, detailed observations, in standard settings, distributed throughout the day. These observations were made by teams in a New England town called Orchard Town—its identity is still a mystery—and in five farming and herding villages throughout the world. In Mexico, Kenya, India, Japan, and the Philippines, as well as in New England, hundreds of hours of observations were made.

In all six cultures, boys differed from girls in the direction of greater egoism and/or greater aggressiveness, usually both. The difference varies greatly from culture to culture, presumably in response to different degrees of inculcation of gender role. Even more interesting, the girls in one culture may be more aggressive than the boys in another. But the direction of the difference within any culture is always the same. In other words, studies of children who are not fully socialized to their cultures underscore gender differences in the areas of aggressiveness and nurturance.

It may be argued that the children in Whiting's studies had nevertheless been trained; they ranged in age from three to 12. Furthermore, all of the six cultures may well be sexist.

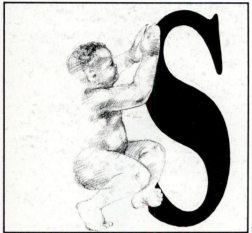

till, we can go younger. Annelise Korner has spent many years studying newborn infants, and one of her central interests has been sex differences. She, as well as other investigators, has found that at birth boys show more muscle strength—greater head lift in the prone position, for example—while girls show greater skin sensitivity, more reflex smiles, more taste sensitivity, more searching movements with their mouths, and faster response to a flash of light.

But before we resort to this indirect accounting, it behooves us to consider another category of evidence: the sort of evidence that comes from studies of hormones, behavior, and the brain.

The idea that humoral factors secreted by reproductive organs influence gender differences in behavior is very old; castration has long been used in attempts to reduce aggressiveness in animals and men, and systematic experimental work demonstrating that this works has been available since 1849. The question is no longer whether hormones secreted by the testes promote or enable aggressive behavior, but *how*, and also: What else goes on in a like manner?

The principal male gonadal hormone in mammals is testosterone. It belongs to a chemical class known as steroids. The steroid class includes the two principal female reproductive hormones: estradiol—the key estrogen in humans—and progesterone, the gestation-promoting substance secreted in massive quantities by the placenta, and in lesser quantities, in the nonpregnant woman, by the ovaries. Estradiol and progesterone, together with the pituitary hormones that regulate them, participate in the determination of the

monthly cycle. Although nothing so fabulous as that exists in males, there is much in common between testosterone's mode of action and that of the two female sex steroids.

The brain is the main regulatory organ of behavior, and behavior is that organ's major output; for a molecule to affect behavior it must generally first affect the brain, or at least the peripheral nerves. Sex steroids are no exception. Giving a rat a systemic injection of estradiol (radioactively labeled for tracing) will produce a high concentration of this hormone in certain brain cells—specifically, in their nuclei—within two hours. Twenty-two hours after that there will be a correspondingly massive increase in the tendency of the rat—if female—to respond to stimulation with sexual posturing. What happens in those 22 hours will tell a tale that may very well change the way we look at cell biology, but the tale cannot be told without at least a few more years of research.

Meanwhile, we know, as children like to say, *for sure,* that sex steroid hormones affect behavior, and we know they get around quite well in the brain. Using radioactive labeling, it has been very easy to show not only that they pass from blood to brain, but they concentrate selectively in certain brain regions. That is, concentrations occur in brain regions that play an important role in courtship, sex, maternal behavior, and violence—just the behaviors in which the sexes most differ and the ones most subject to influence by testosterone, estradiol, and progesterone.

Although the way the system works is scarcely understood, there are clues. For instance, injection of testosterone lowers the threshold for firing of nerve fibers in the pathway that leads to the hypothalamus, and as such in all likelihood mediates an excitatory influence on sexual and aggressive behavior. This finding gives substance to the action of testosterone on behavior. It is one thing to say that this hormone probably influences sex and aggression by acting on the brain; it is quite another to find a major nerve bundle deep in the brain, likely to be involved in sex and aggression, that can fire more easily when testosterone acts on it than when it does not. A key link in the story has been formed.

But we don't even need to reach so deeply into the brain. Peripheral nerves have now been shown in several experiments to concentrate these hormones. In songbirds in which the male of the pair is the singer, testosterone is concentrated in the motor nerves to the syrinx—the bird's voice box—and this is almost certainly part of the reason testosterone promotes song, which is a male courtship pattern. In female rats, injec-

Among male prison inmates,
the higher the adult testosterone level,
the earlier the age of the first arrest.

tion of estradiol increase the size of the region of sensitivity of the nerve to the pelvic region, even when that nerve is detached from the brain; this is presumably part of the mechanism that makes the female susceptible—some of the time, anyway—to male advances.

Such is the view of the physiologist, which is, not surprisingly, pretty unrelenting. What is a bit surprising is that someone like Alice Rossi has accepted it. Rossi is a family sociologist. After years of distinction in her field, she became dissatisfied with 19th-century sociologist Emile Durkheim's dictum that only social facts can explain social facts and began to take seriously the notion that at least some social facts might be explained by biological ones. She has become adept in reading the biological literature, and when she reviews it for her sociologist colleagues, she does not attempt to conceal from them her belief that some of the observed gender difference in social behavior—for example, in parenting—is attributable to causes in endocrinology.

In reviewing the well-known sex difference in nurturing behavior—obvious particularly within the family, and in all cultures—Rossi has accepted the possibility that it may have its roots partly in hormonal differences. She has defended this viewpoint in several recent articles, in the scholarly as well as semipopular literature.

From a hormonal perspective, nurturance has not been as well studied as aggressiveness, in some ways the antithesis of nurturance. In many studies of humans and other animals, testosterone at least clearly enables and perhaps directly increases aggressiveness. While no one with any experience in this field thinks that there is a simple relationship between testosterone and aggression, most people now accept that some such relationship does exist.

To take an example, although repeated studies of aggression and testosterone in prison inmates have produced a confused picture, one intriguing discovery stands out: Among male prison inmates, in one very good study, the higher the adult testosterone level, the earlier the age of the first arrest. That is, the men who had the highest levels had been arrested youngest, in early adolescence. In another study, the level of testosterone in male juvenile delinquents was correlated with their level of observed aggressive behavior.

This finding brings us to one of the most central facts about the gonadal hormones: They rise very dramatically at adolescence. From very low levels during early and middle childhood, testosterone (especially but not exclusively in males) and estradiol and progesterone (both especially but not exclusively in females) all rise to adult levels over the course of a few years, and the female monthly cycle is instituted. Few studies have measured hormones and behavior in the same individuals, but it is likely that adolescent behavior—and its gender differentiation—is influenced by these massive hormonal changes. Gender differences in fat, muscle mass, and the pitch of the voice, all of which contribute to gender-specific behavior, are determined in large part by the teenage boy's rise in testosterone.

One could conceivably leave the picture here, stress the similarity between the sexes in neurobehavioral plan, and suggest that evolution made a single beast with a single twist: an infusion of different hormones, coming from the gonads, just at the moment of reproductive maturity, just when we would expect the genders to begin to be really different.

The difficulty with this neat picture is that we have overwhelming evidence that the sexes differ in their behavior long before puberty, when previously we had thought that there were not enough circulating sex steroids to make the difference.

There is increasing evidence that the accounting may lie deep in the brain. In 1973 it was shown for the first time that male and female brains differed structurally. In the most forward portion of the hypothalamus, male and female rats differed in the density of synaptic connections among local neurons. Furthermore, castration of males just after birth would leave them with the female brain pattern, and injection of testosterone into females—likewise just after birth—would give them the male pattern.

To say that this study by Geoffrey Raisman and Pauline Field "rocked the neuroscience community" seems an extreme statement, yet I believe it to be accurate.

Scientists concluded that the basic plan of mammals is female—unless told to be otherwise.

There are several reasons. For one thing, it was the first demonstration that the brains of the sexes differ, in any animal. For another, the difference was in a region where it should have been—a region concerned with the brain's regulation of the very gonadal hormones we have been looking at. But most impressive of all, to those who knew the field, was the demonstration that sex hormones, circulating *at birth*, could change the brain. One of the most interesting experiments of the kind produced "pseudo-hermaphrodite" monkeys by administering male gonadal hormones to female fetuses before birth. As they grew, these females showed neither the characteristic low female level of aggressive play nor the characteristic high male level but something roughly in between.

or these reasons, investigators had, before 1973, already begun to talk about a change in the brain by male sex hormones around the time of birth; to put it crudely, a masculinization of the brain. But the involvement of the brain was only speculative until the report of Raisman and Field, which then gave the phrase its first genuine meaning.

That, as it now appears, was only the beginning of the story. A few years later, Dominique Toran-Allerand did a tissue-culture experiment—with brain slices in petri dishes—in which she watched the process in action. She made thin slices of the hypothalamus of newborn mice—of both sexes—and kept them alive long enough to treat them with gonadal steroid hormones, including testosterone. Her brief paper, published in *Brain Research*, shows the stunning results in photomicrographs. The cells in the slices treated with testosterone show more and faster growing neural processes than with the testosterone-free solution. In effect, she was able to watch as testosterone changed the newborn

brain. Her work did not imply that the faster, more florid growth made the testosterone-treated hypothalamus *better*—only different.

For these and a variety of other reasons, the community of scientists working in this field concluded that the basic plan of the mammalian organism is female and stays that way unless told to be otherwise by masculine hormones. That this was not a necessary arrangement was shown by the sexual differentiation of birds, in which the opposite seems to be true; the basic plan is male, and the female course of development is the result of female hormones. But the mammal story was becoming clear: The genetic signal for masculinity, from the Y chromosome, did its work on a female structural plan, through masculine hormones.

It is only natural to doubt whether such generalizations are applicable to that most puzzling of all mammals, the one that does research on its own nature. My own doubts in the matter—formidable at the time—were largely dispelled by the investigations of Anke Ehrhardt and her colleagues, first at the Johns Hopkins School of Medicine, later at the Columbia College of Physicians and Surgeons. Ehrhardt has spent years studying the condition and clinical treatment of certain unfortunate "experiments in nature"—anomalies of sexual and psychosexual development. In one such set of anomalies, known as the adrenogenital syndrome, a genetic defect produces abnormally large quantities of the sex steroid testosterone. For girls with the syndrome, masculine levels of the hormone are floating around in the blood throughout gestation, until the time of birth. Shortly after birth the condition can be corrected, so that it is presumably only in the prenatal period that the hormone can have its effects.

At age 10 these girls are psychologically different from their sisters and from unrelated controls. They are described by themselves and by their mothers as doing less doll play, being more "tomboyish," and expressing less desire to marry and have children when they grow up. Whatever value judgment we choose to place on these phenomena—I am inclined, for the moment, to place none—they seem to be real. They have been repeated by different investigators with different samples and even with different syndromes that amount, hormonally, to much the same thing. Taken together with the increasing animal evidence, these findings suggested to Ehrhardt and her colleagues—and to many others as well—that humans too could experience psychosexual differentiation, affecting both behavior and the brain, as a result of masculinizing hormones acting near or before birth.

This possibility received stunning confirmation in a series of discoveries made by endocrinologist Julianne Imperato-McGinley of the New York Hospital-Cornell Medical Center. These had to do principally with the analysis of a new syndrome of abnormal sexual differentiation that defied all previous rules. It was confined to three intermarrying rural villages in the southwestern Dominican Republic and, over a period of four generations, afflicted 38 known individuals from 23 interrelated families. It is clearly genetic but has arisen only recently due to mutation and intermarriage.

Nineteen of the subjects appeared at birth to be unambiguously female and were viewed and reared that way. At puberty they first failed to develop breasts and then underwent a completely masculine pubertal transformation, including growth of a phallus, descent of the testes, deepening of the voice, and the development of a muscular masculine physique. Physically and psychologically they became men.

The physiological analysis undertaken by Imperato-McGinley and her colleagues revealed that these individuals are genetically male—they have one X and one Y chromosome—but lack a single enzyme of male sex-hormone synthesis, due to a defective gene. The enzyme, 5-alpha-reductase, changes testosterone into another male sex hormone, dihydrotestosterone. Although they lack dihydrotestosterone almost completely, they have normal levels of testosterone itself. Evidently these two hormones are respectively responsible for the promotion of male external sex characteristics at birth and at puberty. The lack of "dihydro" makes for a female-looking newborn and prepubertal child. The presence of testosterone makes for a more or less normal masculine puberty.

But for present purposes, the most extraordinary thing about these people is that they become men of their culture in every sense of the word. After 12 or more years of rearing as girls, they are able to completely transform themselves into almost typical examples of the masculine gender—with family, sexual, vocational, and avocational roles. Of the 18 subjects for which data were available, 17 made this transformation completely, the other retaining a female role and gender identity. The 17 did not make the transformation with ease. Imperato-McGinley reports that it cost some of them years of confusion and psychological anguish. But they made it, without special training or therapeutic intervention. Imperato-McGinley and her colleagues reason that the testosterone circulating during the course of growth in these men has a masculinizing effect on their brains.

What are we to make of these extraordinary facts? For the immediate future, at least as far as I am concerned, nothing. It is simply too soon. Given present knowledge, for instance, it is not beyond the realm of possibility that the observed differences between the brains of the two genders serve only physiological functions. The brains must be different to exert different control over different reproductive systems, having nothing at all to do with behavioral subtleties. But I think this unlikely. If not now, then in the very near future, it will be extremely difficult for an informed, objective observer to discard the hypothesis that the genders differ in their degree of violent behavior for reasons that are in part physiological. [See Currents, p. 14, of first evidence of differences in human brains.]

If the community of scientists whose work and knowledge are relevant should come to agreement on this point, then it seems to me that one policy implication is plausible: Serious disarmament may ultimately necessitate an increase of women in government. Some women are as violent as almost any man. But speaking of averages there is little doubt that we would all be safer if the world's weapon systems were controlled by average women instead of by average men.

I think it appropriate to end where we began, contemplating the women who have helped unearth these facts. Visualize them in their offices and laboratories, trying to sort out what it all means; how do they handle the dissonance their findings must engender? I suspect that they do it by making a reconciliation—not a compromise—but a complex difficult reconciliation between the idea of human difference and the ideal of human equality. It is one that we must all make soon.

Melvin Konner, a Harvard biological anthropologist, will become chairman of anthropology at Emory University this fall.

THE WAY WE ACT

More than we thought, our biochemistry helps determine our behavior.

BY YVONNE BASKIN

IMAGINE YOU'VE BEEN strolling along a tropical beach all morning, your thoughts wandering. You haven't a want in the world. In just a few minutes, however, a rather single-minded goal is going to drive you indoors.

Deep in your brain, in a tiny cluster of cells called the subfornical organ, blood-borne molecules of the hormone angiotensin are arriving, sounding an alert as they latch onto receptors on the surface of nerve cells. Inside each cell a gene, perhaps newly aroused by the arriving hormone, launches into production. Chemical messengers pour into the tiny junctions between nerves. Ions flow in and out of membrane pores as signals are fired along to the hypothalamus, to a tiny cell cluster there called the paraventricular nucleus. From this cluster of cells deep in the brain, the chemical cascade fans out to rouse your body's stress response by way of your autonomic nervous system. Your adrenal glands begin churning out steroid hormones. Your blood vessels constrict. Your kidneys stop producing urine. The silent message is clear: You're dehydrated. Conserve fluids.

But conservation alone won't solve this problem. It's time to get the organism motivated. So the juices of subfornical cells also speed their message along other pathways to the limbic system and the cerebral cortex, centers of emotion and thought, where neuronal bureaucra- cies filter and interpret the signals. Suddenly you realize, "I'm terribly thirsty! I'd die for a glass of water." And you head straight across the sand toward the nearest cantina.

ARMED WITH A FLOOD of newly discovered chemicals and the techniques of cellular and molecular biology, brain scientists are beginning to track the origins of some of our most basic emotions, drives, and behaviors from the level of genes and molecules to specific nerve circuits and brain systems. What they're finding are the biological underpinnings not only of thirst but also of hunger, pleasure, pain, stress, sexual arousal, and even learning.

"I think that behavior is much more hardwired, much less flexible than people thought," says Candace Pert, chief of the Section on Brain Biochemistry of the National Institute of Mental Health. We carry in our genes, she believes, in the coded instructions for making proteins, an innate personality substrate that influences the way we perceive the world and the way we think, feel, and act in it.

Just a few decades ago, the chemistry of the brain looked too simple and predictable to play such a role. Only three or four neurotransmitters were known, including acetylcholine and adrenaline. Their job, so it seemed, was simply to assist the electrical signals, the one-way flow of information, across the gaps, or synapses, between nerve endings.

41

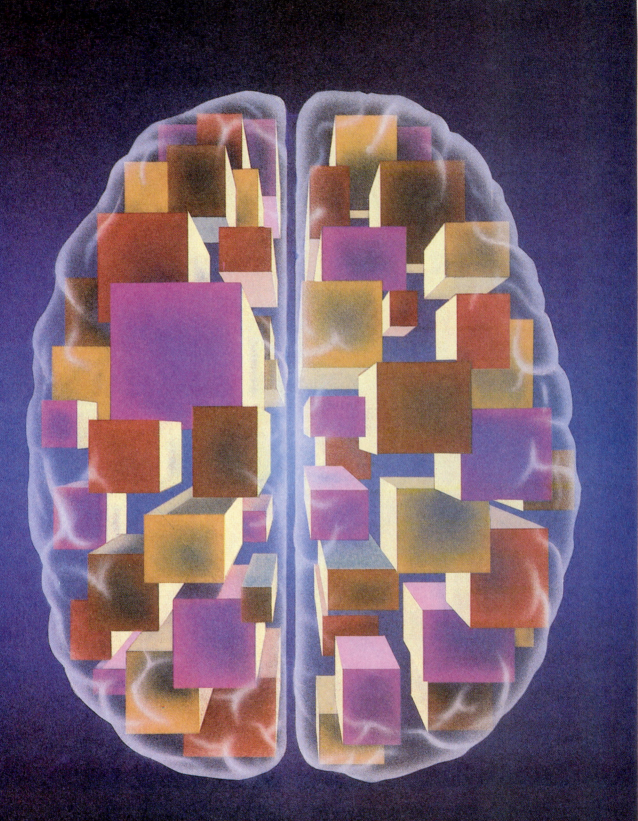

But the newly revealed complexity of brain chemistry has completely revised our concept of what nerves can say and do to one another. The action at synapses now looks more like a committee meeting than a simple one-way relay of orders.

The nerve terminal that is doing the transmitting has receptors listening to its own messages and to chemical back talk from the receiving nerve terminal. At the same time the transmitting terminal may be intercepting chemical messages drifting into the area from the bloodstream or from neighboring nerve endings. All this feedback can change the activity of the transmitting cell as well as that of the receiving one.

Today we know that a nerve cell may also release two or more different transmitters at a single synapse. Or a neuron may switch transmitters. Thus a single neuron can send different messages at different times, depending on what's going on in various parts of the body.

To add to this complexity, the number of known neurotransmitters has jumped to more than 60, and there is no end in sight. Among these is a newly discovered class of protein messengers called peptides, first spotted serving as hormones in the gut, the pituitary, and other parts of the body.

A neurotransmitter may act in classic fashion to encourage or discourage the recipient cell's firing, then disappear in a matter of milliseconds. Or, in contrast, the neurotransmitter may order a long-lasting metabolic change in the receiving cell, perhaps switching on genes that order the production of new transmitters or receptors.

The impact goes well beyond the single nerve cell. For instance, opiate peptides such as the endorphins can sedate, cause euphoria, or kill pain depending on which type of receptor in what brain circuit they reach. Thus no wiring diagram alone is going to tell us how nerve networks that can recognize metaphors or fall in love differ from those that can orchestrate a mean moonwalk or remember your 16th birthday. For that we also need to know what's being said and done at the chemical level.

Major efforts in Pert's and many other

BILL DENISON

Scientific revolutions are very interesting. The way they happen is that most people deny them and resist them. And then there's more and more of an explosion, and there's a paradigm shift.
—*Candace Pert*

labs are directed to mapping the distribution of peptides in the brain and the location of receptors that recognize and respond to them. Neuropeptide receptors are turning out to be especially dense in the limbic system, the emotion-mediating area of our brains, and in structures that filter information from our senses or set thresholds for sexual arousal or pain.

Pert says there is clear evidence that most, if not all, neuropeptides can alter our behavior or our mood. The strongest case for these mood-altering effects can be made for neuropeptides that are the brain's own versions of psychoactive drugs such as morphine, Valium, and PCP.

In fact, all drugs now used to treat mental illness function either by mimicking or blocking the action of natural transmitters. Working to define the transmitter and receptor systems that underlie specific mood states and drives should help in designing new drugs to treat disorders like depression, schizophrenia, drug addiction, and obesity. To Pert, the research also suggests that we

have within us the capacity to alter our own physiology without drugs. "The study of emotions," she says, "is very ambitious and exciting. If we figure them out, we figure ourselves out."

Pert and immunologist Michael Ruff, also at the NIMH, recently reported finding receptors for Valium on cells of the human immune system, which defends against infectious disease and cancer. They speculate that this link between an antianxiety substance in the brain and the immune system will provide clues to psychosomatic illness and the way our moods affect our physical health.

Such disclosures are tantalizing, but the crucial next step is to find out just how neuropeptides interact in specific nerve networks to evoke distinct moods or behaviors. That's a tough order because the human brain is a dense thicket of hundreds of billions of nerve cells, each capable of forming anywhere from 1,000 to 500,000 synapses. At any given time, a neuron is talking with dozens to thousands of other neurons at synapses along its vast network of branches. It must compile and average out all the incoming signals before it decides whether to fire and at what rate and what neurotransmitter to release.

But before researchers can begin to work out circuitry and chemistry in useful detail, they must have some idea where to look in the vast black box of the brain. The search for the molecular origins of behavior in creatures with simpler nervous systems is yielding some tantalizing results. Molecular biologists working with the sea snail *Aplysia*, for example, have already succeeded in linking certain features of the animal's reproductive behavior directly to the activities of specific genes and the peptides they encode.

The life of this undistinguished slug is largely devoted to eating and reproducing. The latter behavior is a fixed-action pattern, an innate ritual that's not open to change or learning. Scientists had already isolated a peptide called egg-laying hormone, ELH, that when injected, triggers parts of this ritual. Their next goal was to use genetic engineering techniques to isolate the gene that encodes this behavior-provoking substance, then find out exactly what nerve circuits ELH activates to evoke behavior.

Richard Axel at Columbia University College of Physicians and Surgeons cloned the ELH gene and got a surprise. The gene's DNA sequence actually codes not just for the single peptide he was seeking but for a much larger polypeptide, which can be chopped into smaller segments—ELH and at least five other peptides. (Many peptides in the human body seem to be cut in the same way from polypeptides.)

This raised a fascinating possibility. Perhaps all the behaviors in the innate egg-laying ritual, not just the few triggered by ELH, are orchestrated by the peptide products of a single gene. Axel's group and researchers at Stanford and the University of California, San Francisco, have found three active peptides made by this gene and have tied them directly to two pieces of the ritual.

The polypeptide containing ELH is produced in the bag cells, two clusters of nerve cells that sit atop one of the snail's major nerve bundles. When the bag cells fire, they release at least three peptides

Everything we do has a biological and chemical explanation, but we're not going to understand that for an exceedingly long time, if ever. Freud thought he understood it, but not quite at the level of the synapse.
—*Richard Axel*

cut from the polypeptide. One, ELH, travels via the bloodstream to excite the muscles of the animal's reproductive duct, making them contract and extrude the egg string. A second peptide stimulates the bag cell that produced it, keeping it excited so that it continues to fire and release peptides. Both ELH and the third active peptide identified so far also excite other nearby nerve cells, causing them to pour out a different array of peptides.

So the complexity continues. Cloning of the DNA from this newest set of neurons in the chain has turned up even more polypeptide genes that seem to code for this secondary cascade of neuropeptides.

These peptides may be responsible for completing the ritual: *Aplysia* stops walking and eating, its heart and respiratory rates rise, it grabs the egg string in its mouth and begins waving its head back and forth; it pulls the string out of its

duct and winds it up; finally it sticks the whole thing to a rock.

"Our next task is to figure out, as we did in ELH, which of the peptides are indeed released and what their biological activity is," Axel says. "We're not there yet." To find out what each peptide does, he must stick microscopic electrodes into the neurons in *Aplysia*'s well-mapped neural circuits, drop a peptide on the neuron, and record whether the cell fires or ceases firing. Working on live animals, he hopes to discover whether the peptide causes the head to wave, for example, or the heart to race.

Few of our behaviors are likely to be as closely orchestrated by our genes, as inaccessible to learning and conscious control, as *Aplysia*'s egg-laying ritual. And yet humans in every culture share a repertoire of innate and stereotyped emotional expressions—smiles, frowns, tears, laughter (although the provocations shift with culture and learning). Psychologists such as Paul Ekman at the University of California, San Francisco, are exploring the possibility that these largely involuntary facial movements actually spark changes in neurons that alter our moods, heart rate, and other body operations.

We also know of at least one example in mammals where the injection of a substance triggers a stereotyped response, just as the injection of ELH provokes a snail. That substance, as we saw in the opening scenario, is angiotensin. "If you inject angiotensin, people actually get the sensation of thirst," says Larry Swanson, a neurobiologist at the Salk Institute. "I think it's really the first example of a real behavior with cognitive parts where we know what triggers it. We've actually got a hormone."

Researchers in England discovered in the 1960s that in a dehydrated animal the liver releases into the bloodstream a polypeptide that's cut up to produce the peptide hormone angiotensin. That hormone constricts blood vessels to keep fluid loss from lowering blood pressure. It halts urine production. It causes thirst. To cause this sensation, of course, it must act on the brain.

"So the next question was, Exactly where does it act in the brain?" Swanson says. His lab and others recently answered that question by tracking it to the subfornical organ (SFO) above the hypothalamus. Blood vessels in this tiny cluster lack the special membrane qualities that keep neuropeptides from entering most brain cells. When you infuse angiotensin directly into the SFO, the brain responds just as it would to actual fluid loss. "I think it's the best example of getting a foothold on some actual circuits in the brain that underlie the coordination of the visceral response and the behavioral response," Swanson says.

One of those circuits, a particularly interesting one, involves the stress response centered in the paraventricular nucleus (PVN) of the hypothalamus. There a cluster of cells produces corticotropin-releasing factor (CRF), the peptide the brain uses to launch the classic hormone cascade of stress—the release of pituitary hormones that cause the adrenal gland to pour out steroid hormones. Your heart races, you breathe harder, your stomach tightens, you are infused with nervous energy. When the steroid hormones reach a certain level in the blood, they tell the brain to stop the chain of command that's releasing them—a classic negative-feedback regulatory system.

When Swanson's team removed the adrenal glands from rats, eliminating the steroid hormones and thus the negative-feedback response, the PVN did as expected. It stepped up the stress alert to make the pituitary increase hormone release. But it did this in an unexpected way: It not only stepped up CRF production but also began making two new peptide hormones, vasopressin and angiotensin, both already known to stimulate pituitary hormone release. Swanson believes the steroid hormones act directly on the genes in the paraventricular nucleus nerve cells to speed the production of pituitary hormones.

Molecular biologists collaborating with Swanson, Michael Rosenfeld of the University of California, San Diego, and Ronald Evans of Salk, are transplanting synthetic genes into mice to study how peptides and steroid hormones influence the genes inside the nuclei of nerve cells.

The most intriguing possibility opened

RENE SHERET

The most exciting and challenging prospect in neuroscience for me is understanding how and where genes are activated to allow the human brain to develop normally.
—*Larry Swanson*

up by this work is that the brain systems underlying some of our most basic moods, drives, and behaviors don't always respond the same way to the same situation. Their response—and perhaps your anxiety level or blood pressure—will depend on your hormonal state. The innate underpinnings of personality remain, but the thresholds for triggering pain, pleasure, depression, anger, or even memory are reset by chemistry.

"Instead of thinking of nerve circuits as fixed anatomical circuits that always do pretty much the same thing, there's a metabolic or biochemical plasticity, a real chemical dynamic in brain circuits that is probably different to some extent in different people," Swanson says. "There are CRF cells in other parts of the brain, like the cortex and the limbic system that are thought to be involved with cognition and motivation and to affect feelings and moods." The emotional centers of the brain have circuits that talk directly to the PVN, providing a way for

anxiety, worry, and thought to provoke changes in blood pressure and other body systems.

"So now, if you take chronic stress—putting someone under stress for weeks or months where there are chronically high levels of steroid hormones in the blood—the person may be exposed to the same stimuli as before, but now since the biochemistry of this circuitry has changed somewhat, they're going to start at least physiologically responding differently," Swanson says. And they begin to pour out more or less of various neurotransmitters.

"Now the big question is, you take two groups of people and subject them to the same chronic stress, and some people thrive and some people can't take it," Swanson says. "We really would like to know if there's something different about the biochemistry in the limbic and hypothalamic circuits in people that can't handle stress."

Perhaps some individuals are born with genetic quirks that affect the biochemistry of these circuits and leave them innately predisposed to depression, severe anxiety, ulcers, and hypertension when they encounter pressures or setbacks. By defining the links between genes, brain chemistry, and behavior, we may learn ways to intervene and protect ourselves from stress.

This research has also yielded clues to the long-suspected link between stress and the biochemical events in the brain that underlie learning and memory. The steroid hormones that come into play when we encounter stress can also alter the activities of nerve cells in the hippocampus, a brain region known to play an important part in learning and memory, says Bruce McEwen of the Rockefeller University. These cells are loaded with steroid hormone receptors, and prolonged stress exposes the receptors to steroids, actually killing some of those cells and destroying a feedback circuit that normally helps turn off the stress system.

But stress may in fact enhance some types of learning. It's well known that we learn best when we're alert and attentive and somewhat aroused by the experience or lesson. And when we're severely aroused—horrified, frightened, grief-stricken—the experiences are often carved indelibly into our brains.

"If you stop and think about what you really remember—when your mother died, for instance—it's associated with just a tremendous emotional response at the same time," Swanson says. "That's something that only happens to you once, but you'll remember it forever. And there're a lot of people who think this tremendous surge of steroid hormones feeds back on the hippocampus and in this way jacks up the memory formation process."

Exactly how this might happen, no one knows. But several stress-related peptides do seem to be candidates for a part in the system. In rats, infusions of the pituitary hormone adrenocorticotropic hormone (ACTH) will enhance certain types of learning. In humans, Dutch researchers determined years ago that a nasal spray of vasopressin seems to improve performance on long-term memory tests.

These are tantalizing leads to follow. But before the molecular mechanisms of learning and memory can be worked out in detail, researchers must know if there are different kinds of learning and memory and where to look for their traces in the vast circuitry of the brain.

Working separately, Mortimer Mishkin of the National Institute of Mental Health and Larry Squire of the University of California, San Diego and the Veterans Administration Medical Center have already identified two distinct types of memory: Skill or procedural memory stores habits or "how to" functions and conditioned reflexes. Fact or declarative memory stores faces, dates, numbers, and the sorts of things you usually say after, "I remember...." (It's this second type that fuels our thought, colors our world view, and contributes to our sense of self.)

Skill or reflex memory has been easier to track to the molecular level since virtually all organisms share some capacity for it. In several instances stored memory traces in rabbits have been tracked to a speck of tissue in the cerebellum, a brain region that controls motor functions. The memories are conditioned respons-

JEANNE STRONGIN

Our own work has taught us that there are usually multiple brain sites that are involved in a process. There's no single substance that's going to be solely responsible for anything. I think we tend to oversimplify the systems in our need to make them approachable.
—*Bruce McEwen*

es, such as an eyeblink reflex. When Stanford neurophysiologist Richard Thompson destroys that tiny bit of brain matter, his trained rabbits no longer respond on cue, even though they're still perfectly able to blink their eyes.

Two research teams working on conditioned reflexes in the marine snails *Aplysia* and *Hermissenda* have already proposed cellular mechanisms that might explain this type of memory. While *Aplysia* can't change its egg-laying ritual, it can learn to alter some of its other behaviors. In both snails, researchers have found that, after training, there are membrane changes in nerve cells that leave the neurons more excitable or primed to fire with less provocation the next time around.

Such mechanisms may explain the short-term storage of conditioned responses, even in humans, but they're not

likely to explain our unique ability for long-term factual memory: how you remember your favorite teacher's face and cheery voice and the multiplication tables she taught you 40 years ago.

Eric Kandel and James Schwartz at Columbia have suggested that this second type of memory may require the enhancement or repression of the activity of specific genes, which can make new proteins that change the functioning of the cell.

But other scientists believe that if, as we suspect, each cell with its perhaps 500,000 synapses participates in the storage of many memories, a genetic change is too global and crude a way to store all the bits of factual information we pack into our cortex in a lifetime.

"How can you change synapse number 9,742 and at the same time synapse number 62,121 without changing any of the others if you're turning on genes?" asks Gary Lynch of the University of California, Irvine.

Without waiting for someone to pinpoint the trace of a stored factual memory in the brain, Lynch has proposed a mechanism for permanent changes at the synaptic level that he believes could underlie this type of learning.

Bursts of high-frequency electrical stimulation can cause some nerve cells in the cortex and hippocampus to remain more responsive to this stimulation for weeks or even months. The phenomenon is called long-term potentiation (LTP), and its involvement in memory has long been suspected. Lynch theorizes that during LTP, an enzyme called calpain is activated at the excited synapse. Calpain attacks the protein skeleton that shapes the nerve cell membrane, exposing hidden receptors at the synapse, reshaping the branches of the cell, and even creating new synapses.

The mechanism could explain the findings of University of Illinois neurobiologist William Greenough, who's shown that when rats learn, their nerve cells sprout more branches and form new synapses. Lynch has tested his mechanism by perfusing the brains of rats with a substance that blocks calpain. Just as he predicted, this impairs the rodents' ability to learn cognitive tasks. The rats are

RENE SHERET

I think the question of how human cognitive operations are carried out is going to be one of the great scientific playgrounds for people, ranging from philosophers to cognitive psychologists to basic neurobiologists like me.
—*Gary Lynch*

still able to learn new conditioned reflexes, however.

"The next stage for the field is to say, 'Okay, now you've got this [possible mechanism]. Put it in a circuit and let's see what kind of memory comes out,'" Lynch says. "Let's go now to the next level of analysis, which is the circuits and the systems level.

"In the next 20 years we will no longer be dodging human cognitive operations," Lynch predicts. "We went into classical conditioning because that's what we could study. Okay. But the moment is on us now, I think, where we will no longer be avoiding the properties like human associative memory."

He's not alone in his prediction. "I think the biggest area of challenge in neuroscience in general is to integrate the behavioral and psychological with these incredible new discoveries in the biochemical area," Pert says. "I'm no longer interested in studying merely the brain. I'm now ready to study the mind. And I think it's now possible to do." ∎

THE HOLY GHOST
PEOPLE

Why do they take up poisonous serpents, handle fire, and drink strychnine?

by Michael Watterlond

Photographs by Mike Maple
Woodfin Camp

For the Holy Ghost people of Appalachia, it is a fragile fabric that separates this world from the next.

They are serpent handlers.

They take up poisonous snakes in church—timber rattlers, copperheads, even cobras—and they drink strychnine. They handle fire, using coal oil torches or blow torches. And they speak "with new tongues." They lay hands on the sick, trusting that—God willing—the sick shall recover. And when necessary, they cast out devils in Jesus' name.

"We live in the world, but we are not of the world," they say repeatedly during their twice-weekly church services, as though this were the statement that most distinctly defines them from us.

That these people are of another plane is unquestionable. They exist wholly in the thin, almost dimensionless region of "hard doctrine," of "getting right with Jesus" and most importantly of what they offhandedly call "this thing" or "this."

"This" is the featureless article of language they use to encompass the fiery, dramatic, even deadly practices that set their religion, their lives, and their select social grouping apart from most of Christian culture.

They belong to a variety of independent, fundamentalist sects called loosely Jesus Only. And they belong specifically to churches that subscribe to a doctrine based on what they call "the signs" or "the signs following."

The basis for these doctrines is a stone-hard reading of the last few verses of the Gospel according to Mark and other passages in the New and Old Testaments as presented in the King James version of the Bible, an English translation published in 1611.

In the pertinent section of Mark, Jesus has already risen from the tomb and appeared to several characters, including his disciples. As he is about to ascend, he issues these final pronouncements:

Mark 16:17 "And these signs shall follow them that believe; In my name shall they cast out devils; they shall speak with new tongues;

Mark 16:18 "they shall take up serpents; and if they drink any deadly thing, it shall not hurt them;

they shall lay hands on the sick, and they shall recover."

The Book of Daniel, in which Shadrach, Meshach, and Abednego are cast into the fiery furnace, is the basis for fire handling.

The fundamentalist serpent handlers take these passages as absolute. That these verses in Mark do not appear in the earliest extant texts is of no importance to them at all. Only the King James Bible counts. It acts as a major initiator of personal action, behavior, and decision making in their lives. It defines them.

Mary Lee Daugherty, formerly a professor of religion at the Univer-

Ray McCallister of the Church of the Lord Jesus in Jolo, West Virginia, handles a canebrake rattler, even though he has frequently been bitten. Snakes represent the devil: "If we are fully right with Jesus," says one church member, "we are supposed to have power over the devil."

sity of Charleston, estimates that there are now about 1,000 members of serpent-handling sects in West Virginia. She says numbers have dwindled recently because high unemployment has forced many members to migrate to urban areas. Since no organization links these congregations, a total member count would be guesswork.

Though there are local laws against handling dangerous animals in public in many states where serpent-handling churches exist, the laws aren't always strictly enforced. There are congregations in most areas of Appalachia, stretching from West Virginia south through Kentucky, Tennessee, the Carolinas, and into Georgia. Migrations from hill country into some of the urban areas of the Midwest have led to serpent-handling churches in nonrural areas such as Columbus, Cleveland, Flint, Indianapolis, and Detroit. The Full Gospel Jesus Church of Columbus, under the leadership of Willie Sizemore, has purchased and reno-

vated a building in one of the city's industrial areas.

George Hensley, who began the practice of snake handling in rural Tennessee around 1909, could not have predicted its spread to urban environments. Hensley, a Holiness circuit preacher, died of a snake bite near Atha, Florida, in 1955. He is not revered by these people and is not considered to have been a prophet of any sort. His death, however, does illustrate a point one frequently hears in Jesus-Only congregations: The Bible says to take up serpents; it doesn't say they won't bite.

"Make sure it's God," a deacon

Willie Sizemore, founder of the Full Gospel Jesus Church of Columbus, Ohio, lets flames from a coal oil torch touch his face to show he has God's anointing.

warns. He holds the microphone close to his lips like an entertainer. His hefty coal miner's shoulders straighten as he whips the mike cord away from his feet. "Only God can do it. Not me. Not you."

The loud, mechanical sounding buzz from the white pine serpent box makes his point unmistakable. The box this afternoon contains four timber rattlers and a rosy, velvet-textured copperhead.

"Death is in there," he says. "Don't go in the box unless it's with you."

By "it," the deacon means "the anointing"—the protection and spiritual direction of God that is manifest in what believers report as physical and emotional sensations.

"It's different for everyone," according to Sizemore. "Some people get a cold feeling in their hands or in their stomachs. Some don't."

Investigators in the past have reported that members say the anointing has a different and, for them, recognizably distinct sensation for each sign. The anointing to handle serpents may appear as a tingling, chilled feeling in the hands. An anointing to drink strychnine may appear as a trembling in the gut. The reports vary just as the sensations vary.

The deacon's warning about acting on the signs only if the anoint-ing is present is a typical part of services, and the saints, as the members call each other, enthusiastically applaud. As he turns from the pulpit, the underlying rhythmic drum beat that has throbbed subliminally in the background becomes distinct and powerful. It is joined by electric organ, electric guitar, tambourine, and a room full of the clapping hands, stomping feet, and hearty, frantic voices of 40 saints.

As the service gets underway, the

loud, insistent singing. Most songs are belted out in four-four time, and each lasts as long as 20 to 30 minutes. After a few songs there will be requests for prayers or healings and testament. The prayer requests may be for "sinner children" or for members of the church who are sick or injured. There will be more songs before the sermon. Services last from two to five hours depending on the time of year and work schedules in the mines.

The signs may show themselves at any time during the service but are most apt to be manifest in association with the driving rhythms of the music. The enthusiasm may verge on violence. One woman slumps to the floor, "slain in the spirit," they say. As she trembles in front of the pulpit, other saints close in on her screaming, "JESUS! JESUS! JESUS!" in her ears.

"I saw one man get up and run around the inside of the church more than 50 times," says sociologist Michael Carter of Warner Southern College in Lake Wales, Florida, an experienced observer of the sect.

Members wail and shake and lapse into the unintelligible, ec-static "new tongues" of glossolalia. Each member has his or her own style of speaking. As one saint sails into a new oration of tongues, another clamps his hands to her head and speaks in tongues himself; the ecstasy spreads like contagion. "He's translating," Carter observes.

There are two camps of psychological explanation and description of such services. Some researchers theorize that the wild activities are attempts to transcend reality, while others believe the point is self-actualization. Possibly both are right. It takes only a brief conversation with participants to learn that their daily life is one ongoing seance. They see God's movement and directives in every action, object, or thought.

Jerking as though his head were being battered by some unseen opponent, one brother moves across the floor toward the canister of coal oil next to the pulpit. He lights it quickly and thrusts his hands into the fire as though he were washing himself in flame. Next to him a young woman has been dervish-like for several minutes. She continues spinning under the tent of her long brown hair for nearly half

Sizemore, originally from West Virginia, started the Columbus church in 1968. He later bought and renovated the building with tithes and offerings from church members.

saints stand, clapping with the music, and walk slowly toward the open area between the pulpit and the first row of pews. The movement forward and together is called a "press." There is some feeling that the spiritual power of the group is concentrated by this gathering together. Should a member be bitten by a snake or "get down on strychnine," the gathering of saints around the victim is also called a press. Members refer to this communal praying and support of the stricken person as a "good press."

The services themselves have an informal structure that begins with

"I'm just as afraid of serpents as anybody. I'm afraid when I'm in the flesh."

Rayford Dunn was bitten on his hand by a cottonmouth moments after this picture was taken in Kingston, Georgia. Not only did he go out to eat afterwards, he returned to church next day and handled a rattler and a water moccasin without getting bitten.

an hour. In the back, the children play tic-tac-toe, practice spelling exercises, or sleep, unconnected to the proceedings.

Investigation into psychological and sociological aspects of fire and serpent handling has been conducted sporadically since the 1940s. A paper presented last year by Carter and sociologist Kenneth Ambrose of Marshall University in Huntington, West Virginia, at the Fifth Annual Appalachian Studies Conference, attempted to determine the satisfaction church members derive from such activities. They interviewed members of an urban congregation to compare the rewards of church versus non-church activity.

Results of the study indicate that taking part in the signs gives these people personal reward equalled in no other aspect of their lives. Participation in "signs of the spirit" were statistically evaluated by Ambrose and Carter to reveal the highest level of satisfaction for mem-

bers when they spoke in tongues. Handling serpents and handling fire were also rated highly, while drinking strychnine—clearly the most deadly sign—provided more shallow levels of satisfaction.

"When you drink strychnine," members say, "you're already bit" —your fate has been decided. Strychnine, commonly a white or colorless powder, causes a warm feeling in the gut, tingling sensations, and muscle spasms. In poisonous doses—15 to 30 milligrams for a human—the spasms can be severe enough, as the serpent handlers say, to "snap muscles right off the bone" and stop the heart. However, it is possible to ingest a considerable amount of strychnine and not exhibit the symptoms of poisoning. The drug does not accumulate in the body because it is rapidly oxidized in the liver and excreted in urine. The likelihood of developing a tolerance to it is remote.

While members of serpent handling churches—as well as most Je-

sus Only churches—forego worldly diversions such as films, television, and politics, they do hold down jobs. Sizemore, for example, is a factory worker. But they consider mingling with the world on the job part of their earthly burden.

Since most members have had to face stern criticism and even ostracism by friends and relatives—including husbands and wives at times —they are even more strongly pushed into this cluster of supportive friends at church, where they speak of themselves as the chosen people. The social and psychological bonds are reinforced more or less constantly by hugging, touching, kissing. This creates a rich, meaningful world for them—a sense of being special.

Also, the pastor rides herd spiritually on the congregation. During service he will approach a member he suspects (or "discerns," as they would say) is backsliding, or going to other churches. He will preach to that member eye-to-eye, only the microphone between them, and talk in generalities about worldliness, sin, or traipsing around.

Preacher Bob Elkins of Jolo often gives sermons lasting up to an hour and a half.

"I don't hold with people going from one church to another," says Brother Sizemore.

It is sometimes a strenuous task for the outsider to pry himself loose from all this music and high spirits and remind himself that these people take poisonous reptiles out of the countryside, bring them into their churches and drape them over their bodies, wear them in bundles on their heads. While the churchgoers are enthusiastic and emotional and committed, they do not appear to be disturbed and certainly not suicidal.

"I'm just as afraid of serpents as anybody," one 22-year-old West Virginia man says. He has attended these churches since childhood and has left the church his mother attends in recent years because that congregation has stopped handling serpents. "I'm afraid when I am in the flesh," he explains, "but when it is the spirit, there's nothing. I'm just not afraid."

He pulls up his sleeve to illustrate the critical point he wants to make: that these serpents are real and that their venom is real.

"It bit me here," he says, pointing to his wrist. "And it swelled up so much that the skin just pulled apart up here."

"When Richard died," one member says, "his whole arm split open from the shoulder down to the elbow."

Richard was Richard Williams. He died in 1974 after being viciously bitten by a huge eastern diamondback. Like most members who suffer bites, Williams refused medical aid and waited for fate to reveal itself.

The people of this church still talk about Richard Williams' anointing and about the serpent-handling feats he performed. Pictures on the walls of the church show him with his face in a mound of snakes; lying with his head resting on them like pillows, stuffing them into his shirt next to his skin. In a photo of Williams and the snake that killed him, it appears as if he is holding the felled limb of a tree rather than a snake.

"What really killed him was that the serpent got his vein when it hit the second time," one member says.

"You just can't tell," Willie Sizemore says, "you just have to make

To mix the strychnine solution, a knife tip is dipped in the white, odorless powder and swirled in a quart jar of water. Strychnine drinking is rare, and members almost never swallow the whole quart.

sure you have the anointing."

The folk myth that individuals who suffer repeated snakebites develop an immunity to the venom is viewed skeptically by Sherman A. Minton, Indiana University School of Medicine microbiologist and toxicologist. Minton says that such immunity is developed rarely and only when regular, gradually increased doses of the venom are administered. He points out that many people have allergies to venom, making successive bites more painful and causing greater swelling, asthma, and other symptoms.

As one snake expert puts it, however, the chances of dying by snakebite in the United States are comparable to the probability of being struck by lightning. One 10-year study showed that 8,000 venomous bites occur each year resulting in an average of only 14 deaths.

There are many theories about why snakes strike the saints infre-

quently. It is possible that given many warm-bodied targets pressing closely around it, a snake lapses into a sort of negative panic, a hysteria that makes it unable to single out one target.

Some observers have reported that church members' hands feel cold to the touch after handling fire or snakes. "I have felt their hands after serpent handling or fire handling," says Ambrose, who has observed these services for 15 years. "Their hands are definitely cold, even after handling fire." This would correspond with research in trance states involved in other religious cultures. It would also account for the vagueness of memory, almost sensory amnesia, that researchers have reported in serpent handlers as well as fire handlers. In his doctoral dissertation at Princeton University in 1974, Steven Kane reported that in North Carolina serpent handling congregations, young women were known to embrace hot stovepipes without injury or memory of the event. It has also been suggested by some observers that cold hands on

the body of the snake would camouflage the touch and prevent it from feeling the handler.

Retired sociologist Nathan Gerrard, formerly of the University of Charleston, observed serpent handlers for seven years in the 1960s. By administering portions of a psychological test to measure deviate personalities, Gerrard concluded that serpent handlers had healthier attitudes about death, suffered less from pessimistic hypochondria, and generally seemed better adjusted in certain ways than "conventional" churchgoers he used as a control group.

However, one of Gerrard's conclusions at the time was also that serpent handling represented a sop to desperation. He called them the "stationary working class" and attributed their stern doctrine to highland ignorance and poverty —a fatalistic creed that offered death and salvation as the only way out of West Virginia. Since that time, however, Jesus Only churches have spread out of Appalachia as economic hardships pushed followers into urban centers perched

on the edge of the Midwest.

Also, the members of the Full Gospel Jesus Church of Micco, a creek-bank town about 10 miles from Logan, West Virginia, are distinctly not the archetypal mountain folks. They come to church in well-polished, late-model automobiles and dress like middle-class people in most parts of the country.

While it may be difficult for outsiders to say that it is simply common faith that keeps these groups together, that would be the first thing they would say themselves. And this is a self-definition that has been immensely important to Western civilization.

"You can clearly see early Christianity as having very strong sectarian overtones," says Robert Bellah, a sociologist at the University of California, Berkeley. "Without that at the beginning, there would not have been any Christian church."

"We are not a cult. If Jim Jones had been right with Jesus, those people wouldn't have died."

"Sect religions," Bellah says, "are most apt to occur in relatively low-status groups, relatively low-educated groups where a combination of intense religious experience and rather high group discipline create a kind of separate world in which the people in the sect live.

"They largely reject the surrounding culture," Bellah explains, "rejecting many of the prevailing cultural forms. In other words, the whole round of life tends to be bound up in the sect itself. Social contact is limited by the sect, and the meaning of most things that one does derives from the sect."

Bellah makes the distinction that churches involve a structure which attempts to encompass the whole of society. They include a range of social classes and do not oppose the dominant social power but view themselves as having influence on how that power is exercised.

"The church accepts the culture while working within it," Bellah says. "A sect is exclusive."

It is the current public concern about total-commitment sects that has many people wondering about what have come to be called cults these days.

"'Cult' is really not a sociological category," Bellah explains. "It is a pejorative, popular term that we use for groups that are unfamiliar to our culture." Generally, the word is used to describe groups that are non-American in origin or are aberrantly individualistic—"in that they have been created by some 'kook,'" Bellah says. "Like Jim Jones."

"We are not a cult," Sizemore says forcefully. "If Jim Jones had been right with Jesus, those people wouldn't have died."

And still, outsiders want to know why anyone handles serpents.

"Because it is written," says Bishop Kelly Williams of the Jesus Only Church of Micco, West Virginia. "The main purpose in our doing this is to obey the Word of God." He points out that it really does not matter that the snakes symbolize Satan.

"Now, we don't think that everyone has to take up serpents," Williams says. "It doesn't say that all signs will follow all believers.

"You," he says to a visitor. "You might only speak in tongues. It depends on how God moves.

"Everyone knows that it is the nature of those serpents to bite you,"

he nods toward the buzzing pine box of copperheads and rattlers. "But you saw last night that God gave us a victory over those serpents. They were new serpents. They'd never been handled."

In fact, in a quiet evening before, Williams had gone to the box, lifted out a rattler and held it close to his body. He stared down at the serpent in his palms, smiled calmly for about three minutes, and set the snake back down in the box.

"You've seen that there is no one way to handle serpents," he says. "You been around enough to know that. There's no trick."

The styles of serpent handling are as various as the vocabulary of new tongues. On one Sunday afternoon, several men lift up the box, shake it hard and dump a mass of rattlers and copperheads onto the wooden floor without much caution. One man reaches into the tangle of scales and rattles and pulls up a timber rattler about four feet long. The other snakes, as well as a microphone cord, are tangled up with it, so he just shakes the whole mess until the excess snakes drop off. They coil stunned on the floor, as if paralyzed by the bad manners of it all.

The serpents are passed between hands. Loose copperheads wander around the box, uncertain of any particular route of escape. The heavy beat of gospel music picks up and the floor vibrates, the congregation claps and wails and sings.

In the back row of pews a girl about 11 turns back over her shoulder to talk to the visitor. She is playing hairdresser with another girl and holds an unfinished braid in her hands. She smiles half-heartedly and rolls her eyes heavenward as though her patience were limitless and unconditional.

"Boring," she says, "isn't it?" §

After prayers, members begin singing and playing guitars and tambourines. As the frenzy increases, some dance while others speak in tongues or move convulsively.

Michael Watterlond is a free-lance writer living in Los Angeles.

INFANTICIDE

Why does it happen in monkeys, mice, and men?

by Barbara Burke • paintings by Brad Holland

The murder of a child is the most abhorrent of crimes; even hardened criminals loathe a baby-killer. Our innate affection for the young is so strong that we are drawn to infants of other species—kittens, puppies, newborn foals. The pioneer observer of animal behavior, Konrad Lorenz, noted that any living creature with babyish features tends to trigger in an adult an instinctive urge to nurture and cherish it.

Lorenz argued that we inherited this protective response from our primate ancestors. After all, he wrote in the early 1970s, animals in the wild sometimes kill members of their own species by mistake but never on purpose. And harming the young was the strongest taboo of all.

So when reports that animals in the wild frequently kill their own young began to filter in from the field a decade or so ago, many scientists were bewildered. The first response was to dismiss such killings as pathological aberrations. But in just two decades the body of knowledge about the way animals behave in the wild has been completely revised by a new generation of field researchers—hardy and patient men and women who venture out to observe and live with their subjects. Among their more astonishing findings is that deliberate infanticide is a chronic hazard for rodents, birds, fish, lions, and more than a dozen species of primates. "We are discovering that the gentle souls we claim as our near relatives . . . are by and large an extraordinarily murderous lot," says Sarah Blaffer Hrdy, a research associate in biological anthropology at Harvard's Peabody Museum.

The first clues that monkeys deliberately kill their young came from Yukimaru Sugiyama, who was studying gray langurs, leaf-eating monkeys whose speed and elegance have won them comparison with greyhounds. Langurs generally live in troops of about 25 individuals led by one to three adult males. They were thought to be gentle and sociable creatures that work cooperatively for the good of the group. But in 1967 Sugiyama, a researcher at Kyoto University, reported that male langurs taking over a troop in India killed infants.

When Hrdy learned of this, she wondered if overcrowding explained the langur killings. She knew that rats in crowded laboratory cages killed infants. To find out, Hrdy, then a graduate student in anthropology at Harvard University, went to India. From 1971 to 1975, her observations and those of others led her to reject crowding as an explanation. Instead she proposed that male langurs taking over a troop killed unweaned infants so they can sire their own offspring sooner. A nursing langur is not fertile; by killing her infant and bringing her into estrus, an infanticidal male could sire more offspring than a noninfanticidal male.

The notion that such apparently destructive behavior is programmed by evolution "seems intuitively a bad thing to happen to any species," says Fred vom Saal, assistant professor of reproductive biology at the University of Missouri at Columbia. But many scientists, including vom Saal, now argue that a trait that benefits an individual may thrive—even if it harms the group as a whole.

"There's been a major shift away from the notion of the good of the species to the notion of the good of the individual," says Glenn Hausfater, professor of biology at Missouri. In this view—a tenet of sociobiology popularized by Richard Dawkins in his book *The Selfish Gene*—any trait that enables an individual to have more descendants than others tends to flourish and become part of its population's genetic heritage.

Infanticide could be such a trait: Individual infanticidal males may gain, even though the group may suffer. "Each infant killed lowers the average reproductive success for the society as a whole," Hausfater says. "Nonetheless infant killing is still reproductively advantageous on average for the specific animals that do the killing."

The behavior of the mother seems equally paradoxical. Disturbed as she may be by the slaughtering of her infant, she frequently rewards infanticide by mating with her infant's killer. Dian Fossey, director of the Karisoke Research Centre in Rwanda, has shown how females may benefit from the death of their own infants. A young male gorilla in the process of establishing his own harem may kill infants of a low status female living in a larger group led by an older male. The female then abandons the troop and joins that of the killer. By becoming one of the first to join the young male's group, the female gains high status: She gets better food and more protection, and any young she subsequently bears will carry his genes and also be protected by him. So in losing one infant the female gorilla gains a better chance of having more surviving offspring.

In any case, the mother has no choice. Smaller and weaker than the male, she can sometimes delay infanticide but can seldom prevent it. Some female monkeys with infants tempo-

rarily leave the troop when a new male takes over. Others use sex in an apparent attempt to safeguard an infant by confusing paternity. A pregnant langur may solicit a new male, presumably in hopes that the male will later spare an infant that he thinks may be his. But whenever this strategy fails and her newborn is killed, the bereaved mother only punishes herself further, at least in terms of lifetime reproductive success, if she refuses to mate and replace her dead infant. In fact, an infanticidal male may well be a particularly good choice as a mate.

"It sounds grisly, but if it is advantageous for a male to kill infants of other males, then it's advantageous for a female to breed with infanticidal males," Hrdy says. In fact, some females cut their losses even sooner. Scientists have long been puzzled over why pregnant rodents often miscarry if a new male appears. In the light of infanticide this behavior now makes sense. Why carry pups to term only to have them killed?

Yet the idea that gaining a reproductive advantage is the motive for infanticide is far from proven. The obvious way to test the hypothesis is to see if its predictions are borne out. Presumably, males should kill only unrelated infants; on average, the killer should gain sexual access to the mother sooner than if the infant had lived; the killer should mate, at least some of the time, with the mother; the killing should shorten the period until the killer's own infant is born; and, finally, the infanticidal behavior should tend to be inherited.

In rodents, at least, laboratory studies seem to support the theory. Vom Saal found, for example, that infanticidal male mice stop killing infants about 15 days after mating—presumably a fail-safe mechanism to prevent them from killing their own pups when they are born. At the same time, the males begin to care for the baby mice by protecting them and keeping them warm,

Among birds, infanticide is often by close relatives. It is also the number one cause of chick mortality in many species. When food is scarce, parents may abandon their eggs or even nestlings.

a complete change in behavior.

But data from the field aren't always as clear. It is not easy when studying wild animals to determine which males sire which infants or just how long the normal interval between births is. As Hausfater has shown in a series of computer models, an error of only one or two months in these estimates can totally skew the calculations of how many infants a male can potentially sire.

Some researchers, unconvinced by the reproductive advantage hypothesis, maintain that infanticide is caused by stressful conditions. Phyllis Dolhinow, professor of anthropology at Berkeley, and Jane Boggess, a research associate there, have never seen infanticide in the gray langur troops they are studying in India and Nepal respectively. "I think it is more than a coincidence that those sites where you don't see infanticide are the less disturbed ones," says Dolhinow. "At sites in which infanticide occurs, population densities tend to be very high, and there's more interface between monkeys and humans."

But Tom Struhsaker and Tom Butynski of the New York Zoological Society report that they have witnessed infanticide by males taking over troops among three species of monkeys in the Kibale Forest in Uganda, an undisturbed and uncrowded site.

Nevertheless, Hrdy agrees that the genetic hypothesis is not the *only* explanation for infanticide, even though it best explains the phenomenon in lions and several species of monkeys. Males may sometimes kill to reduce competition for food; they may kill infants to eat them; or they may kill them by accident during intertroop clashes.

Though rarer, infanticide by females also occurs in the wild. Female chimpanzees sometimes kill and eat infants of other females. Female elephant seals may kill strange pups that try to nurse. Dominant female wild dogs, dwarf mongooses, and hyenas may kill pups of subordinate females. In one of the few cases where rodent infanticide has been observed in the wild, the females did the killing, probably to acquire nests for their own infants.

Outside the world of mammals, the killing of kin is common. Male fish sometimes eat eggs they have fertilized, and some species of sharks actually eat their brothers and sisters in the womb. Among birds, infanticide "is often by close relatives," says Douglas Mock, associate professor of zoology at the University of Oklahoma. "And it's the number one cause of chick mortality in many species of birds." When food is scarce, for example, parent birds may abandon their eggs or even their nestlings.

More curious are cases where parents set the stage for the killing but let a sibling do the dirty work. The black eagle, for example, begins incubating the first egg several days before laying the second. When the second chick hatches, its older and stronger sibling will peck it to death. Mock suggests that the second egg is an insurance policy. Some birds can raise only one chick at a time, but if that chick dies, the parents will have lost an entire breeding season. By laying a second egg, the parents hedge their bets.

Mock says that most male birds don't appear to kill strange chicks in order to father their own brood sooner, probably because most birds are monogamous. On the other hand, a polyandrous female will sometimes kill the brood of a male and add him to her harem.

Among some animal species, then, infant killing appears to be a natural practice. Could it be natural for humans, too—a trait inherited from our primate ancestors? When we hear that some mother has killed her own baby, we are horrified and assume she must be deranged. Some killers, of course, *are* sick. A recent study of Canadian homicide figures showed, for example, that nearly half the parents convicted of killing their own children were mentally ill—though it is not clear whether this was cause or effect of the killing.

But human infanticide is too widespread historically and geographically to be explained away just as a pathology or the peculiarity of some aberrant culture. Charles Darwin noted in *The Descent of Man* that infanticide has been "probably the most important of all" checks on population growth throughout most of human history. In fact, there is good evidence for infanticide in 100 hunter-gatherer and agricultural societies.

In these societies newborn babies have been smothered, drowned in jars of milk, starved, or poisoned by opium smeared on their mother's nipples. The citizens of ancient Greece took unwanted infants into the mountains and abandoned them. In 18th-century Europe, so many children were killed when their parents rolled over them in bed—ostensibly by accident—that an Austrian decree in 1784 forbade parents to take their children under five to bed with them. In 19th-century England, parents turned their infants over to professional nurses, often called killer nurses, who made short shrift of the newborns. Eskimos left newborn babies in the snow, while Africans left them in dry streambeds. In France in 1833 more than 160,000 babies were given to foundling hospitals, where most of them died in infancy.

Infanticide is prevalent today in Zimbabwe in southern Africa, where rapid urbanization and the doubling of population over the last decade are fast eroding traditional rural values. "Baby dumping," according to Prime Minister Mugabe, is emerging as one of the country's most serious problems. "Police are picking up babies all over the country," Mugabe says. There have already been 50 reports this year of newborns that have been dumped in toilets, drains, wells, ditches, and on the banks of rivers. Sally Mugabe, the wife of the prime minister, says, "The gods are not pleased with us."

Just as methods vary from culture to culture, so do motives. Often babies are killed because they put too great a strain on a family's limited resources.

This may seem a cruel and inefficient method of family planning, but in cultures without effective contraceptives, where childbirth is safer than primitive abortions, it may appear to parents to be the only way to keep family size in line with family resources. Australian aborigines, for example, sometimes kill babies born during droughts, while some South American Indian mothers kill their ill-timed newborns because they take milk away from their older babies who are still nursing. A number of cultures kill the second-born of twins. Some researchers argue that such killings, which on the surface seem to be motivated by economic considerations, could also be an attempt by the parents to maximize their reproductive success.

Single-parent families can also pose a threat to newborns. Paul Bugos, a Ph.D. candidate in anthropology at Northwestern who has been studying the Ayoreo, a Chaco tribe that lives in northern Paraguay and southeastern Bolivia, says that tribeswomen told his wife, Lorraine McCarthy, about relatives and friends who had killed their infants, either because the father had divorced the mother or had died, or the   feared it was unlikely the man would stay around.

In some cultures closely spaced children and later-born children in large families are more likely to die young than others. The !Kung bushmen of the Kalahari Desert in Africa practice infanticide as a way of spacing births. One study showed that fifth-born and later-born children in Brazil were almost four times more likely to die in in-

fancy than firstborn children.

Being born the wrong sex—namely female—can also be extremely dangerous. Jesuit missionaries reported in the 17th century that the Chinese killed infant daughters by the thousands. The British found female infanticide rampant in India in the late 18th century.

Even though in modern societies

> Some researchers argue that the killing of infants, which seems to be motivated by economic considerations, could also be an attempt on the part of parents to maximize their reproductive success.

girls are hardier than boys, in former times they died suspiciously more often. In the 17th and 18th centuries, death rates in colonial America for girls aged one to nine were sometimes more than twice those for boys, and similar patterns are seen in 18th-century Europe. Sheila Johansson, a demographer at Berkeley, says that by the 19th century, when a monetary society held sway, sons were contributing to raising cash crops, while the daughters' labor

had no monetary value. So girls in poor, rural areas were underfed and overworked. In cities and industrial areas, where girls could find paid jobs, they and their brothers died at more equal rates.

Even today baby girls are killed at birth in some parts of India. And in China, according to a recent news article in *The People's Daily*, "butchering, drowning, and leaving to die female infants . . . has become a grave social problem."

More common today, however, is relative neglect of girls—poorer nutrition and care. Mortality rates for infant females exceed those for males in Bangladesh, Burma, Jordan, Pakistan, Sri Lanka, Thailand, Lebanon, and Syria. In parts of South America, mothers wean girls earlier than boys because they fear that nursing them too long will make the girls unfeminine. Less well nourished, the female children tend to succumb to fatal diseases.

Researchers may not agree on why people kill their young—whether the killers are reflecting some deep biological imperative or making a rational economic calculation—but most believe that infanticide often makes sense for the killer. "Society may call infanticide pathological," says Mildred Dickemann, an anthropologist at Sonoma State University in California, "but that doesn't mean that for the family it's maladaptive."

Some researchers, in fact, have begun to argue that the "battered child syndrome" is really a kind of slow and dilute form of infanticide. Susan Scrimshaw, associate professor at the school of public health at UCLA, suggests that as overt infanticide has become illegal and unacceptable, the practice has merely changed form—resulting in greater suffering than a quick killing at birth. Vulnerable children include those who are closely spaced, later born, female, or who have physical or emotional disabilities. Such children, who might have been killed at birth in the past, are more likely to be abused than other children. Parents may not mean to be cruel; sometimes they are unaware they favor some children over others.

Even defining child abuse is tricky. Anthropologist Jill Korbin of Case Western Reserve, who has done cross-cultural studies of abuse, says it would be exceedingly difficult to set up standards that would apply to all cultures for either optimal child rearing—or for abuse. She points out that many cultures find it cruel or detrimental to development that Western mothers force their infants to sleep alone in separate cribs, while Western mothers find extremely repugnant the custom in many societies of harsh initiation rites, which include scarring the body and circumcision for girls as well as boys.

However it is defined, though, child abuse is not a recent phenomenon. "When we examine the history of humankind, whether from paleontological evidence, documentary accounts such as the Bible, or culture-specific myths and fairy tales, we see evidence of children being mistreated, abandoned, sacrificed, or eaten," writes Robert L. Burgess and James Garbarino in *The Dark Side of Families.*

In a study of 24 two-parent families in rural Pennsylvania, each including at least one victim of abuse, Burgess, Joy Lightcap, and Jeffrey Kurland of Pennsylvania State University found that men were more likely to abuse children than women. That study and some others also suggest that stepparents are more likely to abuse children

than biological parents. Moreover, stepparents who abuse stepchildren apparently are less likely to abuse their own biological children.

But Jim Kent, director of the Children and Family Development Program at Children's Institute International in Los Angeles, suggests that when stepparents or boyfriends abuse children, it isn't necessarily a genetically motivated attempt to hurt a child carrying someone else's genes. It may simply be that a new stepparent, with little or no experience with children, has unrealistic expectations, believing, for example, that a child of a few months can stop crying on demand.

A century ago, the new theory of evolution forced man to give up his view of himself as divinely created to rule the Earth. He has learned, albeit reluctantly, that he too is an animal, the product of evolution. Today the patient work of field biologists is teaching us that we are not, among animals, uniquely depraved and violent. The eminent sociobiologist Edward O. Wilson points out that if we calculate the number of murders per animal for each hour of observation, we "realize that the murder rate is far higher than for human beings, even taking into account our wars." Hrdy adds, "The behavior of animals is determined mostly by evolution, while humans have options for self-improvement in line with their civilized ideals."

To what extent man has inherited a propensity for violence is an open question. If researchers cannot agree on why animals kill infants, much less can they agree about people's motives. But the idea that infanticide may have evolved in animals is giving new impetus to studies of our own violence toward babies and children. That research is unlikely to produce simple answers, but it may help us find the right questions and ultimately make us better understand the strengths and weaknesses of our animal inheritance. S

Barbara Burke is a free-lance writer in Ithaca, New York.

NICE GUYS FINISH FIRST

When dealing with your neighbor, a business rival, or the Soviet Union, the way to get ahead is to get along.

by William F. Allman

Captain J.R. Wilton, an officer in the British Army, was having tea with his fellow soldiers in the mud near Armentières, France. It was August 1915, and World War I had become a trench-lined struggle for barren stretches of countryside. Wilton's teatime was suddenly disrupted when an artillery shell arced into the camp and exploded. The British soldiers quickly got into their trenches, readying their weapons and swearing at the Germans.

Then from across no-man's-land, writes Wilton in his diary, a German soldier appeared above his trenches. "We are very sorry about that," the soldier shouted. "We hope no one was hurt. It is not our fault, it is that damned Prussian artillery."

Enemy soldiers might seem like the last people on Earth who would cooperate with each other, but they did. Despite exhortations to fight and threats of reprisals from their commanders if they didn't, peace often broke out among the German and English infantry. Sometimes there were truces arranged through formal agreements, but many times the soldiers simply stopped shooting at each other, or at least shot where it would do no harm. According to an account by one German soldier, for example, the English battalion across the way would fire a round of artillery at the same spot every evening at seven, "so regularly you could set your watch by it. There were even some inquisitive fellows who crawled out a little before seven to watch it burst."

That such cooperation would occur among their soldiers may have been surprising to the World War I high command, but not to Robert Axelrod. In fact, Axelrod says, the results of a computer tournament he conducted suggest that cooperation among the troops was very likely. Axelrod, a professor of political science and public policy at the University of Michi-

gan, is studying a simple but revealing game well known among game theorists and political scientists. Called the Prisoner's Dilemma, it gives two players an opportunity to cooperate or not cooperate with each other in a single exchange.

Though the game has been studied for some 30 years, there is no strategy that is best in all circumstances. Axelrod, however, wanted to know if there was a strategy that was better if the game were repeated over and over again. So he recently invited authorities on the Prisoner's Dilemma to go head to head with each other in a computer tournament. The winning strategy was one of the simplest in the tournament. And that strategy, to Axelrod's and almost everyone else's surprise, achieved its victory by being cooperative.

The Prisoner's Dilemma got its name because in the original example, devised in the early 1950s, two accused criminals are given a one-time chance to squeal on each other in exchange for lighter sentences — with the catch that if both squeal they each get longer sentences than if they had both kept quiet. But it can also be applied to a variety of not-so-criminal circumstances where two players can either defect on each other or cooperate.

For example, suppose you strike a deal with someone that involves the exchange of goods — say, a sack of food for a sack of money. You arrange to meet and exchange sacks, never to see each other again.

At first it seems like a good deal. But suppose the other person leaves an empty sack? If you don't get money for your food, you can't pay your rent. You also realize there is a chance for you to make a little extra money. If the other person leaves a sack full of money, you could leave an empty food sack. That extra money could pay for Grandma's operation, a noble cause that would ease your conscience a little. Besides, you're never going to see the other person again. So you protect yourself from coming away empty-handed and maybe help Grandma by leaving an empty sack.

It seems logical. But when you finally exchange sacks you find, not surprisingly, the other person has followed your line of thinking, and both of you wind up with empty sacks, no better off than you were when you started. So it would seem that in fact the best move is to cooperate and leave a full sack. That is, of course, as long as the other person is going to leave a full sack. Which he might not. And even if he did leave a full sack, Grandma's operation would be one step closer if . . . .

The game in Axelrod's tournament was similar to that of the food-and-money example: Contestants were asked to create a computer program that will generate either a *C* for cooperate or a *D* for defect. The difference was that in Axelrod's tournament the game would be played over and over for about 200 moves. If both programs produced a *C*, they each received three points. If both produced *D*, they would get only one point. If one offered a *C*, however, while the other generated a *D*, the defecting program got five points; the cooperating program got what is known as the sucker's payoff, a big fat zero. Each program was pitted against the others, as well as a clone of itself and a program that generated a *C* or *D* randomly.

The 14 contestants in Axelrod's tournament included psychologists, political scientists, mathematicians, economists, and sociologists, all of whom had worked on the Prisoner's Dilemma. The winner was the shortest program in the contest—a four-line program submitted by Anatol Rapoport of the University of Toronto called TIT FOR TAT. TIT FOR TAT's strategy is simple: Its first move is to cooperate, then it does whatever its partner did on the previous move.

Axelrod then held a bigger tournament. He wrote up the results of the first tournament, including a discussion of why TIT FOR TAT won and why the other programs didn't. The contestants from the first tournament were invited to try again, and advertisements were placed in several computer magazines. This time Axelrod received 62 entries from six countries.

One entry, called TRANQUILIZER, started out by being cooperative and then occasionally threw in a defection, hoping that other programs would tolerate its transgression. Another, TESTER, started with a defection to gauge how the other program would react.

These innovations, however, weren't enough. TIT FOR TAT won again. Rapoport was the only person to submit it, despite an explicit rule that anyone could enter any program, even if authored by someone else.

TIT FOR TAT might be a good way to win a computer tournament, but will it work in real life? Axelrod thinks so. Many interactions among animals, people, and nations can be thought of, in a general sense, as a Prisoner's Dilemma. From deciding whether to ask the neighbors to dinner to setting trade tariffs, there are many instances where partners run the risk of being defected on (the neighbors never return your dinner invitation) and are lured by the advantage of defecting (a higher tariff on imports means your cars sell better at home).

A lawyer at the U.S. Supreme Court is applying Axelrod's findings to competition and anti-trust laws in business. A Stanford University professor of family law is looking at how couples in divorce suits often use a TIT FOR TAT strategy when dealing with each other. Robert Calfee, a professor of education and psychology at Stanford, recommends teaching TIT FOR TAT in grade school. "It's a technology, a formal-

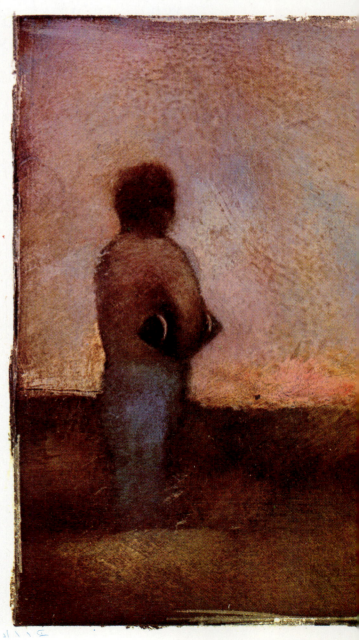

64

"TIT FOR TAT is a technology, a formalized way of dealing with others in society. Nothing in our schools teaches that."

ized way of looking at how to deal with others in society," says Calfee. "What do you do when you're mad at someone you love? Nothing in our schools teaches that."

Axelrod thinks nations have much to learn from his tournament, too. "Today, the most important problems facing humanity are in the arena of international relations where independent, egoistic nations face each other in a state of near anarchy," he writes in his book *The Evolution of Cooperation*. "Examples can include arms races, nuclear proliferation, crisis bargaining, and military escalation. Of course, a realistic understanding of these problems would have to take

into account many factors not incorporated in the simple Prisoner's Dilemma formulation. Nevertheless, we can use all the insights we can get."

What makes TIT FOR TAT a winner? For one thing, it is what Axelrod calls nice; it is not envious of another program's scores and never defects first.

Of all the principles involved in fostering cooperation, not being envious is perhaps the most difficult for humans to grasp. "In my classes, I often have students play the game for several dozen moves," says Axelrod. "I tell them the object is to score well for themselves, and it shouldn't matter whether they do better or worse than the other player. But the instructions don't work. They inevitably compare their score to their partner's. And this leads to envy, which leads to defections, and both players wind up with lower scores than they would have had if they had cooperated in the first place. A better standard for comparison is to ask, 'How well am I doing compared to someone else in my shoes?'"

One reason people are envious of their partner's score is that most people are used to playing what are called zero-sum games. In a zero-sum game the only way to get ahead is to take something away from your opponent, and the less your opponent gets, the more you get. Chess, poker, and just about every other parlor and board game are of the zero-sum type. In a nonzero-sum game the players are still trying to get the most points, but often they can do better if others do better as well. The closest thing to a nonzero-sum parlor game is charades, at least when the players aren't divided into teams.

The Prisoner's Dilemma is also a nonzero-sum game, which is why TIT FOR TAT had the highest cumulative score among all the programs in Axelrod's tournament *even though it never outscored any of its partners one-on-one*. In fact, since it defects only as many times as its partner defects, it can't do better than tie.

Parlor games may be of the zero-sum variety, but much of life is not. The arms race is a deadly nonzero-sum game. Recent research suggests that the explosion of only 1,000 nuclear weapons—the United States and the Soviet Union each have more than 10 times that many—over major cities could create a nuclear winter that would destroy most of life on Earth. "I think both sides realize it's a nonzero-sum situation," says Ralph Earle II, who for six years served as a U.S. negotiator for the SALT II treaty. "It doesn't much matter which nation fires first, the end result would be self-destruction."

Members of Congress engage in a nonzero-sum game as well. A lawmaker, for example, has no reason to be reluctant about helping a colleague. The threat to a senator's reelection comes from challengers within the state, not from another senator. Likewise the short-term gain of writing a bad check to the neighborhood grocery might be superceded by the long-term loss of the convenience of shopping there.

In their book *Getting to Yes: Negotiating Agreement Without Giving In*, Roger Fisher and William Ury of the Harvard

Negotiation Project teach a similar lesson. One stumbling block in negotiations, they write, is that it "often appears to be a 'fixed-sum' game; $100 more for you on the price of a car means $100 less for me." Why bother to invent new options for negotiation, a person might ask, if all the options are obvious and I can satisfy you only at my own expense? Rather than arguing over fixed positions, Fisher and Ury say, it is more valuable to try to develop an objective way of deciding what is a fair agreement. Divorcing parents, for example, might work out the rules of visitation privileges together before any court decision is made on who gets custody of the children.

TIT FOR TAT may never do better than its partner, but it's no sap, either. It immediately answers a defection with a defection. Thus while in any single round of the Prisoner's Dilemma game there is a chance for a great payoff at the expense of a partner, in reality that payoff disappears when the same partners play the game over and over and one of them is using TIT FOR TAT.

For example, against a program that defects every move, called ALL-D, TIT FOR TAT will get no points in the first round while ALL-D gets five. In each successive turn TIT FOR TAT and ALL-D get one point each. But TIT FOR TAT and ALL-D must also face all the other programs in the tournament, and TIT FOR TAT will do well with programs that cooperate, scoring three points each round. In a 10-move tournament between two ALL-Ds and two TIT FOR TATs, for example, an ALL-D will score 14 points when playing with each TIT FOR TAT. Each TIT FOR TAT will score nine points with the ALL-Ds. But the ALL-Ds will score only 10 points when playing with each other. The TIT FOR TATs, on the other hand, will score 30 points with each other, and thus each score a total of 48 points in the tournament. The ALL-Ds will score only 38 points.

Axelrod also changed the structure of the tournament so that the programs mimicked animals or plants competing in an environment. The first round of the tournament started with an equal number of representatives of each strategy. For the next round, the number of representatives using each strategy was dependent on how well the strategy did in the previous round. If a program scored well, more copies of it played in the next round; if a program did poorly, copies were removed. Those programs that took advantage of other programs scored very well at first, but they soon died out along with their victims. TIT FOR TAT, once again, came out on top.

In fact, Axelrod found that even if the environment contains nothing but ALL-Ds, a few TIT FOR TATs can invade and eventually take over the whole "colony." And because two TIT FOR TATs always do better with each other than with ALL-Ds, and never do much worse than ALL-D does with itself, once TIT FOR TAT is established, it stays established. "It appears," says Axelrod, "that the gears in the evolution of cooperation have a ratchet."

TIT FOR TAT maintains its respectable score by cooperating with the other nice programs and quickly responding to the mean ones. "One of my biggest surprises," says Axelrod, "was understanding the value of provocability. I came to this project believing one should be slow to anger. The computer tournament demonstrates that it is actually better to respond quickly to a provocation. If you wait, there is a danger of sending the wrong signal."

If your upstairs neighbor suddenly starts practicing his tap dancing lessons at midnight, for example, it isn't very effective to simply bury your head in your pillow, hoping that

"If you look in a supermarket at similar brands of cereals, they all have the same price. That's not just a coincidence."

eventually he will stop. If you don't react immediately, not only will he not be aware you are angry, but he may take your silence as a sign of approval. If you finally do accost him for keeping you awake all those nights, he may be more confused than apologetic.

Delayed reactions can have more serious repercussions. The United States, for example, is installing Pershing and cruise missiles in Western Europe as a response to the Soviet Union's deployment of SS-20 intermediate-range nuclear missiles. But as Earle points out, the Soviets have had nuclear missiles, albeit less sophisticated ones, aimed at Western

Europe since the early 1960s. The Pershing deployment, while touted as a reaction to a provocation, is so much after the fact it gives the impression that the United States is escalating the arms race.

Similarly, in 1979 there was a great outcry from some politicians about the presence of Soviet troops in Cuba, despite the fact that the troops' existence had been known for more than 15 years. The Cuban Brigade, however, was cited by some as an example of Soviet perfidy, and the already deteriorating relations with the Soviets eroded further, culminating in a halt in the Senate ratification of the SALT II treaty after the the Soviet invasion of Afghanistan.

When Earle asked a Soviet diplomat why the Soviets had entered Afghanistan knowing that their actions would result in nonratification of the treaty, the Soviet responded that the United States had purposely sabotaged the ratification of the treaty in the Senate by suddenly bringing up the Soviet troops in Cuba. Regardless of the merits of the SALT II agreement or reasons behind the Soviet intervention in Afghanistan, the delayed response to the Soviet troops in Cuba was apparently seen by some Soviets as being a provocation rather than a response because of its late timing.

One danger of quickly responding to every defection is what Axelrod calls echoing. If two strategies playing TIT FOR TAT get out of sync, they wind up taking turns defecting on each other, leading to a computer version of the Hatfield and McCoy feud. The way to avoid this in the real world, says Axelrod, is that while responding quickly, respond perhaps slightly less forcibly than the provocation. For example, if the Warsaw Pact nations suddenly move three army divisions into East Germany, the NATO countries should respond with a troop mobilization of their own. But since the Soviets might not see that the NATO response was a result of their actions, NATO should mobilize perhaps only one or two divisions to keep the situation from escalating.

While TIT FOR TAT is quick to anger, it is also quick to forgive. As soon as another program shows a willingness to begin cooperating again, TIT FOR TAT takes them up on it. Several other nice programs in the tourney didn't do as well as TIT FOR TAT because once the other player defected they would defect for the rest of the game, squelching any cooperative overtures by the other side. Another reason TIT FOR TAT was successful was that it didn't try to be too clever. Its strategy is transparent, and it quickly becomes clear what kind of response a particular action will elicit. One strategy was so hopelessly complex it finished last, worse than the program that simply cooperated and defected at random.

Having a clear, consistent strategy is important in real life, too. People often get back at their spouses for something without telling them why. While it may provide some satisfaction, it doesn't do much to prevent the problem from recurring. Handing out praise or complaints to employees may be a good strategy for a business manager, but if it's done inconsistently, the workers may later take a lack of praise or com-

If lovers regard their lives as individual outcomes, they have a greater chance of breaking up.

plaint as a sign of dissatisfaction or approval.

Because their decisions are often affected by a variety of pressure groups, nations have similar problems demonstrating a consistent policy. For example, according to Herbert York, a long-time negotiator in the talks on the comprehensive ban of nuclear weapons testing, one difficulty in making treaties with other nations is that the treaties have to be ratified by a two-thirds vote in the Senate. This caution, says York, was employed by the country's founders to avoid foreign entanglements, but it is out-of-date in a world where Soviet missiles are only minutes away. The U.S. position in arms negotiations often changes, he says, more to try to sway key Senators or military officials in the United States than persuade the Soviet Union. Because the U.S. position can shift without apparent reason, the Soviets may not get a clear sense of how their actions affect U.S. thinking.

During the SALT I negotiations, for example, U.S. officials proposed limiting each country's anti-ballistic missile system to one that would be stationed around each capital city. The Soviets readily accepted, since they already had such a system protecting Moscow. But the U.S. officials realized that it would be difficult to convince the American people to fund an ABM to protect only Washington, D.C. The U.S. negotiators then proposed eliminating ABM systems altogether. The Soviets complained that were being offered a new proposal on something to which they had already agreed. The talks bogged down.

Cooperation is not just for the chronically friendly. The most self-centered individuals, upon looking at the tournament results, might conclude that using TIT FOR TAT is a good way to further their own interests. The World War I trench soldiers were in a state of war, but there was a general willingness, as the infantrymen leaving the front told their replacements, to "live and let live."

What is important in nurturing cooperation, says Axelrod, is not friendship, trust, and formal agreements but rather the durability of a relationship. As long as the parties involved know that they will be engaging in similar deals in the indefinite future, cooperation can evolve all by itself.

Diamond dealers, for instance, successfully conduct millions of dollars of business with a verbal agreement and a handshake. A study of the records of one manufacturing company showed that fewer than a third of its business agreements were policed by legal contracts.

The enforcement for these relations, says Axelrod, comes from the future. The diamond dealers, like other businesses, know they will be dealing with each other over and over. According to a businessman in one study, "If something comes up, you get the other man on the telephone and deal with the problem. You don't read legalistic contract clauses at each other if you ever want to do business again."

The perception of the future is also important in relationships. A wedding ceremony, for example, provides a symbolic affirmation that a couple is committed to being together far into the future. "People who live together without being married tend to see themselves as individuals rather than a joint venture," says University of Washington sociologist Pepper Schwartz, who with colleague Phillip Blumstein has published a ten-year study of American couples. "It undermines the commitment, and they are less likely to pool resources. And if people see their lives in terms of individual outcomes, a couple has a greater chance of falling apart. Cohabiting couples split up much more often than married couples."

Whether it's a personal, business, or international relationship, as soon as it's clear that the game is about to be over, the strategy often changes from TIT FOR TAT to "nobody knows you when you're down and out." According to one study, "Once a manufacturer begins to go under, even his best customers begin refusing payment for merchandise, claiming defects in quality, failure to meet specifications, tardy delivery, or what-have-you. The great enforcer of morality in commerce is the continuing relationship." A study of Gypsies in California found that while they rarely paid their doctors' bills, they promptly paid city fines for breaking garbage regulations. Apparently, says Axelrod, the Gypsies knew they had to deal with the city on an ongoing basis; there were plenty of other doctors around.

The more times the players know they will see each other, the greater the atmosphere for cooperation to develop. The 1973 Israeli withdrawal from Egypt's Sinai Peninsula was arranged to be done in stages that coincided with Egyptian efforts to normalize relations with Israel. This increased the times the two would have to interact with each other, promoting cooperation. The World War I trench soldiers' tacit cooperation arose because, unlike most wars, the troops were stationed so that the enemies faced each other day after day; they knew that the same people they shot at one day would be shooting at them the next. According to one soldier, "It would be child's play to shell the road behind the enemy's trenches . . . but on the whole there is silence. After all, if you prevent your enemy from drawing his rations, his remedy is simple: He will prevent you from drawing yours."

In fact, adopting a strategy designed to damage your partner's chances for survival can be very dangerous. One of the reasons for the Japanese attack of Pearl Harbor, says Axelrod, was that economic sanctions imposed by the United States for Japan's intervention in China made them think their power could only diminish in the future. Instead of relinquishing their interests in China, they chose to attack the United States before they became weaker. The same principle applies to the idea of trying to win the arms race by, as some people advocate, spending the Soviet Union into bankruptcy.

There are times, of course, where promoting cooperation is the last thing you want to do. Businesses have long recognized the value of cooperation, which is why anti-trust laws exist. But the real problem, says Carl Huber, who has written on the legal applications of Axelrod's work in the *Yale Law Review*, is that cooperation can evolve without direct dialogue

"The Soviet Union and United States will both be here a long time—or neither of them will be."

between companies. "If you look in a supermarket at similar brands of cereals, they all have the same price. That's not just a coincidence; all the manufacturers know the best thing is not to cut prices." Similar cereal prices may be due to competition, he says, but it is difficult for legal bureaus that monitor anti-trust violations to distinguish between tacit collusion and a common response to a tough competitive environment.

One way to prevent businesses from cooperating, says Axelrod, is by changing the game. The military, for example, usually takes bids on the manufacturing of specific airplane parts. Because only a few manufacturers do the specialty work required to make such parts, they repeatedly find themselves bidding against each other. This repeated bidding can encourage the companies to engage in subtle forms of cooperation, leading to higher prices, even without direct communication. The solution, says Axelrod, is to invite more companies to bid on such jobs. The fewer times the companies meet, the better the chances that they will remain competitive.

You don't need a corporate strategy to benefit from cooperation. In the animal and plant kingdoms, where the maxim of "survival of the fittest" would seem to preclude helping another organism, cooperation is rampant. Lichen is a combination of fungi and algae—a plant/plant co-op; ants guard acacia trees that serve as their home and provide food; mating sea bass, which are hermaphroditic, take turns being the male and the female.

Fig trees are pollinated only by a certain species of fig wasp that fly from tree to tree laying eggs in the figs. If the wasp lays too many eggs in one fig, however, an indication that she has not pollinated very many trees, the tree stops the fig from growing, thereby destroying the eggs.

In coral reefs there are many species of small fish that pick parasites off larger predator fish. These "cleaner" fish are even allowed to forage inside the open mouth of the large fish. What keeps the relationship stable (and the cleaner fish alive), is that each small fish has its own territory, and the large fish line up, as biologist Richard Dawkins puts it, "like customers at a barber's shop." The closed environment ensures both fish that they will be playing with the same partner again. In the open sea, says Axelrod, these relationships do not exist.

Such a closed environment, says Axelrod, also exists with the United States and the Soviet Union. Earle agrees: "It's as if you live on one end of a block, and at the other end lives a neighbor who is an unpleasant, unsociable bully. But he has a nice house and a good job, and he's not going to go away. It doesn't make much sense, therefore, to get up every morning, stand in front of his house, and yell 'Go to Hell.'"

"People have a very difficult time with the perception of the future," says Axelrod. "But it's clear that the Soviet Union and the United States are going to be here for a long time," he says. "Either that, or neither of them will be here."

Perhaps the biggest stumbling block in fostering cooperation is that nations and people sometimes fail to recognize the nature of the game they're playing. Fisher and Ury tell a story of an American father tossing a Frisbee with his 12-year-old son in Hyde Park in London. It was the early 1960s, and few British had seen the strange disk in action. A small crowd had gathered to watch. Eventually one of the onlookers came up to the father. "Sorry to bother you," he said. "Been watching you a quarter of an hour. Who's winning?" Ⓢ

*Meet George, who should be happy but isn't.
Four therapists offer four solutions.*

THE SHRINKING OF GEORGE

BY PERRY TURNER
ILLUSTRATIONS BY ANDREA EBERBACH

HAVE YOU EVER thought about going to a therapist? How would you pick one? You could ask your doctor—maybe he has a friend from medical school who's "just great with problems like yours." Or maybe you have a brother-in-law who went to one that "works wonders. Miracles, in fact."

Well, you can probably assume that this individual trained in some kind of accredited program, but unless you do a little investigating, you can't expect much else—least of all a bearded, taciturn gentleman given to pronouncing *w*'s as *v*'s. Your childhood memories, as darkly suggestive as they might seem to you, interest many therapists not at all. Some will want to know what you think about on the bus ride to work; others will want to know where you sit. You might get one who asks you to imagine you're the bus driver, or the bus.

All told, 250 kinds of therapy are practiced today. A few have endured long enough and helped people enough that they've achieved mainstream status. You're about to see some in action.

The scenarios that follow are largely the production of four Washington, D.C., area therapists. Each reviewed the predicament of George, an unhappy fiction, and then offered a solution. The therapists came recommended to the writer by the same kind of sources most prospective patients would turn to: friends, doctors, and a local psychiatric society.

GEORGE'S CASE

George is 31 years old and has been married for five years. He has a bachelor's degree in economics from Purdue and works as an administrator in a state government office that manages small business development. In his spare time, he plays bassoon with several community orchestras; he currently averages two performances a month. His wife, who is 30, is four months pregnant with their first child.

George came in complaining of insomnia, "testiness," and anxiety caused by fantasies about another woman and by fears that he would prove inadequate as a father, husband, and musician.

George reports no history of significant acute or chronic physical illness. He takes no prescribed or over-the-counter medications. His last physical was seven

**One day
when George plays
his bassoon
at a noontime concert
in the park,
his wife, Ann,
comes to listen.
So does Laura,
the woman he
fantasizes
being in bed with. . .**

71

months ago; all findings were normal.

His childhood was "as happy as anyone's," he says, and his parents were loving and fair. There is no mental illness in the family. He has one older sister, a bookkeeper in another city, with whom he maintains a friendly, though not close, relationship. They "got along well enough" while growing up. He recalls her taunting him while he practiced his bassoon but quickly adds that he must have sounded "pretty bad back then." His mother, a housewife, was a quiet, passive woman whose principal disciplinary tactic was a doleful look—this she used mostly when George neglected to practice his bassoon and when his sister dated unsuitable boys. George's father, an engineer, was very protective of his wife and often referred to her when correcting his children's behavior, as in, "This is really going to disappoint your mother." She died the year after George entered college. His father is now retired and living in Tucson.

George began playing bassoon in fourth grade. In college he considered majoring in music, but in his third year his father suggested he major in something practical because he "could always do music at night and on the weekends." At the time this seemed to George reasonable advice; he showed a modest talent for economics and graduated with a B+ average and a minor in music. He got his current job two months out of school.

He met his wife, Ann, in the cafeteria of the building they both work in. Ann coordinates state programs for drug dependency. Although she plays no musical instruments, she enjoys classical music and attends all of George's performances. She is very excited about having a baby, according to George, and plans to stop working for six months after it is born and then return to work on a part-time consulting basis.

About seven months ago, a new typist named Laura started working in George's office. Laura, a poor typist and a very pretty young woman, behaved quite seductively around George. He found this amusing at first and planned to tell Ann about it—they had always prided themselves on sharing more of

A behavioral therapist invites George to do some role-playing: he acts the part of Laura, the woman who provokes him.

their lives than other couples. The night he planned to tell her they had a fight—George thinks it had to do with who would be using the car that evening, but he can't remember with certainty. He ended up not telling Ann about Laura, and he remembers feeling a moment of satisfaction in keeping this part of his life to himself. He and Ann made up shortly, but he "never got around to telling her" about Laura, who over the ensuing weeks made it progressively clearer to George that she wanted to sleep with him.

About two months after she had started working in his office, George played a noontime concert in a nearby park with a quintet made up of several coworkers. Laura and Ann showed up, though separately. When he saw them, he felt suddenly humiliated by his "artistic pretensions," as well as the ungainliness of his bassoon and the amateurishness of the group he was playing in—he adds that playing outdoors made him feel even more foolish. Subsequently he began making excuses not to practice, and he dropped out of one of his musical groups, claiming it wasn't serious enough. One night, having awakened at 4:00 A.M., he resolved to get his life in order: the next day he began suggesting to Ann that they start a family, and he asked a coworker to complain about Laura's performance to the office manager and see about getting her transferred. Within three weeks, Laura had been reassigned to an office on another floor and Ann had conceived.

But George didn't feel any happier,

and he began to grow frustrated. He started waking up regularly in the middle of the night and could not fall back to sleep. He feared Laura would discover he had engineered her transfer and considered taking her to lunch to "set the record straight"; he soon abandoned this idea, as it made him too nervous. He grew irritated at his wife's "sickliness"—she was by this time frequently nauseous—and he began taking different elevators to avoid running into her at the office. He threw himself into his music and decided that if he was going to make anything of himself as a musician he would need a new bassoon. But there was no extra money now that a baby was on the way, which aggravated his "testiness" with Ann.

He did run into Laura several times at work and was disconcerted because she continued to behave seductively around him, though now he wondered if she was mocking him. One night while making love to Ann he fantasized he was with Laura, and subsequently he has been unable to stop doing this whenever he and Ann make love.

George sought help three weeks after the fantasies commenced. He spoke of finding the "self-discipline" to be a good husband, father, and musician. He does not want to resent his child as an intrusion in his life, but fears that he might. And he wants to sleep through the night.

BEHAVIORAL THERAPY

You might not remember much from your college history class, but throughout life your mind remains far more absorbent—and tenacious—than it sometimes needs to be. And that can be a problem: illnesses like phobias, compulsions, and obsessive thinking, a behavioral therapist would submit, are some of the unhappier results of learning a lesson too well.

Say, for instance, you see a rat scurrying into the kitchen of a certain Italian restaurant. You might choose to avoid frequenting that restaurant for awhile, but then find yourself avoiding other Italian restaurants as well, until eventually you stop going out to eat at all, dreading the worst.

These kinds of associations, according

to behavioral therapists, are forged deep in a primitive portion of the brain, the hypothalamus, beyond the mediating forces of reason. The only effective treatment, these therapists maintain, is a program of relearning, one that extinguishes maladaptive physiological responses and establishes more adaptive ones. Behavioral therapists hold that little can be gained by seeking out hidden psychological motivations, when observable behavior is itself so revealing and so readily repaired.

"What I would first try to do," says psychologist Marcia Chambers, "is 'operationalize' George's complaints—get him to define them as specifically as possible. What does 'self-discipline' mean? Does 'testiness' mean he can't sit in a chair for more than three minutes, does he lose his temper more quickly?

"Once we had defined behaviors he would like to change, I would have him monitor what he's doing that's a problem. In behavioral therapy, everything is measurable and you can see change. It's important for the person to see the change visually, so clients chart their progress on lots of different kinds of graphs and three-by-five cards.

"In George's case, probably the easiest behavior to monitor would be sleep—what time he wakes up, and either how many times he wakes up in the middle of the night or how long those times were.

"Sometimes just monitoring a behavior makes it drop out—it just stops happening. For instance, one of the best ways to lose weight is to write down everything you eat."

Once the problem behaviors had been pinned down and George was plotting their frequency, says Chambers, "I'd teach him a relaxation technique, because you can use that in so many different ways. There's tensing and loosening of muscles, deep breathing, and something called autogenic relaxation—thinking about individual muscles and relaxing them, from ankles to scalp.

"Often when we do muscle relaxation, people's minds will still race, and you have to teach them to relax their minds. I have them imagine a very peaceful scene—the beach or the mountains—

For his cognitive therapist, George keeps a detailed journal of his emotional upsets and the thoughts that led to them.

using all their senses. Once they come out of their relaxed state, I have them talk about it: What did you see? What were you doing?—that kind of plants it in their head. And when I try to get them into it again I can use those descriptions.

"I would spend maybe four sessions teaching George relaxation. A very deep relaxation takes 30 to 35 minutes.

"Once he'd learned that, we could really use it for many different things. For instance, what I could do is once he's very relaxed, have him think about being in bed and having sex with Ann. And then see if he could do it again at home. You first have to train him to have positive thoughts about being with Ann; it gives him a good feeling, and you want to get as much 'positive' in him as possible. So if he starts thinking about Laura, he could signal to me—by closing his eyes tighter, or moving his elbow—and I'd say, 'Stop—think about Ann.' If he can't get into an 'Ann scene' or gets anxious in it, I could get him back to the neutral relaxing scene I taught him earlier, and then ease him back into thinking about Ann."

With practice, George would come to relax when he made love to Ann, and the deeper his relaxation, the higher his resistance to distress—to thoughts of Laura, specifically. As Chambers points out, "It's physiologically impossible to feel relaxed and anxious at the same time."

Chambers might also help free George from his anxious deadlock with Laura by giving him a few lessons in the art of conversation. Role reversal, for instance, with George playing Laura and Cham-

bers playing George, would teach him firsthand how different conversational gambits would be likely to affect Laura, and how he could keep their encounters comfortable. "She's going to be around for a long time," observes Chambers, "so George might as well learn how to deal with her."

George could even use Laura as a fulcrum for lifting his musical inclinations out of the doldrums. "Every time he talks to her, he could reward himself by putting aside $5 toward a new bassoon," Chambers suggests. "The reward should be something he could come up with himself. If he can't, I could help him come up with some. Also punishers: the classic one is to write a check to the organization you like least. So if he was supposed to do his relaxation five nights a week and he only did it three, he would have to write a $5 check to, say, the National Rifle Association every time he missed."

By the 16th or 17th week, Chambers would see if George could get by with less intensive therapy: fewer sessions a month, more modest rewards and punishments. She would teach him progressively faster relaxation methods ("I can do it to myself in a minute," she says). And she would encourage him to devise his own incentives, especially ones that he could work into his day-to-day routines, such as taking Ann to dinner after a week of faithfully practicing his bassoon. "My goal," she explains, "is to put myself out of business."

COGNITIVE THERAPY

It's a rainy day, and you're standing in a packed bus. Everyone is dripping on everyone else and pretending not to notice, when all of a sudden you feel the tip of someone's umbrella prodding you in the ankle. You'd like to turn around and glare at the slob, but you don't have enough room even to do that. As the bus lumbers on, the umbrella digs deeper, until finally, at the next stop, you shift away and turn to fix your assailant with your fiercest expression.

You find yourself glowering at a blind lady with a cane.

The next time something is driving you crazy, see if it's not you sitting in the driver's seat. Unfounded assumptions, interpretations, and suspicions, say practitioners of cognitive therapy, if carried to a self-defeating extreme, can make you miserable, anxious, or enraged. In fact, these therapists contend that whatever you feel, good or bad, is a reaction not to the world around you but to your thoughts about it—thoughts that may pass through your mind so rapidly, so automatically, you aren't even aware of them. That's why a cognitive therapist won't be satisfied if you come to him and say, "I'm depressed because I lost my job"; he'll want to know what importance you attach to being unemployed. Then he'll instruct you in how to keep your thoughts from declaring mutiny on your peace of mind, so that "I lost my job" doesn't lead you to conclude, "I should never have been born."

Each session, as George recounted the bad moments of the week before, cognitive therapist Dean Schuyler would mark off three columns on a lap-sized blackboard and jot down the critical events and the accompanying thoughts and feelings. He might, for example, record the noontime concert episode this way: *Laura and Ann at concert/"I'm a lousy musician and just fooling myself"/Humiliation.* He would also get George to track his responses in a journal between sessions, either at the time of, or as soon as possible after, an emotional upset.

Schuyler claims that careful monitoring would soon reveal how George's thoughts—thoughts he might not have even been aware of—were setting off feelings of distress. "The therapy," says Schuyler, "would then consist of disputing these thoughts," a process dramatized in the following exchange between Schuyler and George (who appeared via the writer).
S: *What is so bad about thinking of someone else while making love to your wife?*
G: *Your marriage is a hoax—this person [Ann] isn't who you wanted.*
S: *So what if your marriage is a hoax?*
G: *Well—then you're destroying someone's chances for happiness because—you bound her into this arrangement under false pretenses.*
S: *So what if you did that?*

George's family therapist gets a detailed history of the relationship between George and his wife, going back to the beginning.

G: *It's hard enough for each person in the world to be happy—why drag someone else down with your lies?*
S: *Okay—so all of this miserable stuff that you're doing has resulted from your having thought about someone else while making love to your wife?*
G: *No, no, but—*
S *(smiling a little):* *Certainly that seems to be what you've been saying.*
George's proxy ended up feeling like a melodramatic fool, but Schuyler points out that "cognitive therapy is mostly done in an atmosphere of extremely good humor, and in fact *that,* I think, has real benefit for a depressed or anxious individual, because what it does is really counteract his usual mood.

"But it's not for everyone. The people who do best in cognitive therapy are the kind who do best with psychoanalytic therapy: psychologically minded, generally bright, verbal individuals who are comfortable dealing with concepts and looking at themselves.

"For George to get relief from the symptoms presented, six months of once-a-week therapy is not an unreasonable expectation."

FAMILY THERAPY

Read enough literature on family therapy and you'll come to doubt that old saw, "You can't go home again." According to these therapists, it's more like, "You can never quite leave home at all." Despite your intentions, you might be scotching your chances for happiness by reenacting in your adult relations all the old attachments, compromises, resentments, and evasions you became so proficient in as you grew up.

There are plenty of different strains of family therapy available, and while some are less interested in childhood relations than others, most have in common the goal of getting the patient to gain insight into and control over how he affects the people around him and how they affect him. Family therapists believe that a patient can best master his problems when he takes a step back and sees himself as part of a whole system of forces acting on one another, like atoms in a complex molecule. Some therapists prefer to see all the members of a household, either alone or together; others will work with just one member.

"What I would do in the first session," says family therapist Joseph Lorio, "is talk to George a little bit about the presenting symptoms, maybe for as little as 10 or 15 minutes. Then I would get a history of the relationship between him and his wife, going back to when they first met, and how the relationship developed, what the big events in it were, and how they each reacted to those events. I would be looking for any changes in the relationship's tone that could have been significant as a trigger for stirring up the anxieties that he has.

"The other thing I would try to do the first session is get a more detailed picture of George's 'extended family'—the family that he comes from." For every patient, Lorio sketches out a three-generation family tree: each family member is described by character traits, accomplishments, responsibilities, emotional, social, and physical impairments, age at death, and cause of death. Before each session, Lorio tacks the chart to the wall so that he and the patient can refer to it. "You may not be able to trace the origin of the problem directly to the extended family," says Lorio, "but almost always you can trace to the extended family the way the person reacts to the difficulty. I always keep that in the background—always a context for what's happening here and now."

Lorio would also try to involve Ann in the therapy as soon as possible. "I may see George alone the first two times and then try to get his wife in by the third session. I might then spend one session just with her, or see the two of them together, then see her individually, then go back to seeing them together—just depends on what the problem is and how they're dealing with it."

Once Ann had come in, Lorio would sketch out her family tree as well. "George's interest in another woman—his 'passing fancy'—this could very well be a reaction to some emotional preoccupation of his wife's that he perceived, perhaps not even consciously, such as with her pregnancy. If you asked him, 'Are you aware that your wife has distanced from you?' he might say no. But if you took a history of what's going on in his wife's family right now, you might find that her mother was just diagnosed with a serious disease like breast cancer, so she's reacting to that, and he's reacting to her reaction, and he's not even aware of that; he ascribes [his fantasies about Laura] to something inside himself, some inadequacy in him as a man—that he's not ready to be married or have kids. Clearly what's happening is he's just at an anxious phase right now with his wife. And a child represents a new level of responsibility, which can evoke anxiety and other symptoms, physical and emotional.

"Usually just talking about these problems with the two of them would take a lot of the steam out of the anxiety, calm things greatly. You can let them know that when families are in this kind of situation, her distancing from him is pretty typical. And when he understands what's going on between him and his wife, he can understand that what he's reacting to is her distancing, and that what he needs to do is be more available to her emotionally.

"The key thing is to change from being an emotional reactor to a better observer. The better you can observe and learn about the interplay between self and relationships, the less you react emotionally to it and the faster you make progress.

"Oftentimes people like him with just six sessions feel less anxious, calmer, better in control of their lives. But he could be in therapy a year or two, or even longer, if I could get him to bridge his cur-

Once faced squarely, his psychoanalyst believes, George's painful emotions and memories will lose their power to torment him.

rent situation to his extended family. For instance, the history mentions his mother being behind his practicing. I would want to explore some of that. It's not unusual for many creative and artistic people to have mothers who are a real strong influence and generator of creativity. And the fact that his mother died—I would want to know how he reacted to that.

"One of the things George needs to do eventually is develop a closer, more emotionally substantial relationship with his mother's siblings, and through that, continue to learn about this person who was his mother—who she was, how she got to be who she was, the family that influenced her and therefore influenced him. The same is true for his father and his father's family. This is one of the best ways for him to understand who he is and how he got to be who he is.

"That's a more long-term effort. Every person who ends up with a long-term success at some point has to do something like that with his or her own family.

"The most important part of the therapy doesn't happen here in my office," says Lorio. "It happens between sessions, between the patient and whoever is important to him. The relationship with the therapist is not important; it's almost like the therapist is a kind of consultant. Sessions here are sort of like coaching, or checking up on how they're doing with their relationships."

PSYCHODYNAMIC THERAPY

If you've never given it much thought, your idea of a session with a psychiatrist might resemble a scene between Elizabeth Taylor and Montgomery Clift in *Suddenly Last Summer:* the doctor doggedly scrutinizing the feelings and memories of the patient, who reacts with reticence, horror, and relief in turn. Lots of pacing and twisting of handkerchiefs.

Welcome to psychodynamic therapy, Hollywood style.

It is not, of course, always dramatic, or even entertaining. In psychoanalysis, the oldest form, it can get tedious. But with its emphasis on emotions, especially those the patient takes pains to conceal or suppress, it can be wearing.

On the surface, little is required of the patient—no behaviors to practice, lists to compile, relatives to visit. Psychodynamic therapists maintain that intellectualizing projects like these only encourage patients to block out unconscious feeling, and blocking out feeling is what caused the symptoms in the first place. Once faced squarely, the thinking goes, painful emotions and memories will lose their power to torment the patient, and he will be free to abandon neurotic, defensive behavior.

To show what George might have to face, psychoanalyst Robert Winer mulled over the case history and came up with the following impressions.

"I'm struck by the kind of work George does, to begin with—he manages other people's development, but he's having some problem managing his own. It's sort of like that cliche, 'Those who can, do; those who can't, teach.' Then there's his complaint of 'testiness'—the more I thought about that word, the more it struck me that that's not a word that somebody would use about himself. People call *other* people testy, but since he's saying it about himself, I'd think he was reporting someone else's complaint about himself. And that goes along with some other things in the history—how quickly he accepts his sister's view that he wasn't a very good bassoon player. And his childhood was 'as happy as anyone's'—*that* struck me as an odd statement; it implies some oversensitivity to other people's opinions, something in his early family life about keeping up with the Joneses.

"He says his parents were 'loving and fair.' Well, 'fair' isn't a word a person normally uses to describe his parents, unless fairness was some kind of an issue. It may be that the parents were overly fair, so that all the normal sibling rivalry and aggression got buried by the mother insisting that 'no one should get angry and you're both to be treated fairly.'

"It sounded to me like the mother was the one who ran the home. His father says, 'This is going to disappoint your mother,' as if he can't stand up for himself or say, 'You're making me angry.' And that makes me think of George having as a model a father who is frightened of assertion, who to a degree hides behind his wife's skirts, and has failed to make claims for himself on life. He tells George to major in something practical 'because he could always do music at night'—well, the 'because' struck me as oddly evasive. You wouldn't major in something practical *because* you could do music at night but because you need to earn a living.

"And George shrugs his shoulders and says, 'Yeah, I can always do music at night.' He sort of ambles along through life; he doesn't reach out very far or for very much. Like the way he meets his wife: there he is in the cafeteria, and lo and behold, there she is, so he decides to marry her. You wouldn't expect him to go outside to look for someone. You assume with someone like this that he's terribly afraid of what it means to be assertive or aggressive.

"George is in so many ways such a little guy—not sure of himself as a man, not feeling like a substantial, solid person, having to rely on other people's opinions of himself—and here he is, playing the bassoon, one of the largest instruments in the orchestra, as if it's something for him to compensate with. And his wife's pregnancy and sickness seem to be contributing to a further deterioration of his sense of manliness, so he decides to compensate by getting a bigger and better bassoon.

"This is getting me to think about the baby representing some further injury to his sense of masculinity. That's unusual—becoming a father usually helps men feel more phallicly potent, more full of

George's goal: to be a good husband, father, and musician. He does not want to feel that his new baby is an intrusion in his life.

themselves. In George's case, it's more as if Ann's growing and he's shrinking. The history says that he and Ann had always prided themselves on 'sharing more of their lives than other couples'—well, when people make this claim you don't necessarily feel that that's all that healthy. Some people 'share more of their lives' because of some fear of independence or having competing interests. There may be some excessive clinging in this relationship, which makes it very hard to tolerate the arrival of a third party, like a baby. You wonder if he feels some threat to his security with his wife.

"And the whole business of getting Laura transferred represents an overriding concern with his own security and a lack of a reasonable effort to be concerned with someone else's. Laura is nothing to get nervous about. She's being flirtatious, that's all. She's entitled to that in life. He can always say no. It's not as if she's being flirtatious in the face of his saying, 'Look, I'm a married man, we're not going to have anything happen.' I did think getting her transferred was a strikingly aggressive act for him—though again, it's passively done; like his father, he won't do it himself, he gets someone else to do it.

"Then he starts wondering if she's mocking him. Now that's interesting. I presume she's *not* mocking him. I don't know for certain, but that struck me as a projection—displacing his own contemptuousness, which he can't own up to, onto her. And if he feels contempt toward her, that might in turn be a defense against feeling vulnerable to her, maybe because she's arousing him. It may be that he doesn't feel safe letting a woman arouse him, and I wonder if his wife arouses him, or if he's kept their sexual life at a more dependent, less erotic level.

"And now he becomes obsessed with Laura. Usually obsessions are a way of controlling aggression. You wonder how much anger toward his wife about the pregnancy is tied up in that. And men can experience intercourse with a pregnant wife as an attack on the baby, if they're already feeling aggression toward it, so maybe the obsessive thoughts about Laura are some way of blocking out that aggression.

"He does say that he doesn't want to resent the child as an intrusion, so he has some capacity for self-awareness. And he takes the initiative to seek help, which leads me to think that he also has the capacity to make more active decisions. It may be that just seeing him through the end of the pregnancy will be enough to help him make some kind of adjustment around the baby. But if his goal is to realize himself more fully as a man, given that he's been ducking that all his life," concludes Winer, "you're talking about analysis: four or five sessions a week, probably for several years."

If you can't decide which therapy suits you best, try the therapist your doctor or friend recommends; provided he's experienced and ethical, he won't waste your time if his treatment can't do you any good. And if you're in serious trouble— if you're hallucinating, for instance, or can't stop crying—most any psychiatrist can help by prescribing some standard medication, like lithium, Thorazine, or Elavil.

Drugs like these probably constitute the most solid scientific advance in the treatment of mental illness. But if the proliferation of "talking therapies" suggests a more spotty history of scientific inquiry, it also speaks to our capacity for resourcefulness in the face of anguish and sorrow. ⬛

Perry Turner, a copy editor at Science 86, *is now working on a novel in which George is kidnapped by four different bands of gypsies.*

*The demand for therapy
has increased 400 percent
in three decades.
Does it work?*

TESTING THE TALKING CURE

BY NIKKI MEREDITH
ILLUSTRATIONS BY STEVE GUARNACCIA

PSYCHOTHERAPY HAS BECOME such an established accessory to contemporary American life it's easy to forget that it was not always so. As recently as 1957 only 13 percent of the population had sought some kind of psychological counseling in their lifetimes. That number is now almost 30 percent—or 80 million people—at a cost of over $4 billion annually.

This increase signifies a substantial change in popular attitudes toward psychotherapy, once considered the exclusive province of the very rich and the very disturbed. The new class of mental health patients has been created in part by the well-documented *Sturm und Drang* of social change, such as the breakdown of families, and in part by a standard of living free enough from physical hardship to accommodate a quest for emotional fulfillment. Thus, the great majority of those seeing therapists these days are not afflicted with severe and intractable mental illness but are more likely to suffer from problems associated with "normal" living.

Nonetheless, most who find their way into a therapist's office are truly unhappy, beleaguered by depression, anxiety, phobias, or some other distress from the long list besetting the human race. The variety of people and maladies for which they seek relief has spawned a profusion of new treatment techniques. There are more than 250 brands of therapy now on the market, including not only offshoots of traditional individual, group, and family therapies but a multitude of others. The labels suggest that it is possible to convert almost any activity into therapy: work therapy, jogging therapy, breathing therapy, pleasant experiences therapy, soap opera therapy, and, for those not interested in such here-and-now pursuits, past-lives therapy.

While each treatment form has its champions, the therapies considered most credible by professionals are supported by well-developed theoretical formulations and have some sort of traditional pedigree. Freudian psychoanalysis, the antecedent of them all, is the best known but, in fact, one of the least practiced. The analyst and his couch, so often parodied in the media, is in reality accessible only to those sufficiently healthy to withstand the reliving and "working through" of early and often painful stages of their lives and sufficiently wealthy to pay for four or five sessions a week for the two to 15 years that it might take.

Most conventional therapies fall into two classes: psychodynamic—the most widely dispensed form of treatment—and behavioral. Psychodynamic therapies, though much less intense than psychoanalysis, are based on the same principles and therefore delve into such things as unconscious motivation. Behavioral therapies are derived from learning theory and focus on retraining behavior. Instead of looking for hidden causes, behaviorists guide their patients in changing their everyday actions and thoughts.

In recent years, abbreviated versions of the major therapies have gained in popularity. Brief therapy ranges from a single session to as many as 20, but generally the goal is to provide support, minimize weaknesses, and reinforce psychological defenses—with a minimum expenditure of time and money. (One of the first practitioners of brief therapy was Freud. Composer Gustav Mahler, suffering from impotence with his wife,

All 250 therapies treat the one syndrome shared by all patients: demoralization.

was treated successfully by Freud in a single four-hour session.)

The use of drugs has also increased in recent years, winning adherents among both psychodynamic and behavioral practitioners. There is mounting evidence that some drugs are useful in treating particular kinds of depression and anxieties and especially when used in conjunction with therapy.

As would be expected, the profusion of patients and therapies has been accompanied by a growth in the supply of mental health professionals—in 1975 there were 60,000 therapists in the United States; currently there are 160,000—and also an increase in the number of disciplines they represent. Psychiatrists, once the dominant force in the field, now must share clients with an ever-growing stock of psychologists, social workers, and a mix of other practitioners such as psychiatric nurses and clergymen. In fact, the largest portion of the nation's therapy is now practiced by nonpsychiatrists, who charge significantly less for their services: the median cost for psychiatric professionals in private practice is $90 a session; psychologists take in an average of $65; and the going rate for social workers, who outnumber psychiatrists by almost two to one, is $50.

The competition for patients and for insurance reimbursement has sparked fierce territorial disputes between professional organizations, each claiming its members have unique, superior attributes. In fact, varied as their training may be, the distinctions in actual practice are not as great as the acrimony would suggest. The differences in therapists' methods are determined more by their personalities and therapeutic ideologies than by their academic backgrounds. One bona fide difference is between those licensed to prescribe drugs—namely psychiatrists, who are physicians—and those who can't. Some nonmedical therapists circumvent this limitation by associating with a psychiatrist who will prescribe for their patients.

The unfettered growth of the psychotherapeutic enterprise faced its first serious challenge in the late 1970s when the Carter administration and Congress con-

A primer on the professionals

Your favorite confidante, Aunt Martha, has left town. You need someone to talk to and have decided that perhaps it would be best to see a professional. Which one should you choose? All the titles sound the same. But basically they fall into two categories: type of training and type of therapy used. The terms **therapist** and **psychotherapist** really don't tell you anything about qualifications or method of therapy. Psychiatrist, psychologist, clinical social worker, psychiatric nurse, and counselor are terms that explain how the person was trained and what their focus is. Psychoanalyst, behavioral therapist, group therapist, and any other kind of therapist are descriptive titles that tell what kind of therapy or approach will be used. Any professional can receive training in any type of therapy.

Psychiatrist is probably the term heard most often. A psychiatrist is a medical doctor who has done a residency (three or four years) in psychiatry. Different from psychology, psychiatry includes psychopharmacology (the mind and drugs), management of hospital patients, neurology, psychopathology, and psychotherapy. Because they are physicians, psychiatrists are the only mental health care providers allowed to prescribe drugs—an important difference if the patient has, for instance, manic-depression—but many other therapists work in conjunction with a psychiatrist who will prescribe for their patients. However, because most of their training is in hospitals, psychiatrists are familiar mainly with severe mental illness, not everyday problems such as mild anxiety and depression. Many psychiatrists, however, have gone on to receive additional training in psychotherapy.

Psychologists who specialize in psychotherapy and diagnosis are called clinical psychologists. They have Ph.D.'s in clinical psychology, which includes work in basic psychology, psychopathology, psychotherapy, and research. They have had at least a one-year internship in a mental health care setting and must pass a state examination. About 45,000 of the therapists practicing in the United States are psychologists. Says psychologist Sol Garfield, "Whereas psychiatrists, as physicians, are more inclined to view psychological disorders as diseases or illnesses, psychologists tend more to view them as learned patterns of behavior, or habit disorders."

Clinical social workers and **psychiatric social workers** handle a growing segment of the mental health care market. The former travels to a variety of sites, while the latter works in a traditional office. For accreditation they have to have at least a master's in social work and two years' experience in a clinical setting. Most states require an examination. Social workers emphasize seeing the patient as a part of her environment.

Although all registered nurses can work in a psychiatric setting, some have continued their schooling and received a master's or doctorate in psychiatric nursing. These **psychiatric nurse specialists** can be certified by the American Nursing Association in either adult or child and adolescent psychiatric nursing. The only mental health specialists besides psychiatrists who have a medical background, their approach is to see body and mind as a whole.

Any of these professionals can be skilled in one or many of the few hundred therapies available.

The oldest type of psychotherapy is psychoanalysis. **Psychoanalysts** have been trained at one of many institutes throughout the United States and Europe. Although most are psychiatrists, psychoanalysts can be psychiatric nurse specialists, clinical social workers, or psychologists.

There are also marriage and family therapists (specialists solely in that therapy), mental health counselors, pastoral counselors, and others who have all been well trained, sometimes with the same course work. With more than 160,000 qualified therapists in the United States alone, there is fierce competition among the professionals. Since fees can vary by more than $50 a session, insurance coverage is the focus of the war over patients. Each type of therapist tries to get a state license or accreditation, often necessary for coverage. Qualification for licensing and accreditation differs from state to state, as does insurance coverage.

Everyone adds something different to the profession. As Daniel Goleman, psychologist and behavioral science writer for the *New York Times*, says, "All but the most adamant of psychotherapists will acknowledge that the competence of a given therapist depends more on his training, experience and innate ability than on his academic credentials or license."

Where to go from here? Call local mental health clinics, ask friends for recommendations, or call local professional associations. Relationships with therapists are intimate. If they are not willing to discuss their methods and fees in advance, call someone else. They should help, not confuse. Don't be afraid to ask questions. Aunt Martha would be proud. —*Heléne Ross*

---

sidered instituting national health insurance and needed to decide what kinds of therapy to include. With Reagan's election, the prospect of national health insurance with or without psychiatric benefits faded along with the government's interest in regulation, but the continued rise in health costs has had its own regulatory effect.

Psychotherapy has been one of the fastest growing segments of total health costs, and therefore has been targeted for substantial cutbacks from the insurance industry. Many companies have limited expenditures by requiring practitioners to justify extended treatment to a panel of professionals and by putting arbitrary ceilings on benefits. Federal employees, for example, once had excellent Blue Cross mental health coverage that paid 80 percent of any sort of treatment up to $50,000. Now their best Blue Cross coverage pays 80 percent of only 50 visits a year.

There is an assumption that mental health services are more vulnerable to cutbacks than other medical services because there is less scientific evidence to support them. "People in science would like to believe evidence drives public policy, but it doesn't always," says Gerald Klerman, former administrator of the federal Alcohol, Drug Abuse, and Mental Health Administration. One example of this is the fate of prison therapy programs. Conventional wisdom has it that psychological rehabilitation efforts in some prisons were discontinued because they didn't work. However, it appears that no treatment program for adult offenders had been fairly tested, according to the National Academy of Sciences.

While science may not drive public policy, policy seems to be driving science. For as unwelcome as mental health cutbacks and the prospect of government regulation have been to practitioners, both have encouraged research. There are signs that the enormous gap between treatment and scientific study has begun to narrow. "We now have the methodology to conduct credible psychotherapy studies," says John Docherty, former director of research at the National Institute for Mental Health. "From a research standpoint, the field is the healthiest it's ever been."

The erratic history of systematic research got off to an explosive start in 1952 when British psychologist Hans J. Eysenck published a review comparing the improvement rates of a group of "untreated" neurotics with the improvement rates of groups that had been treated with psychoanalytic or eclectic (mixed treatment) psychotherapy. He reported that 72 percent of the "untreated" group improved, while only 64 percent of the group treated by eclectic therapy and 44 percent of the psychoanalytic patients got better.

At the time, psychoanalysts were quite popular and were cranking out reports of spectacular successes. Eysenck's study, though widely criticized, served to challenge this long-enjoyed complacency, and systematic research became a serious pursuit.

Despite the subsequent invalidation of Eysenck's work, many of the points for which he was criticized—issues of bias and methodology—have continued to weaken therapy research. He was accused of selecting only studies that would prove his point and of comparing studies in which the key variables were too disparate. For example, there was no way of determining if the illnesses of the treated and untreated groups were comparable in severity. Moreover, the studies Eysenck compared did not use a uniform definition of improvement. Critics also pointed out that many of the "untreated groups" were cared for by general practitioners and thus actually received some therapy, i.e., attention, reassurance, and suggestion. (To this day, the problem of setting up a placebo-free study baffles researchers.)

The pattern established by Eysenck and his critics continued for the next few decades. Every study was followed by an attack on the findings and research methodology, which was then followed by another study with different findings, which was also attacked, and so on. The result was a collection of studies whose findings canceled each other out.

The impasse was broken in 1980, when psychologists Mary Lee Smith, Gene Glass, and Thomas Miller published the results of an analysis of 475 studies revealing that the average patient who received therapy was better off at the end of treatment than were 80 to 85 percent of comparable patients who did not receive such treatment. Having considered only studies meeting minimum standards of controlled trial research—those including a control group—the researchers concluded: "Psychotherapy benefits people of all ages as reliably as schooling educates them, medicine cures them, or business turns a profit."

Although the Smith study is considered the most comprehensive and bias-free ever done, it created an impasse of its own. All the therapies examined, psychodynamic or behavioral, got comparable results for the treatment of all disorders. This despite dramatic differences in philosophy and procedure.

While upsetting the proponents of various therapies, the findings confirmed the ideas of those in the field who believe that it is the general rather than the specific aspects of therapy that produce change. Psychiatrist Jerome Frank, one of the most respected spokesmen for this point of view, says that all therapies share features that are effective at treating a syndrome shared by all patients: demoralization. Regardless of their complaints, he says, patients feel helpless, unable to cope, depressed, guilty, and worthless.

The elements contained in every therapy that are effective in treating this condition, says Frank, include a special relationship in which the therapist expresses concern and engenders trust; a special setting—the therapist's office—that is seen as a sanctuary; and a conceptual framework that, in addition to providing an explanation for the patient's behavior, offers hope that the treatment will relieve the suffering. And all therapies produce a degree of emotional arousal and an increase in patients' awareness of alternatives.

From all indications, most practitioners are not very flexible. Researchers have found that few therapists, regardless of their treatment philosophies, vary their techniques to meet the needs of individual patients. But it may be that specific treatments are crucial. "A major theme of research now is the development of specificity," says Docherty. "It is the increasing focus on specific factors that is leading to definitive answers."

The National Institute of Mental Health is now funding several projects that seek to compare specific treatments for specific disorders. Although the results are not yet available, one of the most ambitious is a rigorously controlled study on the treatment of depression. The study compares the success rates of cognitive therapy and interpersonal therapy, both of which have done quite well in preliminary trials in the treatment of depression, a malady that afflicts more than eight million adults annually. Cognitive therapy teaches patients to modify thoughts that produce feelings of unworthiness, frustration, and hopelessness. Interpersonal therapy, on the other hand, uses more traditional techniques and focuses on relationships and social functioning. The improvement rates of the two therapies will be compared to a group receiving antidepressant drugs.

Identical trials are being conducted at three research sites—University of Oklahoma, University of Pittsburgh, and George Washington University—thus getting a much larger sample of patients than is generally feasible and also providing simultaneous replication.

Researchers in this collaborative study have gone to great lengths to standardize treatment because in many earlier studies it has been almost impossible to define exactly what therapy was administered. Even among therapists within the

More than 250 brands of therapy are marketed today. Their names suggest that it is possible to convert almost any activity into therapy.

The case of the moody car salesman

You can't talk about a cure in psychotherapy until you've defined what the illness is. To make that process easier, the American Psychiatric Association publishes a field guide of sorts called *Diagnostic and Statistical Manual,* Third Edition. *DSM-III* attempts to describe every mental illness in terms so unequivocal, so objective, that any two therapists, regardless of which forms of treatment they dispense, will, after examining a given patient, arrive at exactly the same diagnosis. To get a feel for how a therapist might use the *DSM-III,* first consider this case history, from an APA teaching guide called *DSM-III Case Book.*

A 29-year-old car salesman was referred for evaluation by his current girl friend, a psychiatric nurse, who suspected he had a mood disorder, even though the patient was reluctant to admit that he was a "moody" person. Since the age of 14 he has experienced repeated alternating cycles that he terms "good times and bad times." During a "bad" period, usually lasting four to seven days, he sleeps 10 to 14 hours daily, lacks energy, confidence, and motivation—"just vegetating," as he puts it. Then he abruptly shifts, characteristically upon waking up in the morning, to a three- to four-day stretch of overconfidence, heightened social awareness, promiscuity, and sharpened thinking—"Things would flash in my mind." Occasionally the "good" periods last seven to 10 days, but culminate in irritable and hostile outbursts, which often herald the transition back to another period of "bad" days.

In school, A's and B's alternated with C's and D's. As a car salesman his performance has also been uneven; even on "good days" he is sometimes perilously argumentative with customers and loses sales that appeared sure. Although considered a charming man in many social circles, he alienates friends when he is hostile and irritable.

DSM-III-style diagnosis is largely a matter of excluding illnesses that don't apply and seeing what's left. So the therapist evaluating the car salesman would begin by asking himself, Does the patient suffer from some organic illness that could be causing these symptoms? If the answer were yes, the diagnosis might be primary degenerative dementia with depressive features (*DSM-III* diagnosis number 290.13) or organic affective syndrome (number 293.83). Since there's nothing in the history to in- dicate a physical illness, the therapist would go on to ask, Does he have any psychotic symptoms, like hallucinations? That might indicate schizophrenia with a superimposed atypical mood disorder. Because the salesman seems untroubled by visions or delusions, the therapist might next wonder if the problem is manic-depression. The trouble with that diagnosis, according to *DSM-III,* is that the patient must be seriously depressed or manic for at least two weeks, or manic enough to be hospitalized—ruling out the salesman. Well then, the therapist might ask himself, how long has this moodiness been going on? If it's less than two years, he could have adjustment disorder with depressed mood (number 309.00). But the salesman has been riding an emotional roller coaster for a good 15 years, which leaves two possible diagnoses. One is dysthymic disorder, a low-grade depression, but patients with that condition never experience the bursts of energy the salesman feels. So the diagnosis ends up number 301.13—cyclothymic disorder, the APA's terminology for chronic moodiness.

There's no question that the diagnoses in *DSM-III* sound wonderfully—sometimes comically—precise. But are they really objective? Like earlier editions, *DSM-III* never manages to escape accusations of ideological bias. For instance, the recent proposed addition of "self-defeating personality disorder," a diagnosis employed by Freud and his followers, rankled feminists, who feared that it was conceived with repeatedly battered women in mind—a "blame-the-victim" approach not justified by research on domestic violence.

Even if he harbors no such reservations, a therapist turning to *DSM-III* for help will only get so far: the book won't tell him what caused the problem or how to fix it. Though a precise diagnosis would seem to suggest an equally precise treatment, experienced therapists find that patients who are really motivated to change will often improve regardless of the form of treatment they receive. According to Robert Winer of the Washington Psychoanalytic Institute, "Patients well suited for the rigors of daily psychoanalysis can make better-than-average use of once-a-week therapy." And Dean Schuyler, a consultant at Sheppard and Enoch Pratt Hospital in Baltimore, says the best candidates for his brand of treatment—cognitive therapy—are those who would be considered well suited for psychoanalysis.
—*Perry Turner*

---

same school there is so much variability in the methods used that it is often said there are as many therapies as there are therapists. To overcome this, professional therapists hired for the project were trained to use the same methods—a process that is now more consistent because of the recent development of treatment manuals—and then monitored by supervisors. Further, each therapy session was recorded so it would be possible to analyze the extent to which the actual therapy conformed to the program.

Measuring outcome has been another dilemma. Many studies use very different measures of treatment success—ranging from the objective, such as rehospitalization, to the subjective, such as the patient's sense of well-being. The collabo- rative study uses a much more complex and sophisticated system. Multiple tests measuring a variety of factors such as symptoms and social functioning are completed at various junctures before, during, and after treatment. These evaluations are done by the patients themselves, "significant others," therapists, and independent evaluators who are blind to the type of therapy administered.

Collaborative study researchers are also able to take advantage of a completely overhauled and more standardized diagnostic system, though new evidence suggests that other patient variables, such as personality type, may be more important than diagnosis in predicting the success of particular thera- pies. In preliminary research, Ann Simmons and George Murphy of Washington University in St. Louis used a test called the Rosenbaum Learned Resourcefulness Scale to measure patients' preferred methods of coping. They have had success in using the results to identify which patients will be responsive to cognitive therapy and which will be responsive to drugs.

Some researchers, however, believe that the clinical trial method—even when exhaustive attempts are made at specification and standardization—miss crucial information about the individual characteristics of each patient as well as the nature of the therapist-patient relationship.

John Curtis and George Silberschatz

Therapy offers
the hope that we
don't have
to be crazy,
and that may be
invaluable.

are codirectors of another research project funded by NIMH designed to overcome the limitations of the clinical trial method. Their work, called process research, involves examining, in minute detail, what happens in each session during the course of a subject's therapy. "Going into the session and examining what happens in this detail is like basic cellular research in medicine, where people might spend years studying cells, the nature of cells, and the interaction of cells," says Silberschatz.

Curtis and Silberschatz are testing the effectiveness of a form of psychodynamic therapy based on a theory called control mastery. Oversimplified, control mastery means that the patient defines goals and is taught to invalidate beliefs that stop him or her from achieving those goals.

Four years into the five-year study Curtis and Silberschatz have found a high correlation between patient progress and the appropriateness of the therapists' interpretations. In tracking this, however, they have also witnessed enormous fluctuations in the behavior of therapists, all of whom are highly experienced. "Therapists will be on, then they'll be off, they'll be up and they'll be down," says Silberschatz. "We've seen bad therapies where the patient was not doing well and then, almost by accident, the therapist suddenly got on the right course and the patient got better. Then the therapist reverted to the old pattern and the patient got worse."

Silberschatz and Curtis are hopeful that the results of their study will help therapists become more consistent. "If we continue to show this high correlation over many, many cases," says Silberschatz, "it has enormous implications for training."

While none of the current research has yet resulted in major breakthroughs and there is still little hard evidence, the body of work is beginning to reveal nuggets of information that may one day lead to bigger answers. One of the questions remaining, however, is the extent to which these answers will be listened to by practitioners. In 1984, psychologists R. Bruce Sloane and Fred R. Staples

wrote, "There is little evidence that any findings of any outcome study have had much influence on the *practice* of psychotherapy...."

Dianna Hartley, a researcher at the University of California Medical Center in San Francisco, believes that this inattention to research is in part due to the limited applicability of what findings there have been, even when they are positive. "If a study is published which says out of a sample of 100, 50 patients got analytic therapy, 50 got behavior therapy, and 70 percent of the patients got better, that doesn't really tell me much about the patient I'm seeing at three o'clock. The results haven't been broken down in a way that's useful to clinicians dealing with individual patients."

The work will eventually alter the practice of psychotherapy, Docherty argues. "There really has been a revolution in psychotherapeutic research," he says, "in its methods and its power to determine clinically relevant findings. But it takes a long time for findings to penetrate practice; that's true for medicine as well."

In the meantime, many of the people who are treated do not get better, and one of the criticisms leveled at psychotherapists is that they continue to dispense treatment in the absence of improvement. But historically, medicine has always had the problem of caring for people who have diseases for which there is no known cure.

And as it is most often used in this country, psychotherapy is a last resort. Contrary to myths, therapy is not the first choice of individuals in trouble but usually the last, after they have tried everything else. The average time lapse between the first symptoms of alcoholism and seeking help is five years; for those with panic attacks, 12 years. People suffer with anxiety and depression anywhere from six months to two years before seeking help. It is perhaps the way in which psychotherapy represents a last chance that is its most important contribution. To borrow Jerome Frank's concept, the very existence of therapy may play an important role in treating the demoralization of society. Perhaps we can never evaluate the symbolic role therapy plays, but the belief that we don't have to be depressed or anxious or crazy, the hope that there is always a way out, may be invaluable. In their summary of the contribution therapy makes to people's lives, researchers Smith, Glass, and Miller conclude: "Of the levers that can move society forward, psychotherapy is only one. It may not educate so well as schools; it may not produce goods and services so well as management science; it may not cure illnesses so well as medicine; but it reaches a part of life that nothing else touches so well." ▪

Nikki Meredith is a former psychiatric social worker who now makes her living as a free-lance writer.

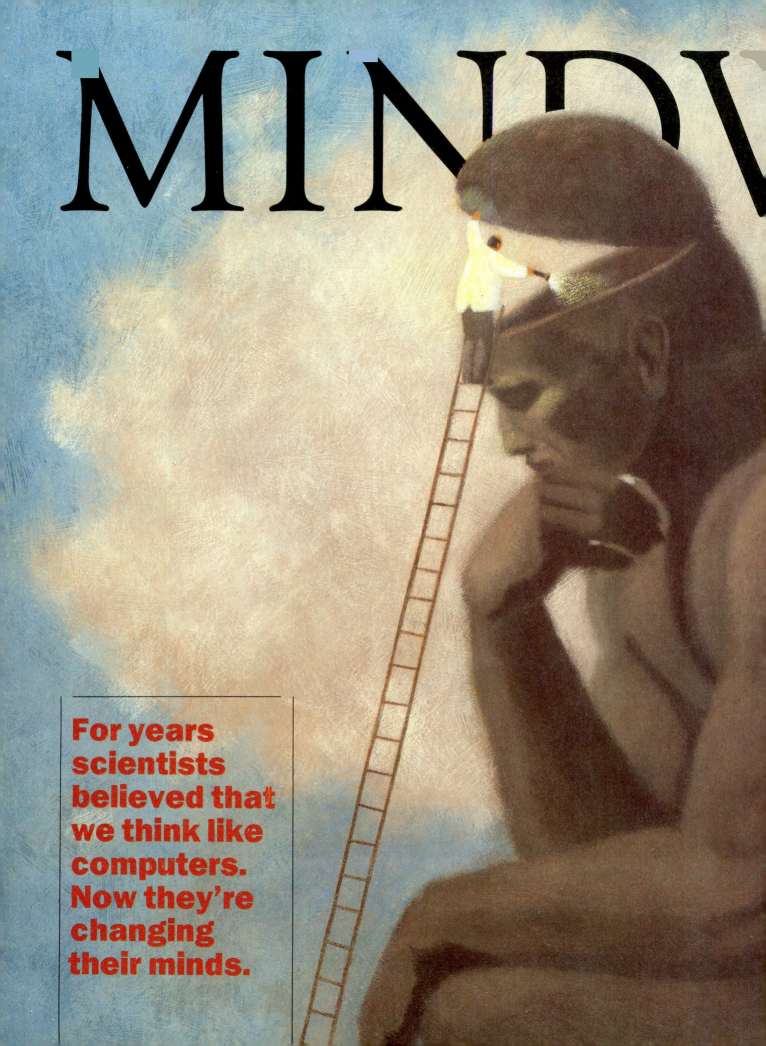

MIND

For years
scientists
believed that
we think like
computers.
Now they're
changing
their minds.

ORKS

BY WILLIAM F. ALLMAN

TERRY SEJNOWSKI, wearing the face of a proud father, smiles over the noise. A tape recorder is cradled in his lap, wailing. *Naaaaeeeemmooo-ch-ch-ch-ooooeeeenananaaaahhh*, the high-pitched voice drones, filling the room with a crazed mantra of chants, coos, and clicks. "What we're hearing is the first training session," Sejnowski shouts above the cacophony. "It's basically producing random sounds." The voice belongs to NETtalk, a machine Sejnowski created, a machine that is learning to read aloud.

After a minute or so the wail begins to take on order, the long vowel sounds broken up into smaller bits by consonants, a sound not unlike what you might hear in a nursery: *Mamamammamaamamaa-mamamamamamamama*. "The first thing it discovers is the distinction between vowels and consonants," says Sejnowski. "But it doesn't know which is which.

ROB COLVIN

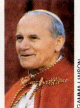

Which of these are bachelors? Everyone may answer differently, but if all the members of a category share common attributes, why do some members appear more representative than others?

Why is it so hard to understand names over the telephone? Partly because we comprehend only about 70 percent of the words we hear—our minds fill in the rest according to the context of the conversation. Since an unfamiliar name in a telephone message has no context, it usually has to be spelled out.

So it produces an 'ah' sound for vowels and an 'm' sound for consonants. It babbles."

The steady stream of chatter suddenly stops, then begins to sputter again in bits and pieces, a verbal hopscotch over the quiet. *Mop. Chi-ah-nee. Eee. Eee. Nib ah pon toe nee.* "Something really strange happens here," says Sejnowski. "Hear the difference? It's discovered the spaces between words. It now talks in bursts of sounds, pseudowords." Still incoherent, the voice rambles on, but the rhythm is somewhat familiar, short and long bursts of vowels packed in consonants, a crude, mechanical "Jabberwocky."

"What you just heard was the result of about an hour and a half of training," says Sejnowski. "What we'll hear next is what happened after we left it on overnight, reading the same text over and over for 10 hours." Sejnowski beams as the voice from the box spills words into sentences; the timbre still mechanical, the inflection a little out of kilter, but the diction a few steps into the human side of the world. *I walk home with some friends from school*, says the machine. *I like to go to my grandmother's house. Because she gives us*—the machine pauses, struggling—*candy.*

In a world where computers control satellites, play expert chess, and help locate mineral deposits, creating a machine that reads aloud seems somewhat prosaic—especially since several such machines already exist. But to Sejnowski, the importance of his creation is not what it does but how it does it.

Sejnowski, a cognitive neuroscientist at Johns Hopkins University, is interested in minds, not machines. He is trying to figure out how our minds perform the enormously complicated tasks that most of us take for granted, like reading aloud. He feels, as do a growing number of psychologists, neuroscientists, linguists, computer scientists, physicists, and even philosophers, that the answers to many questions about thinking will not be found using the conventional model of how our minds work. That model was developed hand in hand with the digital computer and its symbolic, rule-based method of processing knowledge. Computers have produced many insights into how we think, but researchers like Sejnowski feel that on a fundamental level, the marriage of machine and mind is not a happy one.

Instead, Sejnowski and a handful of other researchers are experimenting with a new way of modeling the mind. And they are testing their ideas on machines that are inspired by the brain itself, machines that are made with many neuronlike units connected with each other to form vast networks.

The researchers get their inspiration from complex systems—systems that, while made of simple elements, display complicated behavior when those elements come together in large groups. "Suppose you put two molecules in a

box," says California Institute of Technology physicist John Hopfield. "Every once in a while they collide, and that's an exciting event in the life of someone studying molecular collisions. If we put 10 or even 1,000 more molecules in the box, all we get is more collisions.

"But if we put a billion billion molecules in the box, there's a new phenomenon—sound waves. There was nothing in the behavior of two molecules in the box, or 10 or 1,000 molecules, that would suggest to you that a billion billion molecules would be able to produce sound waves. Sound waves are a collective phenomenon."

Might such collective phenomena exist in our brains? And if so, might they be tied somehow to our cognitive abilities? Our neurons may be sluggish—they're roughly 100,000 times slower than a typical computer switch—but what our brains lack in speed they make up in hardware—or wetware, as it is sometimes called. A brain has from 10 billion to a trillion neurons in it, and each neuron is connected to anywhere from 1,000 to 100,000 other neurons. These individual neurons, not very bright by themselves, form a grand conspiracy to produce many of the phenomena of our minds.

Collective action is the power behind the new brain-inspired machines. Often called neural networks, they are quite unlike conventional digital computers. They have no central processors that operate on a few bits of data at a time; instead, the machines act on all the data at once, bringing the entire system to bear on a problem. The system's memory is spread throughout the network, not housed in a separate area as it is in digital computers. And the machines are not run by large programs that specify rules and operations to do a particular task but instead create their own pathways to solve problems.

The neural networks are so new that few have actually been built. Sejnowski's NETtalk is only simulated, existing in the digital gyrations of a conventional computer, the silicon wet nurse working frenetically to produce effects that would take NETtalk, if incarnate, only one-tenth the time to produce. But the networks have already piqued the practical interest of companies such as AT&T Bell Laboratories, whose scientists are hoping to use them to solve problems like finding the best ways to route wires on microchips and lay out telephone networks.

But most importantly, the researchers and their machines are beginning to change the way we are thinking about thinking. Rather than trying to break down cognitive processes into rules, operations, and tasks, the scientists are using their machines to study how our brains might generate rules, recognize patterns, and adapt. They are not so much trying to take minds apart as trying to put one together. They call themselves connectionists.

IS THE POPE A BACHELOR?

IN A ROOM at The Computer Museum in Boston rests a monument to the power of conventional computers. The monument, a computer built by MIT graduate students, plays an unbeatable game of tic-tac-toe. It's made out of Tinker Toys.

That a bunch of Tinker Toys can play a wicked game of tic-tac-toe illustrates the essence of computers. To be sure, many computers are sleek and shiny and fill a room with a quiet hum as they make blips of light dance across a video screen. They are incredibly fast, have vast memories, and work tirelessly. But the theory behind the workings of these computers is no different from that behind their Tinker Toy brethren. That's because the real power of computers lies in the fact that many tasks, from playing tic-tac-toe to preparing the company payroll to controlling the orbit of a satellite, can be reduced to a set of rules operating on a set of symbols. And if it's rules and symbols you're working with, then speed, a vast memory, and endurance count for a lot. In that game, nothing can compete with a computer. Not even brains.

But our brains can sometimes make the most powerful computers in the world look like bozos. We can, for example, recognize our mother. Right after she's had her hair cut. Or permed. We can understand the speech of a cabbie from Boston or a tugboat captain from Baton Rouge. We can recognize something as a chair, whether it's a Chippendale, a bean bag, or a throne. Wee con undrestin wrds efen wen theh ar misssppld. Or fill in the blanks when l t rs are missing. Many of us can recognize, right away, what this is:

And if we can't, once we are told there is a dog in the center we usually can't help seeing it whenever we look. When we hear "Shall I compare thee to a summer's day?" we don't expect a weather report. When someone asks us if we know Bob Thompson, who plays the trumpet in the school band and lives on Maple Street, we answer yes, but his name is Bill, not Bob, he plays the trombone, and he moved away six months ago. When given the sentences "The fly buzzed irritatingly on the window. The man picked up the newspaper," we know what is about to happen.

We take this kind of mental work for granted, but computers can't even come close to doing it. It's conceivable, however, that given the correct rules and enough data and time, a computer could eventually perform these tasks. The real question is whether our minds do it the way that a computer would do it.

Some computers, for example, can play chess better than 99.9 percent of the people on the planet. They do it, basically, by rapidly examining every potential move, one after another, and choosing the most effective one. This is no small feat, for in a typical chess game there are millions of possible moves to examine in order to look ahead just a couple of moves.

Human chess players, even the ones who can beat the computers, don't appear to do it that way. First of all, their neurons simply work too slowly. "We usually solve problems—such as recognizing a face—in a few hundred milliseconds," says connectionist David Rumelhart, a psychologist at the University of California at San Diego. "If the brain works serially, then it only has time for a few hundred serial steps. And it's laughable to try to write a serial program that does anything interesting in a few hundred steps."

But even if brains worked faster that might not be of much help, because humans are just simply awful at using rules. Given a problem, they seem to use almost everything but rules to try to solve it. In one study, for example, psychologists Daniel Kahneman of the University of British Columbia and Amos Tversky of Stanford University gave people the following biographical sketch of Russ: "Russ is 34 years old. He is intelligent but unimaginative, compulsive, and generally lifeless. In school, he was strong in mathematics but weak in social studies and humanities."

The psychologists then asked their subjects to rank which is more likely: that Russ is an accountant; that Russ plays jazz for a hobby; or that Russ is an accountant who plays jazz for a hobby. The subjects said it was most likely that Russ was an accountant, a reasonable assumption. But they also said that it was more likely that Russ was an accountant who played jazz than that he simply played jazz for a hobby. Since every member of the group of jazz-playing accountants is also a member of the group of jazz players, the probability that Russ is in the former group can't possibly be greater than the chance he is in the latter.

This example doesn't mean we are stupid, it just means that we aren't terribly good at using rules—in this case the rules of probability—to

Some examples represent a particular category better than others, as demonstrated by the incongruity of the "birds," above, perched on the windowsill.

What distinguishes the top group of symbols from the bottom group?

D O R Q U P G B J C S

V F A L T X E Z H N K

solve problems. Instead we bring other mental processes to bear on a problem, and in many cases we are tenacious about keeping them. Confronted with an unknown situation, we often depend more on cues and patterns—such as Russ's accountantlike personality—than rules to guide us in making a decision.

Pattern matching, of course, is in a broad sense based on rules. The rules of the traditional cognitive approach, however, involve manipulating symbols one after another. The question is whether our minds work with those kinds of rules, or whether we use rules of a different kind, rules that arise from the fact that our minds reside in our brains.

Consider the idea of categories. According to George Lakoff, a linguist at the University of California, Berkeley, putting things in categories is a major part of our thinking process. We categorize when we recognize, for example, that the animal coming toward us that looks a little like a lion, but has striped fur and no mane, is probably something we might want to avoid anyway. We also put things in a category when we think of processes: a rock can be thought of as belonging in the category of "things good for hammering with" not because it looks like a hammer but because it shares some qualities with hammers, such as hardness and wieldiness, that make it effective to crack open a walnut.

Lakoff, who has recently written a book called *Women, Fire, and Dangerous Things*—the title comes from an Australian aborigine category that contains all those items—says that the traditional ideas of categories don't really apply when we think. This traditional view defines categories as a collection of objects that share common properties. The traditionalists believe that since these objects and their properties have an independent existence, they can be represented by rules and symbols. This type of category would be very much at home in a computer.

But some categories, like colors, are not simply part of the outside world; they're also part of our brains. Our perception of the color red, for example, results from certain neurons in our brains firing at specific rates. "The reds we see form a category," says Lakoff, "primarily because we have brains that turn a wide range of wavelengths into a single concept."

Furthermore, if all the things in a category are there because they share common properties, he says, then it follows that no single item should be more representative of the category than another. One pencil, for example, should represent the category "pencil" as well as another. But that principle doesn't always seem to apply in our everyday experience.

Anthropologists Brent Berlin and Paul Kay took a collection of color samples, like the kind found in paint stores, and showed them to people around the world. When asked to point to

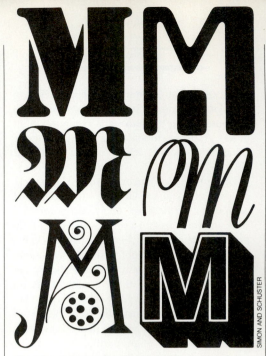

How do we know what these are? They don't fit a single template, but we recognize them all anyway. A computer can't.

the "best" example of the color red, all the subjects, no matter where they were from, picked the same sample. Even people whose language only loosely divides colors into "warm" and "cold" chose the same red as the best example of "warmness." If all the members of the red category share the same attributes, how is it that around the world one red seems more representative than others?

The answer, says Lakoff, lies in our brains. The best example of red is perceived when the neurons for red are firing at their maximum rate, while the neurons responsible for perceiving other colors are firing at lower rates. "Our brains not only determine our color categories," he says, "they also determine what the best examples of a color are."

Colors are not the only categories that have best examples. Psychologist Eleanor Rosch has shown that many of the categories we use contain one member that seems most representative. When we think of birds, for example, we tend to think of something that looks like a robin. Imagine the difference in your reading of the sentence "The birds perched on the windowsill," if the word *birds* were replaced with the word *turkeys*. Likewise, a four-door sedan somehow seems more representative of cars than a jeep does, and Hugh Hefner typifies bachelorhood a little better than Pope John Paul II.

These best examples are called prototypes. We use a prototype dog, for example, to judge all other four-legged—and sometimes three-legged—creatures. "I got into a big discussion with a colleague of mine," says James Anderson, a neuroscientist at Brown University, "about whether a dog with three legs was really a dog. He was arguing that it wasn't, which was amusing, because at the time there was a dog with three legs roaming around the campus.''

Working with a neural network, Anderson is demonstrating the power of using prototypes to make categories. In one experiment he slightly distorted a single pattern various ways, generating a group of related patterns that formed a "category." His neural network was then given the new patterns but not the prototype. When the network was later shown all the patterns, the prototype pattern was the most rapidly categorized—even though the machine had never seen it before. Anderson has had similar results with human subjects.

Using prototypes in a category may be why expert human chess players can overcome their speed disadvantages when playing against computers. When humans consider a chess move, they may recognize the pattern of pieces as similar to patterns seen in previous games and realize that this position may be favorable for gaining control of the center of the board. Of course, using pattern recognition isn't foolproof. Ask anybody who has put out a cigarette in a candy dish.

Lakoff suggests that the link between our body and our mind may influence other facets of our thinking as well. Just as some category members are more representative, some categories seem more privileged than others. According to classical theory, there should be nothing different about the categories "vehicle" and "car." Yet "car" seems to be the fundamental concept around which we organize information. "If I ask you to form a mental image of a car, you can probably do it," says Lakoff. "But if I ask you to form a mental image of a vehicle—not a car or a truck or a plane or a boat, but a vehicle in general, you probably could not do it. 'Car' is a human-sized, basic-level category that fits our abilities to form mental images, manipulate objects with our bodies, and communicate efficiently.''

We tend to use these basic levels when we talk. "We operate at a 'natural' level of complexity," says Anderson. "We say in normal speech, 'Look at that bird on the lawn,' as opposed to 'Look at that organism on the flat area of Kentucky bluegrass, clover, and creeping red fescue.' "

While Lakoff welcomes the connectionists' efforts to bring the brain back into the study of the mind, he is not convinced that their models can duplicate the richness and complexity of all the categories we use. The aboriginal category of "women, fire, and dangerous things," for example, is linked mostly by human imagination. In aboriginal mythology, the sun is the wife of the moon, linking women and the sun; since the sun gives off heat like fire, fire is also included; and because fire is dangerous, the category also contains things that harm. "The result," says Lakoff, "is a category that not only includes stinging nettles and gar fish, but also campfires and grandmothers.''

MAKING CONNECTIONS

CONNECTIONISM STILL HAS a long way to go before it wins over mainstream cognitive researchers. As Stanford artificial intelligence expert Terry Winograd likes to point out, "Connectionism is appealing to some people because it has a higher percentage of wishful thinking." Alfonso Caramazza, a cognitive psychologist at Johns Hopkins, has similar reservations. "It is à la mode," he says, "to appeal to the brain for justifications of a particular position. But can anyone actually show how the fact that we have brains in any way constrains what we believe about the nature of cognitive systems? Until someone can do that, it's just a lot of hogwash, because it creates an impression of understanding when there is deep ignorance."

Sejnowski is generous about the criticisms, and the critics, who can sometimes assume a tone that borders on hostility. "Traditionalists sometimes take the connectionist viewpoint as a personal attack," says Sejnowski. "You have to remember that during the early days of cognitive psychology, behaviorists felt the same way. They held all the university positions and got all the grant money, and computers changed all that. The computer freed the universities and opened up whole new fields of psychology. It was the sword that slew the dragon. But it's a double-edged sword."

Before Sejnowski began working to slay the new, digital dragon, he got his Ph.D. in physics, studying under John Hopfield at Princeton. It was Sejnowski who first got Hopfield interested in how complex systems like the brain work, and, curiously, it is Hopfield, a theoretical physicist, who provided the tools that linked connectionists with brain researchers. The machines and the ideas for them had existed before, but Hopfield gave the new field something every fledgling science needs: numbers.

Hopfield figured out the mathematical equations describing the behavior of the connectionists' neural nets. When talking about these nets Hopfield likes to use an analogy: Consider a countryside laden with hills and valleys. In the valleys lie lakes. If you pour a bucket of water on a hill, it flows down the hill into one of the lakes. No matter where you pour the water, it will eventually come to a place to rest; the system of mountains, lakes, and flowing water will eventually reach a stable state. And just as there are many mountains and lakes, there are many different stable states the system can go to.

It turns out, says Hopfield, that neural nets have contours like the hills and valleys in a countryside; they also have stable states. Imagine, he says, that you construct a neural network from 1,000 students doing their homework in a huge gymnasium. On each student's

Which of these shapes is most different?

Answer: The bottom object— the plain sphere with a small square inside—is the most different, because it is least different. In this puzzle, which takes advantage of our abilities to find cues to guide us in solving a problem, we assume at first that our goal is to look for differences between each object. But each object is different in some way; one has a tiny circle inside, one has stripes, etc. It is only when we realize we should change our initial goal and look for similarities that we realize that the last object, which shares the most characteristics with the other objects, is most alike, and therefore is the most different.

**If one—and only one—
of the inscriptions
on the boxes
is true,
which box
should you open
to find the treasure?**

M.E. CHALLINOR

Answer: Some of the most popular puzzles are, in logical terms, fairly simple, and would be a cinch for a computer. But they are a challenge for us. If the treasure is in the metal box, then the first inscription is true, but so is the second inscription. Since only one inscription can be true, the treasure cannot be in the metal box. If the treasure is in the green leather box, then the second and third inscriptions are true. The only instance in which only one of the three statements is true is when the treasure is in the wooden box.

HOW THE MIND came to be modeled after the workings of the digital computer rather than the workings of the brain has its roots in the early days of cognitive science, when ironically, the idea of an internal mind was having trouble gaining acceptance. Psychology was firmly entrenched in behaviorism, which holds that the science of the mind should be as objective as the science of physics, and limited to an examination of an organism's reaction to the outside world. The concept of an internal mind with intentions and purposes was considered untestable and too soft for a hard science. As the founder of behaviorism, psychologist John B. Watson, wrote in 1913, "The behaviorist, in his efforts to get a unitary scheme of animal response, recognizes no dividing line between man and brute." With that, the behaviorists banished the mind from their laboratories.

The cognitive cartel was finally broken, curiously, not by minds but by machines. The machines had help from philosophers. Philosophers were exploring what is called formal logic, the study of groups of symbols that are manipulated by a group of operations in a consistent way. Using algebra, for example, the equation $f = ma$ can be changed into $a = f/m$ and still be true.

The symbols in formal logic are abstract, but they take on meaning in the real world when ideas are substituted for the symbols: $f = ma$ means something if you realize that f is force, m is the mass of an object, and a is the object's acceleration. That such symbols and operations could be given meaning was a powerful suggestion: if the physical realm of motion and mass can be captured in a set of abstract symbols and rules, then by studying the workings of such symbols and rules, you could also study the workings of the real world.

It was only a small step to extend the analogy to the workings of the mind. Might not our cognitive abilities be formalized as a set of operations on a symbolic representation of the world? If we know, for example, that everyone at a convention is a lawyer and that Jane is at the convention, then we conclude that Jane is a lawyer. But this reasoning could also be expressed formally as symbols and operations—if all p's are q's, and x is a p, then x is also a q. It doesn't matter if it's lawyers or farmers, conventions or state fairs, Jane or Jack, the same rules apply. All we have to do is map the world into symbols, manipulate the symbols, and map the results back onto the real world.

Engineers and mathematicians took the philosophers' work one step further. It was discovered in 1938 that simple electronic on-off switches could be used to do symbolic manipulations, not just number crunching; mathematician John von Neumann showed how such electronic switches could be realized as a working computer. The burgeoning activity came to a head in 1955, when Herbert Simon is said to have told his class at the Carnegie Institute of Technology, "Over Christmas, Allen Newell and I invented a thinking machine." The next year Simon and Newell's computer—called *Johniac* after von Neumann—worked out a proof of a mathematical theorem. Here was the answer to behaviorism's exile of internal thoughts: if machines could process symbols, then certainly minds could too. And the machines were not only an alluring metaphor for the mind, they might actually be a valuable tool to study how our minds work.

Newell and Simon did not feel that their machine actually imitated what goes on inside our brains while we are thinking. "Our theory is a theory of the information processes involved in problem-solving," they wrote later, "and not a theory of neural or electronic mechanisms for information processing." They suggested instead that the workings of the mind might better be approached by studying the processes of thinking at a more general, theoretical level than the level of neurons. The main task was figuring out the proper rules and symbols the mind uses; then you could let neuroscientists figure out how the brain actually produced them.

Thus began a process that would eventually make the connectionists' brain-inspired model of the mind seem like a radical idea. By suggesting that the mind should be studied at a more general level, computer scientists set the agenda of cognitive research for the next 25 years. Here, finally, was a concrete tool, the computer, on which concrete theories about the processes of thinking could be tested. Here was an opportunity to study the mind, applying the scientific rigor of behaviorism while abandoning behaviorists' denial of the mind's internal, purposeful existence. Here, perhaps, was a mirror to our own internal cognitive processes.

The only thing missing was the brain. Faced with the dense, mysterious, and inaccessible mass of tangled nerve tissue, cognitive scientists did what any of us might do when, holding a heavy jacket, we are confronted with a closet full of twisted, intertwined coat hangers. They shut the door.

—*W.F.A.*

desk is a battery, which is connected through an on-off switch to wires that go to the desks of the other students. In each wire is an adjustable resistor, an electrical component that lowers the strength of the current. Also on each desk is a meter that displays on a dial the cumulative strength of all the currents coming in from the batteries of other students. One half of the dial is labeled "on," the other half "off." Now suppose, says Hopfield, that you simply tell all the students to go about their homework and every once in a while look at the meter. If the needle is in the "off" area of the dial, turn the switch off—if it's already off, leave it off. Likewise, if the needle is in the "on" area, turn the switch on if it's not already.

Hopfield discovered that if the vast network of students and switches is turned on, the network will always settle into a stable state, just as water poured on a hill will eventually find a place to rest; that is, after a while all the students who have their switches turned on will have meters reading "on," all the students with their switches off will have dials that read "off," and the system will stay frozen that way. What's more, Hopfield discovered that even though

We have an amazing ability to infer meaning from partial information. After reading this limerick:

There was a young maiden from Kew,
Whose limerick stopped at line two.

it's easier to appreciate this one:

There was an old pirate from Dunn.

there are 10^{300} ways all the on-off switches could be arranged in the 1,000-student network—more than the number of atoms in the universe—the resistors can be adjusted so that there are only about 100 different stable states the system will go to.

Having these stable states, says Hopfield, means the system can function somewhat like our own memories do. When we hear a person's name, for example, we remember information such as what his face looks like, where he works, and even his phone number. Likewise, seeing a face gives rise to a person's name and occupation, and mentioning a workplace might give rise to a name and a face.

Hopfield's system has a similar ability to recall a full range of information from an incomplete input. Suppose, he says, you write down how each student's switch is set in the 100 or so different stable configurations of on-off switches. Then you turn the system off and tell 50 of the 1,000 students to permanently set their switches in a way corresponding to one of those configurations. When the system is turned on again, the other 950 students will eventually fill out the rest of that particular configuration. In other words, five percent of the students—it doesn't matter which—can make the system "remember" the switch settings of the rest of the configuration.

The workings of the student network might seem somewhat mysterious, but Hopfield points out that a person who saw a diagram showing the patterns of water flow over a countryside—but not the hills and valleys—might think the whole process is pretty mysterious

too. But once you realize there are contours, the flow makes sense.

Hopfield also points out that the system has the property of what is known as "graceful degradation"—snipping several of the students' wires will not alter the system's ability to function. This feature is more congenial to brains than to digital computers. "Between the age of 12 and 50, a person might lose three percent of his brain cells," he says. "But the cognitive abilities of that brain will not be diminished; they might even improve. Cut three percent of the wires in a computer and it will grind to a halt."

Hopfield has also discovered that you can create a different set of stable states in the student network simply by changing the resistors on some of the students' wires—changing, as it were, the contours of the network. That also means, says Hopfield, that a neural net can be tuned to solve a particular problem.

Hopfield, working with David W. Tank at Bell Labs, has done just that with a type of problem known as the traveling salesman problem. It commonly crops up in everyday life, from routing genuine traveling salesmen to making airline schedules to designing microchips. Suppose, for example, you had to visit 10 cities spread out in a particular region. How do you find the shortest route to visit them all? You can measure all the routes, but it turns out that for 10 cities there are 181,440 possible routes to choose from. And as the number of cities goes up, the number of possible routes skyrockets. For 100 cities, for example, there are more than 10^{100} routes. Though there are sophisticated programs for solving this problem on digital computers, their basic strategy is simply to measure each route, and that takes a lot of time.

On Hopfield and Tank's neural net, all that needs to be done is to adjust the resistors to represent the relative locations of the cities. Within a few millionths of a second, the machine settles into a stable state representing one of the shortest connecting routes. A typical large computer, even though it has 10,000 more pieces of hardware, will take 10,000 times longer to do the job.

Because there may be many stable states in a neural net, the route Hopfield's machine comes up with won't necessarily be the very best. But it will always be a very good one. Getting a good solution quickly, rather than taking a long time to find the very best, is an appealing model for the way we think. "Biology by and large is not interested in the best things, just things that are pretty good," says Hopfield. "In recognizing faces, for example, the mind can't be too exact." The famous Russian psychologist Aleksandr R. Luria, for instance, described a mnemonist who had such an extraordinary memory that he couldn't remember faces: "People's faces are constantly changing," the mnemonist said. "The different

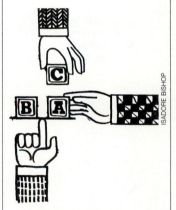

Can you think like a computer? Computers are powerful because many tasks can be reduced to a set of rules and symbols. But if the rules are in the wrong order, computers are helpless. Can you rearrange the rules below so the computer can find the heaviest block?

a. Weigh A against B.
b. Weigh B against C.
c. Weigh A against C.
d. If A is heavier, skip the next three statements.
e. If A is heavier, skip the next four statements.
f. If B is heavier, skip the next five statements.
g. Mark A "heaviest."
h. Mark B "heaviest."
i. Mark C "heaviest."
j. Skip the next statement.
k. Skip the next two statements.
l. Skip the next three statements.
m. End.

Answer below.

Answer: a, d, f, h, c, e, i, b, l, g, m

shades of expression confuse me and make it hard to remember."

Researchers at Bell Labs, who are concerned with finding better ways to route wires between cities and on microchips, are now trying to develop a prototype of Hopfield's machine on a chip. "It's exciting people because it's providing things that are very different," says Bob Lucky, research engineer at Bell. "Then again, it might turn out to be a whiff of a wind."

Connectionism has whiffed a little wind before. Hopfield and his colleagues are sometimes called "new" connectionists, because this type of machine was tried earlier, during the 1960s. But computer hardware then was expensive and somewhat limited, so such machines, often called perceptrons, were relatively simple.

In 1969 MIT computer scientists Marvin Minsky and Seymour Papert wrote *Perceptrons*, a book that provided an elegant mathematical analysis of the machines' abilities. It also poured large buckets of cold water on the movement. Minsky and Papert found that perceptrons, at least at that time, were not very powerful. While they were able to detect patterns, they could not, for example, tell whether a particular figure was continuous or made of separate elements. In an atmosphere of dramatic achievements in digital computing, interest in perceptrons faded.

Looking back, Brown University's James Anderson concedes that Minsky and Papert's book was a piercing—and quite accurate—appraisal. "But their analysis only deals with the most simple level of perceptrons," he says. "The systems we have now, with several levels of modifiable connections and feedback loops, are much more powerful."

With the emergence of multilevel networks and a new mathematical language, connectionists are going at it once again, experimenting with models that, while different from Hopfield's in some respects, embody many of the same principles. Geoffrey Hinton of Pittsburgh's Carnegie Mellon University, working with Sejnowski, has focused on making neural nets find optimal solutions, a little like finding the lowest lake in the entire landscape.

The trick, says Sejnowski, is to avoid getting stuck in a tiny depression between two mountains. "Imagine you have a model of a landscape in a big box," he says, "and you want to find the lowest point on the terrain. If you drop a marble into the box, it will roll around for a while and come to a stop. But it may not be the lowest point. So you shake the box. After enough shaking, you usually find it."

Hinton and Sejnowski use their machine, which they "shake" mathematically, to simulate some the processes of our visual system; their machine can pick out letters or the shape of a coffee cup, for example, in a general scene. The ability to pick something out of a back-

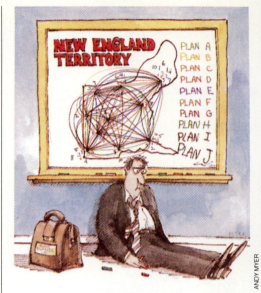

ANDY MYER

In a typical traveling salesman problem, the trick is finding the shortest route between all the cities. To visit 10 cities, there are 181,440 possible routes. For 100, there are more than 10^{100}. Machines modeled after our brains can solve such problems 10,000 times faster than a typical computer.

ground is important for connectionist systems, because it is sometimes desirable to focus the system's attention on a particular aspect of a problem.

Hinton and Sejnowski's machine took over a year to develop, because each connection in the machine had to be planned and built by hand. So they created learning programs that enable the neural nets to develop configurations of connections on their own—programs such as the one that helps Sejnowski's NETtalk learn to read aloud.

NETtalk was born dumb. It had a table of the 53 phonetic symbols commonly used by linguists to represent the sounds of speech, and it could use these phonemes to drive a speaker to make sounds. But it didn't have any rules telling it how to match written text with the correct phonemes to make words. It did, however, have rules on how to *learn* to pronounce words. Between the place where the text goes into NETtalk and where the phonemes come out lies a vast filigree of connections that have adjustable strengths, a little like having adjustable resistors in a wire. NETtalk learns by changing these strengths.

For its first training session, NETtalk was given a 500-word text of a first-grader's recorded conversation, as well as the correct phonemes to reproduce the child's speech, painstakingly transcribed by a linguist. NETtalk's connections looked at each part of the text and matched it with a phoneme; the learning program then compared the phoneme the network produced to that of the linguist. NETtalk's program is complex, but its essential principle is such that if NETtalk's phoneme didn't match that of the

Which of these spirals is made with just one line?

MIT PRESS/ART BY HAROLD JIG

Answer: The spirals, which adorn the cover of a 1969 book harshly critiquing brain-inspired machines, provide some solace for the new generation of connectionists. "This was supposedly one of the big problems with the machines, that they couldn't tell when figures were continuous," says psychologist James Anderson. "But you see? You can't do it either. You have to trace the lines with your finger—consciously turning yourself into a computer—to do it." The top spiral is made with one line.

child's, the strengths of the connections that produced that phoneme were altered to improve the match. In the beginning, the strengths of the connections were all set randomly. NETtalk was dumb as stone. After a day of training, however, NETtalk could read a simple text with about 90 percent accuracy—not bad for a tyro.

It wouldn't make sense to look for rules typical of digital computers, such as "When you see an 's,' make an 's' sound," in NETtalk. NETtalk's rules for pronunciation are contained within the myriad connections in the machine. As the letters file through the inputs, they cause the entire network of connections to readjust, chameleonlike, changing shades of computer colors with the appearance of each new typographic background. "The rules aren't put there," says Sejnowski, "they emerge."

Connectionists are using neural networks to study other aspects of our cognitive processes. Psychologists David Rumelhart of the University of California at San Diego and Jay McClelland of Carnegie Mellon University are using a neural net to study how we process language, teaching it, for example, to change verbs from the present to the past tense. Brown's Anderson is teaching his machine to make inferences from ambiguous language. "If you hear the words *bat, ball,* and *diamond,* you think of one thing," he says, "and if you hear the words *bat, vampire,* and *blood,* you think of another." Given the word *bat* or *diamond* alone, the machine will respond with characteristic qualities of animals or geometric shapes. But if *bat* and *diamond* are put together, the machine comes up with *baseball.*

There is at least one indication from the neurosciences that the connectionists might be on the right track. Walter Freeman, a neurophysiologist at the University of California at Berkeley, is working with Berkeley philosopher Christine Skarda to develop models of how the brains of rabbits process odors. According to Skarda, past models say that a particular smell is recognized by comparing a pattern created among the nerves by the incoming odor to some reference pattern stored in the brain. Freeman and Skarda have devised an alternative model, in which a smell stimulates a change in the brain's entire neural structure; a smell switches the brain from one stable state to another, precipitating a set of associated behaviors. The brain, says Skarda, is poised to organize itself into one of a number of different states or to create a new one in response to the external world.

Most of the connectionists' machines are ethereal, existing in the minds of their creators and in their digital computers. It will be some time before Bell Labs or anybody else puts these systems on silicon chips for practical applications. In that respect, the digital computer is still top banana. In fact, it may stay that way,

for it does very well those things that we are horrible at—the beginning of any beautiful friendship. And so what if it doesn't work like a brain? Nobody ever complained about a steam shovel not working like a human muscle.

But as models of the mind, serial digital computers may go the way of telephone switchboards, steam engines, clocks, and pumps—all former aspirants to the role of "model of human cognition." Not that connectionist machines will necessarily take their place. Many researchers, such as Anderson, believe that the mind probably works through a combination of serial, rule-based systems and parallel, connectionist networks.

There is also the lingering question of whether the brain is too complex for something as simple as the mind to ever figure out. Most cognitive scientists doubt that, but then again that's their job. For a while at least, we can savor a little amazement at the thought that countless researchers will spend countless hours trying to divine what is going on in that lump inside our skulls, a lump primarily designed to keep us alive, a lump that insists on going beyond its job description to create symphonies, fall in love, laugh at *I Love Lucy*—and build machines to imitate itself.

There may also be some perverse satisfaction in the fact that something we all carry about with us is so damned inscrutable. As philosopher Richard Rorty once said: "The ineffability of the mental serves the same cultural function as the ineffability of the divine—it vaguely suggests that science does not have the last word." Or as Christine Skarda put it when asked how it is that the great mental chasms between reflex and recognition and consciousness and metaphysics can all be bridged by a blob of stupid neurons strung together and chugging electricity: "Nobody really has any idea. It's just 'wonder tissue.'" S

William F. Allman is a thoughtful staff writer for Science 86.

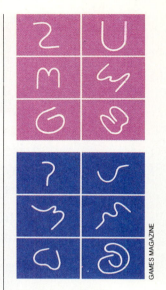

GAMES MAGAZINE

What characteristic unites the figures at top and excludes the other group of figures?

Answer: Putting things into categories isn't always easy, but we're usually a lot better at it than computers. In the top figures, the end lines are parallel.

ROGER N. SHEPARD/STANFORD

Do you see pillars or profiles? Many problems have no absolute answer—something our minds, which can derive completely different meanings out of identical information, are perfectly comfortable with.

THE ROOTS

Does our moral sense arise from emotions or reason? And when does it happen?

BY JOSEPH ALPER

PHOTOGRAPHS BY SUSIE FITZHUGH

IN HER SUBURBAN HOME, 18-month-old Julie was excited when another baby, Brian, came for a visit. But Brian was less than pleased at being with strangers and soon began to shriek and pound his fists on the floor. Almost immediately Julie's delight vanished, her body stiffened, and she looked worried, startled, and anxious. Julie's mom put Brian in a high chair and gave him cookies, but he continued screaming and threw the cookies to the floor. Julie, who usually tried to eat everyone else's cookies, put them back on the high chair tray. Brian's crying continued, and Julie tried to stroke his hair. She then went to her mom, grabbed her by the hand, and brought her to Brian. Julie's mother, concerned over her daughter's discomfort, took Brian into another room.

Julie, whose behavior had been observed and recorded by her mother as part of a National Institute of Mental Health study, was obviously concerned over the distress of her young friend. But she did more than just express concern, she also tried to alleviate that distress even though it did not benefit her in any overt manner. Her actions, in fact, may represent early signs of what is known as prosocial behavior, or behavior for the benefit of others. Many psychologists believe this signals the start of moral development.

Signs of empathy also occur among infants: A nurse dropped a bottle of formula on the floor of a quiet hospital nursery, but aside from the crash of breaking glass, the room remained silent. A little later, one newborn started crying. An

Joseph Alper is a free-lance writer living in Washington, D.C.

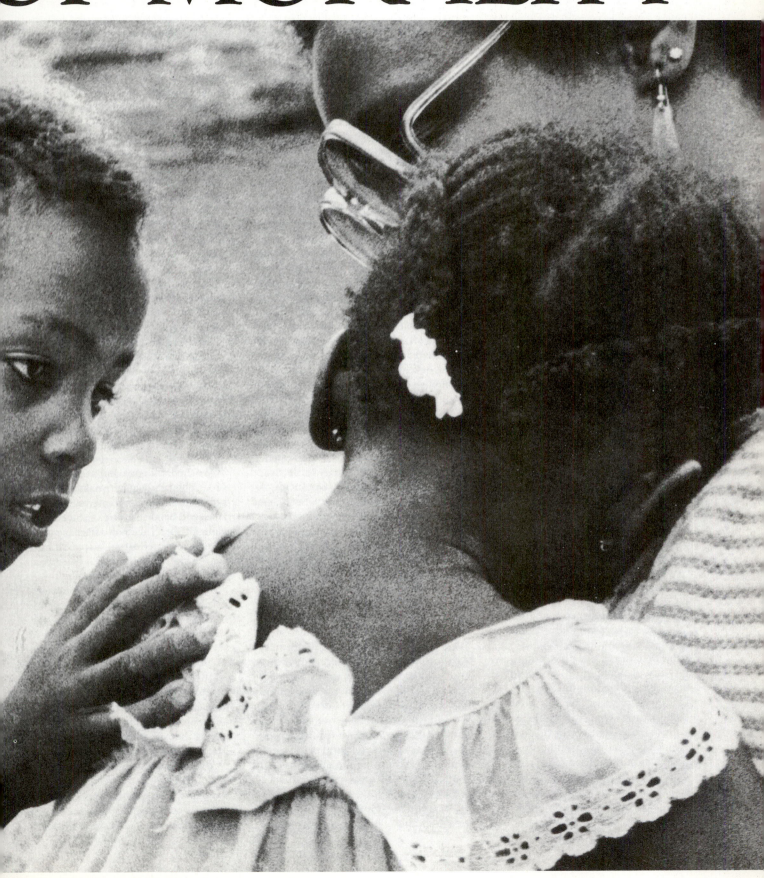

infant in a nearby crib joined in, then two more in the middle of the room. In minutes, the air was filled with the cries of dozens of babies, all demanding comfort.

Among older children the evidence is often verbal and therefore clearer: Freddy had asked his nursery school teacher why his friend Bonnie was not in class. The teacher replied that Bonnie's mother had died. The four-year-old stood quietly for a minute, then said, "You know, when Bonnie grows up people will ask her who her mother is and she will have to say 'I don't know.' It makes tears come to my eyes."

In each of these situations, young children apparently have sensed distress in others and, as a result, become distressed themselves. Feeling someone else's emotions is common in adults; we call it empathy. Only in the past several years, however, have psychologists grown interested in the development of emotion (as opposed to reason) in children. This new area of study reveals that children empathize at a very early age, and some of the investigators believe this behavior is innate, genetically programmed like sucking and crying.

Empathy may do more than trigger a sympathetic response. "The data strongly suggest that empathy is part of the developmental foundation for the child's future system of moral behavior, as well as for social behaviors such as altruism and sharing," says Martin L. Hoffman, developmental psychologist at the University of Michigan.

Marian Radke-Yarrow, chief of the Laboratory of Developmental Psychology at the National Institute of Mental Health (NIMH) and her colleague Carolyn Zahn-Waxler have found that children as young as 15 months show complex empathic behaviors. "Over the next three to six years, depending on the individual, this empathy develops into what we consider moral or prosocial, behavior," says Radke-Yarrow. "Many psychologists still claim, in spite of extensive evidence from several labs, that young children are not capable of moral reasoning."

The NIMH researchers have found much individual difference in the quality of empathy—how sensitive a child is, a toddler's particular style of reacting to others' distress. Nancy Eisenberg, a developmental psychologist at Arizona State University in Tempe, reports similar findings. "Certain qualities of early empathic behavior appear to be associated with certain types of moral reasoning," she says.

Not everyone agrees that moral development starts early in life or that empathy plays a part in it. William Damon, a psychologist at Clark University, believes that the most important aspects of morality do not start forming until a child is adolescent. "It's true young children show empathic behaviors, even sharing, which you might say is a precursor of fairness. But I think a lot of those early signs are just playfulness," says Damon. "Caring is obviously important to any society, but the key question in moral behavior has to do with fairness." He claims that if there are any early indicators of future moral behavior in an individual, they would be the appearance and development of what is called distributive justice—how someone resolves competing claims for goods.

Most psychologists, however, would say that kindness and mercy, and respect for another person's feelings, must be included in a definition of moral behavior, in addition to honesty, justice, and fairness. Biblical writers, Confucius, Aristotle, Kant, Hume, Adam Smith, and Freud have probed the dimensions of moral decision-making and its development without much agreement. It is an issue that no single theory stands much chance of explaining fully.

The first modern-day psychologist to take a crack at explaining moral development in children was Jean Piaget. Piaget directed most of his attention to determining stages of reasoning and intellectual capabilities in children. It was from this perspective of cognitive development that he addressed morality. He believed that children's social maturation, including the ability to make moral decisions, depended on two factors: the acquisition of the rules and patterns governing behavior, and the ability to reason and solve problems using these rules.

In the mid-1930s, Piaget postulated a two-stage development progression based on how children between ages six and 12 interpreted and reacted to various moral dilemmas. The following example is the most well-known:

John was in his room when his mother called him to dinner. John went down and opened the door to the dining room. But behind the door was a chair, and on the chair was a tray with fifteen cups on it. John did not know the cups were behind the door. He opened the door, the door hit the tray, bang went the 15 cups, and they all got broken.

One day when Henry's mother was out, Henry tried to get some cookies out of the cupboard. He climbed up on a chair, but the cookie jar was still too high, and he couldn't reach it. But while he was trying to get the cookie jar, he knocked over a cup. The cup fell down and broke.

Which boy was naughtier and why?

Usually, children younger than 10 replied that John was—he broke more cups. Children 10 and older tended to say that Henry was—he was up to no good when he broke the single cup.

Piaget postulated that younger children are self-centered and do not yet have the cognitive skills to understand the purpose of society's rules nor the ability to use them in a reasoned approach. Thus, they could only make their decisions on objective grounds: who broke the most cups. But around the age of 10, children's cognitive skills reach the point where they can interpret society's rules and become aware of the effects of violating them. They also start using their emerging intellectual capabilities to reach higher level moral judgments, which include motive and intent.

Though Piaget was devoted more to intellectual than to moral development, his work stimulated much of the more specific research on the subject and served as the starting point for Lawrence Kohlberg, a psychologist at Harvard University. Like Piaget, Kohlberg used stories containing moral dilemmas to learn about children's abilities to make moral judgments and to identify styles of reasoning they used to make decisions. This is one of the Kohlbergian dilemmas:

In Europe, a woman was near death from a special kind of cancer. One drug that the doctors thought might save her was a form of radium that a druggist in the same town had recently discovered. The drug was expensive

To say children can't make moral judgments flies in the face of how preschoolers behave.

to make, but the druggist was charging 10 times what the drug cost him to make. He paid $200 for the radium and charged $2,000 for a small dose of the drug. The sick woman's husband, Heinz, went to everyone he knew to borrow money, but he could only get together about half of what it cost. He told the druggist that his wife was dying and asked him to sell it cheaper or let him pay later. But the druggist said, "No, I discovered the drug and I'm going to make money from it." So Heinz got desperate and broke into the man's store to steal the drug for his wife. Should the husband have done that? Why?

Based on the answers to these questions, Kohlberg posited six ordered stages of moral development. In the lowest, decisions are based solely on the likelihood of getting punished for a given action. In the sixth stage, moral decisions are based on one's principles. Two factors promote progression through the stages: exposure to levels of moral reasoning that are immediately higher than one's current level, and new experiences in role taking.

According to Kohlberg, most children up to about age 10 are at stage two. He claims that this is because they do not yet have the logical skills to engage in sophisticated reasoning. Other psychologists have criticized Kohlberg for ignoring the emotional and social roots of morality. In addition, the dilemmas he used to test for development are criticized as too intricate and remote for young children.

"To say that children can't reason, can't make moral judgments on the basis of anything but rules or for self-centered motives flies in the face of what we start seeing in preschoolers," says Nancy Eisenberg. For example, in one study she conducted, 35 four- and five-year-olds were told various stories in which the protagonist had to choose between an altruistic behavior and one that would benefit themselves. One of the stories was as follows:

One day a girl named Mary was going to a friend's birthday party. On her way she saw a girl who had fallen down and hurt her leg. The girl asked Mary to go to her house and get her parents so the parents could come and take her to the doctor. But if Mary did run and get the child's parents, she would be late *for the birthday party and miss the ice cream, cake, and all the games. What should Mary do? Why?*

Nearly all of the children in the study gave answers based on empathic reasoning (as opposed to egocentric) some of the time. Though few used empathic reasoning consistently, Eisenberg suggests they all had the capacity. A sample answer demonstrating altruism might be "Mary should go get the girl's parents because her leg hurts and she needs help."

Kohlberg's theory does not account for this type of reasoning. "Cognitivists don't accept the idea that emotion generated from inside the child plays any significant role in developmental processes," says Hoffman. "And if you discount the idea of empathy, you can't explain the type of behavior Nancy and Marion have observed in young kids."

This is where Hoffman's theory differs from past approaches. He, too, assumes that cognitive development, especially role taking and the ability to distinguish self from others, is necessary for the development of moral behavior. But he also postulates that emotions from within the child, especially empathy, provide the motivation for moral behavior.

Hoffman starts with the belief that empathy is innate. He cites incidents like the hospital nursery scene as support for this idea. He has found in studies that in a group of newborns, more will cry in response to another child's cry than will respond to another equally loud noise. Because an infant cannot differentiate between self and others, distress cues from others are confounded with unpleasant feelings in himself. An 11-month-old girl, on seeing a child fall and cry, looked as if she herself were about to cry, put her thumb in her mouth, and buried her head in her mother's lap as if she were hurt.

Around the end of the first year, children start recognizing themselves as being physically distinct from others. Children at this stage realize when others are experiencing distress but assume that the other's internal state is the same as their own. When Julie fetched her mother in response to Brian's distress, it was because she assumed Brian's emotional needs were the same as hers in a similar situation; most likely, she would have gone for her own mother even if Brian's had been present.

Role taking is part of a three- to four-year-old's experience and continues to be a major factor in the development of empathy. By seven or eight, children are better able to distinguish their own feelings from others' and to choose actions that are appropriate to help others. In addition, they begin to deal with feelings more abstractly. Freddy was extremely precocious, demonstrating this behavior at age four. He felt sad even though his own mother had not died; he had not yet witnessed Bonnie's sadness, but he imagined her future sorrow.

"In the early years of childhood we see expressions of empathy and sympathy and also serious attempts to help, share, protect, and comfort," says Radke-Yarrow. "If that's not moral behavior, then I guess I'm in the wrong field of study."

It is also during early childhood that people begin experiencing empathic guilt—feeling distress when they have been the cause of someone else's discomfort. "As the child learns that he can cause distress in others and that this can cause distress in himself, he will start behaving in ways that don't produce this self-caused distress," Hoffman says.

"Parents can use the child's sense of empathy and empathic guilt to reinforce good moral values," says Hoffman. The point is to discipline the child for wrongdoing, obtain compliance, and at the same time provide an explanation that will induce sympathy for the person being affected by his misbehavior: "You shouldn't call Johnny names because it hurts his feelings, and you wouldn't like it if your feelings were hurt." Radke-Yarrow and Zahn-Waxler found that children of parents who provide explanations for their own behavior have more highly developed empathy.

There are several ways empathy can be triggered, according to Hoffman. In a newborn, the cries of one child can trigger tears and unhappiness in another. This response is probably innate, but later in life whether or not one reacts empathically to a situation depends on one's experience and reasoning ability. One may automatically feel pain upon

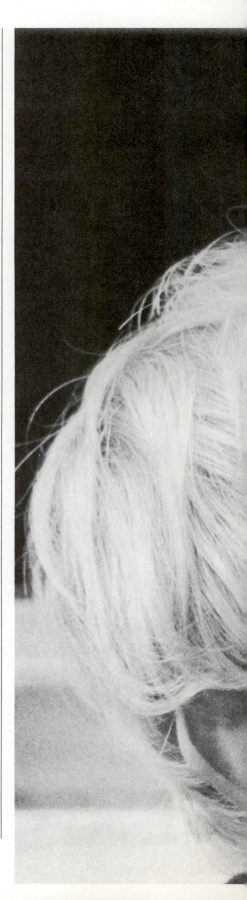

In the earliest years of life,
children make serious efforts to protect and
comfort others who are unhappy.

Why do people go out and help
one another? That's one of the key
questions of human civilization.

seeing someone else in distress because it brings back memories of one's own pain under similar circumstances. Or empathy may stem from the purposeful act of imagining how one would feel if in the shoes of the victim.

The NIMH researchers resorted to an unusual experimental technique that many say has generated the richest data on childhood behavior. "We felt that past experimental methods had some serious shortcomings for studying certain developmental issues such as empathy. Situations that call for empathic behavior don't happen frequently or predictably," says Radke-Yarrow. "With young children, using hypothetical situations to represent real experience has doubtful validity. In real life, children experience events of consequence—real hurts and conflicts." Radke-Yarrow and Zahn-Waxler decided to address the problems by training mothers as research assistants and having each observe her child's behavior in its natural setting over periods of several months. By having day-to-day observations they could monitor continuing development rather than compare behaviors at selected times. This approach also avoids the necessity of getting children to respond to complex stories or questions that they either may not understand or not know how to answer with their limited verbal skills.

In the first of several studies, for example, 24 mothers made systematic observations of distress—pain, physical distress, sadness, fear, anger, and fatigue—occurring in their children's immediate environments. The mothers used portable tape recorders to report their observations. Some of the children began the study at 10 months, some at 15, and some at 20. During the nine months of observation, a researcher came to each home at three-week intervals to check on the mother's reports and carry out some simulated distress experiments. This served as a way of comparing what the children did in simulations with what the mothers were reporting. When the children were six or seven years old the study was resumed for a three-month period.

From a series of these studies the researchers gleaned a basic understanding of patterns and individual differences in

moral development. Children's earliest reactions in the presence of another person's distress were silent, tense standing, agitation, crying, and whimpering; these behaviors accounted for the majority of all responses between the ages of 10 and 14 months. In this early period, the children engaged in some form of helping interaction only rarely.

In succeeding months, the general distress crying waned, occurring very infrequently among the 20- to 29-month-old children. More controlled and positive actions toward the distressed person occurred. At first, these were simple behaviors, such as touching or patting. By age one, all the children in the study showed this reaction at some time. By the latter half of the second year the children were initiating contacts, embracing the victim, seeking help from a third party, inspecting the distress in a more active manner, and giving the victim gifts. "What the children chose to give was not random," Radke-Yarrow says. Sometimes the choice of gift was appropriate for the distressed child, and sometimes it was more appropriate for the comforter.

The studies also revealed that imitation plays an important role in the development of these early behaviors. For example, one mother reported that after she had bumped her elbow, said "ouch," and then rubbed it, her child showed a pained expression, said "ow," rubbed his own elbow, and then rubbed his mother's. The child is still struggling with determining what is the self and what is the other person.

Certain children stood out as being more emotional than others, both in their level of arousal and the way they reacted toward other people. Others had very little apparent emotional reaction and took a more reasoned approach—inspecting, exploring, and asking questions about the situation. Some were aggressive in their interactions—hitting the person who caused a friend's distress, pushing one parent in the midst of a parental quarrel, tearing up the newspaper that had made mother cry. And still other children reacted adversely to the distress, trying to shut it out by turning or running away from the source.

Children who were most outgoing and

emotional at age two continued to display this type of behavior, in a more developed manner, at age seven. Similarly, those who avoided distress by running away behaved in a similar way five years later. However, the data also revealed striking differences in the rate at which each child developed moral reasoning. "Our data showed the value of examining each child individually, because there wasn't much of a developmental pattern when we looked at the group as a whole," said Radke-Yarrow.

In studies at the Arizona State University Child Study Laboratory nursery school, Eisenberg obtained results similar to those of the NIMH group. While analyzing her data, she noticed two groups of children whose style of behaving stood out from the rest. One group of children would give help only when they were asked. These children were generally nonassertive and lacked initiative. At the opposite end of the scale was a group of children who frequently engaged in spontaneous, or unsolicited, sharing. These children tended to be more outgoing, assertive, and social. They also scored higher than average for their ages on moral reasoning tests.

"We see that spontaneous sharing correlates well with preschoolers' ability to make moral judgments," she says. "And I think this relates to the costs involved in that behavior." She argues that it is high-cost behavior when a child gives up something for someone else's benefit. The decision to share spontaneously, because its cost is higher and requires more initiative, is therefore more likely to be a reflection of a child's stronger moral development.

Those researchers who support empathy's role in the development of moral behavior readily say that it is only one of many factors involved in this process. It is nonetheless attractive to speculate that an innate behavior, empathy, is central to behavior so crucial to human civilization—subjugating one's own needs, interests, and desires to those of society, for that is what moral behavior truly is. "That's one of the key questions of human civilization: 'Why do people go out and help one another?'" says Hoffman. "Empathy can provide that motive." **S**

BY RONNIE WACKER

ILLUSTRATIONS BY MATT MAHURIN

EVERYBODY IN THE OLD-AGE home loved Mary Frances. In her late seventies, she was cheerful, undemanding, cooperative. She went out of her way to help other residents in the little Midwestern home, sewing for a woman whose fingers were stiff with arthritis, writing letters for another whose eyesight was failing. She kept up with a large circle of friends outside the institution and was a regular at the kaffeeklatsch. Although a hip operation had left her with a slight limp, and arthritis had settled in her knees, she rarely complained.

When the operators of the home announced that they would have to close and the 45 residents would be relocated to a larger, more impersonal institution, she took the news better than most other patients. "I'm not happy about it," she told an interviewer, "but I'm sure it will work out for the best. There will be things in the new place we'll like better than here." Shortly after the move, Mary Frances was bedridden and listless; in six months she was dead.

After relocation, she lapsed into what psychologists call the first-month syndrome, a common institutional malady caused by a change of environment. She sank into deep depression; she began to complain about the pain in her arthritic knees. For patients who can adjust to new surroundings, the depression lifts, and the frequent complaints of minor pains gradually cease. For Mary Frances, they did not. Her depression deepened into apathy. Some days she wouldn't

Ronnie Wacker is a free-lance writer living in eastern Long Island, New York.

leave her bed. She seemed never to recover her old spirit and finally, one gray day as unpromising as the previous one, she died.

Harry was something else again. The day he entered his old-age home at 81, he complained to a social worker about the racial makeup of the staff. A few weeks later, he drove a volunteer aide out of his room in tears, accusing her of having stolen his false teeth. "You probably hocked 'em!" he shouted at her.

He boasted to everyone around him that he had beaten up his top sergeant in the army 60 years earlier, "and I could do it again if I wanted to, by God!" He refused to bathe regularly and carried so strong a scent of urine that other patients shrank from him in the halls. He proudly attributed this avoidance to their fear of his physical strength.

A bachelor, he was persuaded to enter the home by his only relative, a young woman. She convinced him that he needed close medical attention because of a serious heart condition and emphysema. She helped him move in and at first visited him frequently. But then they had a disagreement over politics, and he ordered her to leave and never come back. She continued to call, but he refused to speak to her.

Eight years after being taken to the home, despite his heart condition and worsening emphysema, Harry roared on, ignoring or feuding with his fellow patients and abusing staff members, who whispered to each other that he was "just too mean to die."

Why did Harry, ill, suspicious, and hostile, apparently thrive in an environment similar to that which felled Mary Frances, originally far healthier and more hopeful? Two University of Chicago psychologists, Morton Lieberman and Sheldon Tobin, became interested in questions like this 21 years ago, when a

study they were doing on stress and the elderly turned up mortality results that surprised them. With disturbing consistency, the "wrong" old people were dying. The surly and paranoid survived, while the cheerful, cooperative, seemingly mentally healthy succumbed.

During the following years, graduate researchers directed by the two psychologists interviewed hundreds of old people, average age 78. It was the first systematic study of the psychology of the very old. And their findings are changing the way in which social scientists look at old age in America.

Lieberman, director of the Aging and Mental Health Program at the University of California, San Francisco, and Tobin, who directs the Ringel Institute of Gerontology at the New York State University, Albany, offer a single basic message: Old age is as fundamentally different from young adulthood or middle age as childhood is different from any of them. It is a separate and distinct stage of life about which we are profoundly ignorant.

Child psychology is firmly established now as a separate and necessary study of one period of the human life-span. But it took a long time for the Western world to recognize that children are not simply small adults, to be dressed in smaller sizes of their elders' clothes and held to the same standards of work and play behavior as adults.

The idea of treating children as adults seems preposterous today, and we wonder why it took so long to recognize the absurdity of it. Lieberman and Tobin suggest that we are at a similar point of discovery about the elderly.

"The old are not just people with white hair," says Lieberman, whose own curling brown hair is beginning to gray at the temples. "They have a unique psychology. We have been treating people 65 to 90 years old as though they were

THE GOOD DIE YOUNGER

After relocation, Mary Frances lapsed into what psychologists call the first-month syndrome, a common institutional malady caused by a change of environment. She sank into deep depression; she began to complain about the pain in her arthritic knees. Problems like these disappear in those patients who withstand relocation and adjust to their surroundings. For Mary Frances, they did not. Her depression deepened into apathy. Some days she wouldn't leave her bed. She seemed never to recover her old spirit and finally, one gray day as unpromising as the previous one, she died.

30, and it's not working very well."

Among the differences that Lieberman and Tobin found:

■ Nice guys may not finish last. Cheerful, cooperative, outward-reaching people may quietly deteriorate and die while their suspicious, aggressive contemporaries bluster on. "Good mental health" in younger people is not necessarily an aid to the survival of the old, especially those undergoing stress such as that suffered during relocation. In fact, attitudes and emotions considered destructive in younger people may actually be beneficial to the old.

"A pinch of paranoia can be quite useful," says Tobin, who recalled the impact of a Chicago opera star on a nursing home. A petite, flamboyant woman in her 80s who affected dramatic shawls accused those around her of conspiring against her. They were jealous, she insisted, and vowed she would expose them in the book she was writing on her life. She never did write the book, but the belief that she had the power to avenge herself on those she didn't trust helped sustain her well into her 90s.

■ Those who approach a stressful situation with the most hope often disintegrate emotionally when they are disappointed. "If hopes are too great," says Tobin, "they can be too easily thwarted." Old people being relocated, already buffeted by loss of their old friends and surroundings, need to establish an identity in their new world. If they bring unrealistic expectations along, they can be crushed by defeat. Harry had so buttressed his identity with myths of his prowess that he was certain he could handle any situation. He was neither too hopeful nor hopeless. Mary Frances, however, accustomed to looking on the bright side, was overcome by the reality of her surroundings.

■ Most vital is a strong sense of continuity of one's self, the conviction that one's personality has not eroded with the passage of time. Older people have less contact with the outside world and therefore less confirmation of their own identity. Without such outside stimulation they resort to different strategies to convince themselves they are still the same people they were when they were young: Harry shouts that he can still beat up his top sergeant, by God! They construct myths, recasting memories of long-ago events, to make themselves hero or heroine instead of a spectator. "That is the biggest task the elderly have, to hang on to themselves and prove that they still are

the same people they were," says Tobin.

At one point, researchers asked old people to describe themselves. A number of them offered decades-old photographs. One woman in her 80s brought out a picture of herself in a bathing suit, shot 40 years earlier. When asked if she did not have a more recent picture, she reluctantly handed over one made the year before, protesting, "It's terrible. It's not me at all."

"Suppose I were to hand you a high school yearbook picture of myself with a full head of hair?" says Tobin, who is balding and offsets it with a full beard. "You'd say I was irrational. There is nothing irrational about an act like that for an old person."

The past is the spring on which the elderly draw to keep parched egos green, Lieberman said. A good case in point is Mrs. Arnold, 77, an active, independent woman. After the death of her husband and a very close sister, she applied to a nearby old-age home where she had friends. The psychologists first tested her

---

People in good mental health may not adjust well to nursing homes.

---

while she was awaiting admission to the home and again three years later.

Both times she agreed to the statement, "I believe I am an important person." The first time, her explanations related to the present: "You should see how many New Year's cards I got." After three years of institutional care she still considered herself an important person, but she went back to the past to justify her feeling: "I have always done the best I could for my family."

Robert N. Butler, of Mt. Sinai Hospital School of Medicine in New York, says Tobin and Leiberman have proven what geriatric psychologists had begun to see in individual patients 20 years ago. In Butler's own clinical work with the very old he has focused on encouraging them to review their whole life. Because the behavior of many old people seems odd, doctors sometimes try to suppress it with drugs. Butler and others encourage changes in public understanding rather than trying to change elderly behavior.

Our culture demonstrates profoundly negative attitudes toward the elderly, says Butler. The old are "gorks," "old crocks," "geezers," "biddies." With very

few exceptions such as *The Gin Game* and *On Golden Pond*, our novels, plays and TV shows usually focus on young love. But as 12 percent of the population is 65 and over, Butler points out, it would be logical to expect that our writing should reflect more of the concerns and interests of that population.

"Our health care systems also have to be changed," he says. Medicare, for example, is set up for acute illnesses rather than chronic care, with no provision for outpatient care or preventive checkups.

The National Institute on the Aging has called for more research on the 85-and-over group and is currently spending $800,000. This is expected to double next fiscal year. The Institute's Deputy Director, Edward Schneider, says that the 85-and-over group—about 2.6 million Americans—is the fastest growing segment of the population and is increasing three times as fast as the total population over 65. It is expected to leap to five million by the year 2000, and to 16 million by 2050. Of this group, 23 percent live in nursing homes and other institutions compared with five percent of those 65 and over.

"The needs of this group will place a heavy burden on the country's economic and health resources," Schneider says. According to one estimate by the National Institutes of Health, the federal government today provides $51 billion in major benefits for those 80 and over.

But how can adequate benefits be offered without a clear understanding of the needs of the elderly? The Lieberman-Tobin studies are the first systematically organized assault on that wall of ignorance. They were based on interviews, reinterviews, and batteries of tests on several groups of old people who were being subjected to stress. Some were leaving their homes to go to an old-age home, some were being transferred from one institution to another, and still others were being involuntarily discharged from institutions into residential settings not their own homes.

The psychologists used as control groups carefully matched samples of people living in the community or those who had lived in a similar institution for one to three years without relocation. Their objective: to quantify what until then had been considered unmeasurable—the functions and personality attributes of hope and reminiscence.

Observing that patients even in well-run nursing homes seemed to deteriorate, the two psychologists brought to-

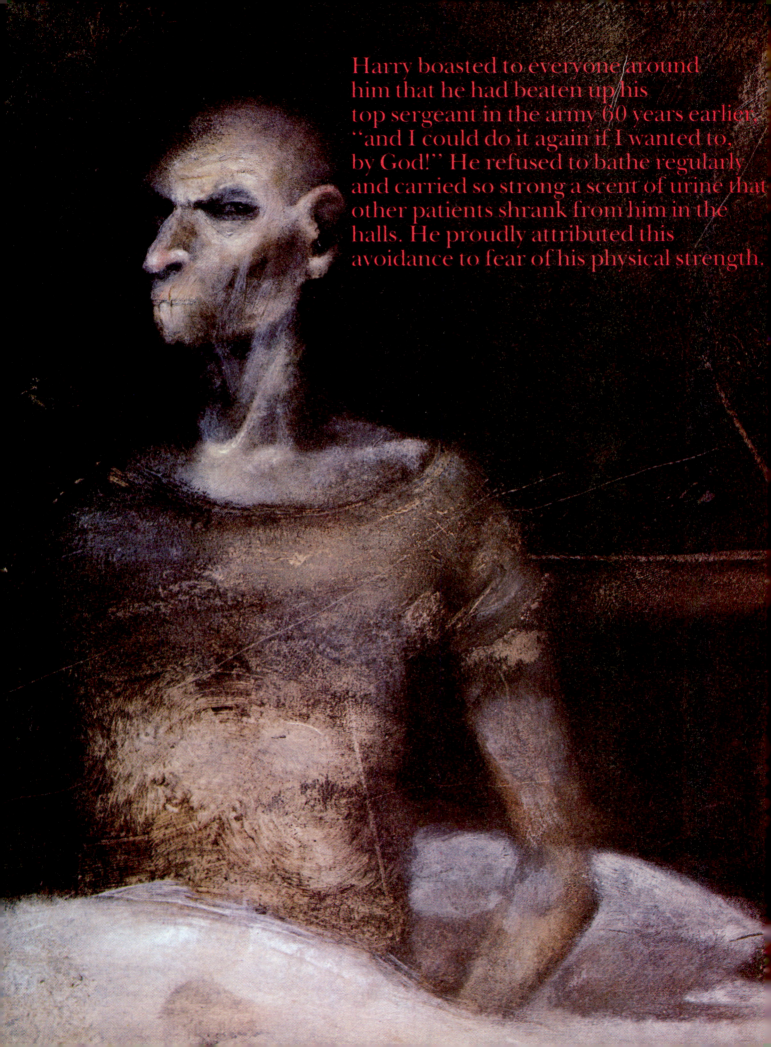

Harry boasted to everyone around him that he had beaten up his top sergeant in the army 60 years earlier, "and I could do it again if I wanted to, by God!" He refused to bathe regularly and carried so strong a scent of urine that other patients shrank from him in the halls. He proudly attributed this avoidance to fear of his physical strength.

gether a team of doctoral students to find out why. They interviewed 85 old people who were about to enter homes and reinterviewed them after they had made the move.

While still involved in this study, the researchers learned that a small public home for elderly widows had closed. The 45 women, aged 61 to 91, were being relocated from the intimate home where Mary Frances had lived happily for three years to a larger, more impersonal institution. They were given an assortment of standard psychological tests designed to assess mental health.

The psychologists found that for many old people, once they are convinced "it's time" to enter an institution, they accept that they will never leave it—they are being sent there to die. And even while on the waiting list, many of the more passive ones begin to do what they believe is expected of them: deteriorate.

"There was an inverse relationship between those who did well on the tests and their subsequent adaptation to the new environment," says Lieberman. "We found that those in good mental health would not be most likely to adjust well. That was the beginning of our education in aging."

Two other studies followed. In all, they interviewed 639 elderly men and women in four different groups in old-age homes and in state hospitals. In each of the studies the lives of the relocated people were followed from one year prior to at least one year following the move. In each group, half the elderly who had been relocated had died or markedly deteriorated within that first year. People who enter old-age homes have an average life expectancy of about six years.

In the largest study, covering 427 elderly patients who were relocated from a state mental hospital to a variety of nursing homes and boarding homes, 18 percent died within a year. But among persons in a closely matched sample from a comparable institution who were not relocated, the death rate was five percent in the same one year period.

One day while Lieberman was visiting one of the homes, the chief nurse told him she felt that one patient would not be with them much longer. He died two weeks later. Lieberman later asked her how she had known it, since there had been no medical indications.

"Brainwaves," the nurse replied.

Consciously or not, the nurse had observed subtle clues that foretold the approach of death. This led to another study, to identify those close to death.

The psychologists selected several tests, including one that required patients to draw copies of designs and another that asked patients to comment on stick-figure drawings of human figures in various positions. The tests were given every three or four weeks over two and a half years. The responses of those who died within one year of the last testing were compared to the responses of those who lived for at least one more year. As people approached death, their copies of the design looked much less like the original. As early as six to nine months before dying, the subjects' designs became disorganized and constricted, the figures smaller, the lines unconnected and poorly articulated. People who, as it turned out, were more than a year away from death got better at copying the designs with each successive try.

A list of personality changes observed among those closest to death could explain the nurse's "brainwaves":

■ Reduced aggressiveness, increased

Among the very old too much hope can be a handicap.

docility.

■ Withdrawal from family and friends, reduced efforts at social contact.

■ Deteriorating performance in repeated tests of association and recognition.

■ Declining introspection. Those in the last downward swing of life were noticeably less interested in contemplating their inmost thoughts and feelings.

■ Frequent use of death symbols in comments on test picture cards: "I see a hooded man with his hands folded and face covered," or "The man is going to drown. He is trying to stay afloat."

Contrary to general expectations, there was no increase in reminiscence as death approached. In general the old fear death much less than younger people, especially those in their 50s. But fear of death is likely to intensify among those who have been removed from familiar surroundings.

One note of caution was sounded about the results of the Tobin-Lieberman studies. Paul T. Costa, chief of the section on stress and coping at the NIA Gerontological Research Center, says the conclusions should be applied only to the special group of the elderly in institu-

tions. The basic personality change to which they refer, he said, does not occur in subjects who remain healthy and live in home situations.

Lieberman replies, "Not all the people we studied were institutionalized, and of those who were, a good number were people comparable to those living in the community. They were residents of old-age homes which they went to more for social reasons than for nursing care. We were studying people under high stress. At one time or another everyone experiences this kind of stress." In fact, among people 65 and over there is a one in three chance that at some point they will be institutionalized.

Lieberman and Tobin's studies also point up a need for more sensitive regulation of the homes and efforts to match the home environment to the individual needs of the patient. Too much attention is paid, Tobin says, to the physical environment in the institutions, and not enough to the psychological needs of their inhabitants. A nursing home for the aged should be a combination of hotel, hospital, and social-recreational facility. "But whatever money there is goes first of all to the hotel and hospital aspects. If there is anything left over, it is doled out for social needs. Still," he shook his head sadly, "they call it a home."

"Perhaps families won't be so quick to pack their seniors off to an institution if the personality changes are viewed not as bizarre, but natural human development," Lieberman says.

If Mary Frances were alive and being relocated right now, what would Tobin recommend to her?

"I'd try to help her to show more aggression, and stand up for her rights. Too often, old people are told to be 'nice' to the doctor, to be 'good' patients. Why? So the institution staff won't be inconvenienced? That's baloney.

"When my mother-in-law went to the hospital, other members of the family told her to be a good patient, follow the doctors' orders and not give anybody any trouble. I called her and told her not to worry about being 'nice' to the doctors and nurses. 'You do what you want to do,' I told her. 'You don't have to be sweet. You want to get out of there? Go. Demand what you want. It's your life.'"

She did, he says, and when she left, feeling a lot better about herself, she went home to her own apartment.

"You know," Tobin says, "these people have not been 90 before. Somebody has to show them how to handle it." ⬛

THE DELICATE SEX

How females threaten, starve, and abuse one another.

BY DUNCAN MAXWELL ANDERSON

THE HEAT of the day is just subsiding as a troop of baboons casually eats its way across the scrubby East African savannah. One female, with a young infant clinging upside down to her belly, pauses every few steps to pull up sedges with her forepaws and nibble them. The infant's fur is jet black, its face bright pink—the signs of a newborn. Like human infants, young baboons have big heads, big eyes and ears, and gently clumsy movements. They are, in a word, cute. The mother seems to peer around nervously at the other baboons as she eats.

Another female suddenly looks up at the mother and starts to grunt maniacally: "Eh-eh-eh-eh!" She jerks her head around to catch the attention of the other animals. Soon they take it up too, until a chorus of females surrounds the mother and infant.

Then there is the whoosh of countless bodies racing through the grass, and the grunts erupt into deafening barks and screams. The mother and infant are buried in baboons. Six females rip and bite,

Duncan Maxwell Anderson is a free-lance writer with a special interest in sociobiology. He lives in the particularly status-conscious city of New York.

BLAIR DRAWSON

Monkeys were once seen as models for
ideal human behavior. It was said that they never kill
their own kind, that they mate freely and without jealousy.
All of these statements are false, it now appears.

frenetically yanking at the infant, as the bleeding mother clutches it and tries to shield it with her body.

A young American woman, notebook in hand, looks on in horror. *They're going to kill that baby*, she thinks. Involuntarily, she starts to move toward the action.

"*Alison!*" a man shouts. "Get the names!" She starts to jot things down: "Mwajuma, with infant Mkia, attacked by coalition of six . . . seven(?) females. Mwajuma's daughter Kichwa tries to intercede, is attacked also; retreats." More than a minute passes.

At last Mwajuma shrieks and bolts with her infant through an opening in the mass of attackers. She takes off across the savannah with a dozen females in pursuit. Primatologist Samuel K. Wasser of the University of Washington and his assistant Alison Starling tear after the females for a quarter-mile, taking notes as best they can.

Back at camp later, the two of them will go over the details: the names of the females who took part in the attack; the fact that several of them were pregnant; that the mother sustained superficial cuts over most of her body and bled profusely from gashes in her nose and wrist; that her infant got only a minor bite on the knee. And that this was the most serious of the 47 "coalition" attacks among females on that day.

This type of incident is not by any means unique to baboons. Among those who study animal behavior, female competition has taken center stage during the last three years. In journals and at conferences, there have been reams of papers presented on the strategies of female animals—most notably, on how they go about sabotaging each other's reproductive cycles: aborting, starving, abusing, and even arranging the murder of each other's offspring. The more familiar offenders include macaques, chimpanzees, gorillas, gerbils, rabbits, wolves, and lions.

Most of us are accustomed to thinking of female animals of any sort as by nature gentle, nurturing, and cooperative.

People can get very worked up over the lives of monkeys. It's clear from the political cartoons in response to the publication of Charles Darwin's *The Origin of*

Species in 1859 that many thought it a grotesque mockery to be told they were relatives of the lewd, coarse apes and monkeys. The mockery probably seemed the more intense because of how much we do physically resemble them.

By the 1960s, nearly all the world's educated people acknowledged our long-armed friends as kin. Meanwhile (perhaps as a consequence) many had begun to see them as models for ideal human behavior: monkeys and apes are vegetarians, it was said; they never kill their own kind; they mate promiscuously and don't get jealous of each other.

All of statements are false, it now appears. In the last two decades field researchers have discovered that despite all our sensational murders and wars, human beings end up killing a smaller proportion of their fellows than do many other vertebrate species. Most fatal violence in primates is the work of males. But to appreciate how much life suppression is going on among nonhuman primates, one must also take account of the ways females scotch each other's reproductive output.

Primatologists like Sarah Blaffer Hrdy of the University of California at Davis were among the first to argue that scientists should pay more attention to female-female competition. Hrdy, who in 1981 wrote a book on female primate strategies, *The Woman That Never Evolved*, feels that if competitiveness is considered an asset among men, then it it must be useful to women as well. "Chauvinists of both sexes have dipped into the social primate literature, taking particular examples to support their positions," she claims.

Apes and monkeys see, hear, and smell the world about the way we do, according to biologists; their brains are complex and are organized as ours are; many kinds of primates live in groups, as we do. They could be seen as versions of ourselves put together with some of the instructions changed, so they came out a little differently. The instructions provide the outlines of an animal's life—where it lives and with whom, what it eats and what eats it, how it reproduces and when it dies. The scientist looks at these factors and gets an idea of the sort of

animal that fits inside. Some young scientists think they can learn enough about the process of life among animals to look at human nature and figure out how it came about and what it's trying to do.

To Samuel Wasser, baboons are a passion, a paradigm for how things work. He is 32, tall, spare, and bushy-bearded; he spends much of the year living in a tin hut in the middle of a grassland dotted with trees in Mikumi National Park in Tanzania. It is there that he has been studying the competitive world of the female baboon.

When Wasser first arrived at Mikumi in 1979, he was shocked to find that females were regularly joining up to form what he calls coalitions—strategic alliances—to go beat up other females. The scientific literature had mentioned this custom, but it was said to be merely an exercise to establish rank. Wasser decided that something more must be at stake, because female rank remained stable despite the aggression. Looking at the situation through new theories of animal behavior, he saw a possible scenario: A female baboon, no matter how dominant, can only raise one infant at a time; if a lot of infants are born in a troop at once, a lot of them die because resources are scarce. Maybe mid-ranking females were trying to keep lower ranking females from having offspring that would compete with their own.

Primatologists had always noticed that in social primates like baboons, macaques, and langur monkeys, females are especially interested in newborn infants belonging to other females and often seem to take turns carrying them around. Even though they sometimes indulge in this pastime over the mother's protests, it was thought the behavior was essentially some form of well-meaning day care, designed to protect the infant, or a form of training for young females learning how to be mothers.

"It's often called 'aunting behavior,' " says Wasser. "The term is awful. Some of the infant handling [by other female baboons] is nasty. It's a type of competition. They're picking kids up, dropping them on their heads. Stepping on them. One mother had her kid handled 40 times in an hour, by maybe 30 different animals. It died of exposure within two months. I even have cases of female infanticide. One mother picked up another's infant and simply bit it in the head."

A female baboon has a pink patch of skin on her rump that swells and reddens in the course of a 30-day cycle, advertising the state of her fertility. Males compete for access to a female in estrus (heat), when she is most fertile. Rival females, of course, can also read the signs on her rump. It so happens that at the onset of estrus, a female's reproductive system is particularly vulnerable to stress. If she is thrashed repeatedly then, her swelling will disappear, and she could fail to ovulate that month.

"In my baboons," says Wasser, "when six or more females are in heat, things get real nasty."

Pregnancy also shows on a female's rump; when a low-ranking animal is attacked in early pregnancy, it could cause her to abort. From her point of view, ovulating or starting a pregnancy when others are in heat just isn't worth it. Rather than lose a valuable year of her reproductive career carrying and nursing an infant that might well get harassed to death, she defers fertility until a less competitive time of year. Her decision to wait things out is presumably unconscious: the hormones her body releases under stress make her reproductive system shut down.

Why should animals get nasty over the issue of baby making? The answer offered by current animal behavior theory is simple: animals and plants have inherited traits that tend to make them have a lot of descendants. One of those traits is competitiveness.

SINCE LIFE forms have been evolving for over a billion years, it is unlikely that creatures tending *not* to reproduce would still be knocking around. And those that tended to direct their bodies and behaviors toward making offspring would become extremely common—and they'd pass along to their offspring any genes that made them the way they are. Com-

petitiveness is one trait that increases the number of one's descendants. "Competitiveness" does not mean unbridled aggression, which would be a waste of energy. Animal behaviorists find that social animals are highly sophisticated: in different situations an individual can be observed pursuing a strategy of cooperation, competition, or merely lying low. However, it will be trying to advance the cause of its own genes' replications at the expense of others'. After millions of generations of life on Earth, anywhere you look you will see animals (like female baboons) that had competitive ancestors and that spend their lives pursuing strategies that help them reproduce.

In her living room, Sarah Hrdy's two young daughters toy with fragile antiques, their mother's clothes, and the visitor's tape recorder as she talks and simultaneously thwarts their tactics as best she can.

"You might say I began to believe in the importance of female strategies," Hrdy says, "because a langur monkey whispered it to me. The first monkey I ever saw in the field was this female who was walking along by herself down a long granite ravine. I was surprised, because I'd been taught that females always stay with the troop. It turned out she was going to join up with a band of males. I wanted to know what was going on."

The gray Hanuman langur of India is smaller than a baboon—males weigh about 40 pounds, females 30, while baboon males and females weigh about 75 and 40 pounds respectively. They scamper gracefully both on the ground and in the trees with a leaping, four-footed stride. Long-term observations of individual animals have made it possible to discern the sometimes subtle strategies of female langurs, whose behavior is generally less showy and aggressive than males'.

Langur living arrangements are basically of two sorts: groups of five to 40 related females and their infants, ruled by a single adult male, perhaps with a few subordinate males, and roving, all-male bachelor bands of up to 60 animals.

Bachelor bands go around trying to take over troops of females by overpowering the dominant, or "alpha" male.

This is not easy, since an alpha male is likely to be a powerful specimen of langur in the prime of life, with long canine teeth. If a bachelor group succeeds, one of them will drive off the other pretenders in his group and become the new troop male. Once installed, he is likely to kill all the suckling infants in the troop, since he is not their father and females are infertile while nursing.

Sarah Hrdy describes the grisly consolidation of power by a new male: "Two older females . . . charged the male to wrest the infant from him. Before they succeeded, the infant was bitten in the skull, and received a gash on his thigh and lower abdomen so deep that the intestines could be seen within.

"This is the only time in my career as a field primatologist that I have ever cried while making observations."

Infant killing by invading males was so horrifying to many other biologists that for years, some claimed the practice was unnatural, a sick response to overcrowding by civilization. However, infanticide as a routine competitive strategy by males has now been found in dozens of mammal species, with more reported every year.

Once the deed is done, the langur infants' mothers, who have grimaced and swatted at the male until now, soon come into estrus, and the murderer impregnates them. Here it would seem that the reproductive strategies of females as a group are being frustrated by males. Why, Hrdy wondered, haven't females voted with their genes and refused?

Jim Moore, then a doctoral candidate in anthropology at Harvard, went to India recently to report on some of the same langur troops. The question of infanticide was on his mind.

"All the females would have to do," he explains, "is say, 'Hey, this guy is infanticidal. *Off* him.' There's no question that a group of females could gang up on a male and kick him out. But they don't."

He began to see some more pieces of the puzzle soon after he arrived. "Some females," he says, "seemed to be encouraging bachelor males to come around." When the troop passed within sight of a group of bachelors, certain females would point their fannies and waggle

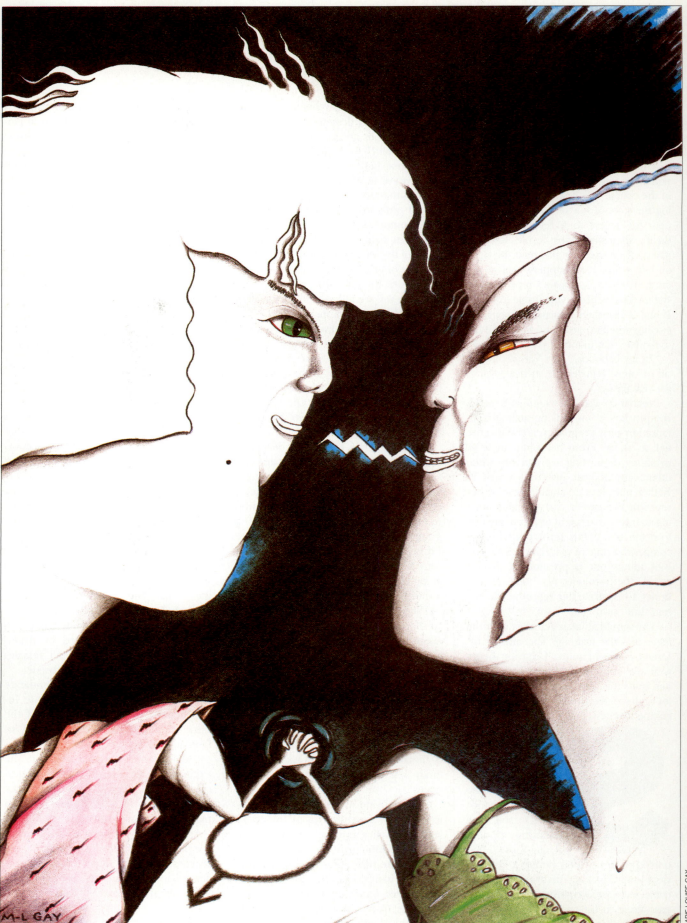

"THE BUSINESS OF COURTING AND MATING IS,
after all, a negotiation process in which each
partner is trying to beat the competition of its own
sex for the best possible deal."

their heads at them in a gesture of sexual invitation called presenting. The same females would sometimes join up with a bachelor band for a couple of days and get themselves mounted by some of the males—and then lead the band back toward their troop. Sometimes the resident male fought the invaders off; sometimes he headed for the hills. When an alpha male was routed, females on occasion got several local bachelor bands fighting for weeks over possession of their troop, and seemed to be egging them on.

"I was watching one of these contests between male bands," Moore recounts. "There was a lull in the fighting, and about half a dozen of the big adult males from each side were sitting on either side of a clearing, panting, chests heaving, clearly too bushed to go on just then.

"Then this female checked things out and walked straight into the middle of the clearing between them and started presenting—but not oriented toward anybody in particular. It seemed to be very deliberate. So the males kind of looked at each other, and then they hauled themselves to their feet and started fighting again."

Why would a female want to bring destruction on her own troop?

"Maybe the females don't all cooperate to prevent infanticidal takeovers because females disagree over the costs and benefits," he says. "The females who've been seen joining male bands to copulate before takeovers didn't have infants. Now, a female *with* an infant sure doesn't want it to happen—but one with no infant at risk might. That would eliminate the infants that would compete for food with *her* future infants.

"These females wean one kid, then start the next. Say a female is between kids—she's about to get pregnant. She'll be pregnant for six months, and then need another eight to nurse the kid. For the next 14 months, she needs peace and quiet—but will the current male hold on? If he's dumped in that time, her kid could get killed by the new guy.

"So for her," says Moore, "maybe it's best to provoke a takeover fight *now*—either you find out your male is still tough, or you get a new male at the beginning of his reign."

RVEN DEVORE, professor of anthropology at Harvard, was one of the first to study how biological drives might be expressed in human societies. In his undergraduate course in human behavioral biology, he finds that a handy illustration of the importance of female strategy and competition resides in television soap opera plots.

"Soap operas have a huge following among college students," he says, "and the female-female competition is blatant. The women on these shows use every single feminine wile."

On the internationally popular soap *Dynasty*, for example, a divorcée sees her ex-husband's new wife riding a horse nearby. She knows the woman to be newly pregnant—so she shoots off a gun, which spooks the horse, which throws the young wife and makes her miscarry. The divorcée's own children are living with their father and this woman; the divorcée does not want this new young thing to bring rival heirs into the world to compete with her own children.

From the products advertised during the commercial breaks on soap operas, there is evidence of competition among women watching the show, according to DeVore.

"Whole industries turning out everything from lipstick and perfume to designer jeans are based on the existence of female competition," he says. "The business of courting and mating is after all a negotiation process, in which each member of the pair is negotiating with those of the opposite sex to get the best deal possible, and to beat out the competition from one's own sex."

What do cosmetic products do for a woman? Pretty much what the commercials promise, says DeVore. They make her look younger and healthier than she is by giving her the big eyes, smooth skin, and ruddy cheeks and lips of a young girl. Makeup makes her look as if she has more potential years of childbearing ahead of her than she really has.

"I get women in my classes saying I'm stereotyping women," DeVore says. "And I say sure—I'm stereotyping the ones who make lipstick a multibillion-

dollar industry. It's quite a few women. Basically, I appeal to students to look inside themselves: What are life's little dilemmas? When your roommate brings home a guy to whom you're extremely attracted—does it set up any sort of conflict in your mind?"

If people like DeVore and Hrdy are right, the possibility of competition among human females—more subtle than the shouting and shoving matches of males—may offer new ways of looking at various aspects of human life.

Sam Wasser thinks there is a lot to be learned about human fertility problems by applying what biologists have learned from the effects of female competition on nonhuman animals. The reproductive suppression of female baboons prompted him to look into the effects of stress on women; he helped design clinical studies with psychologist Mark Pagel at the University of Washington's School of Family Medicine.

"Stress is a very important contributor to reproductive failure in women," Wasser says, "including everything from ovulatory failure, delay of sexual maturation, spontaneous abortion, low-birth-weight kids, prematurity, insufficient breast milk, infant mortality, child abuse—you name it.

"There's physical stress, like malnutrition, overwork, or too much exercise. And psychological stress, such as moving into a new house, can also have a big effect. Ovulation can be suppressed because stress elevates the levels of several hormones in a woman's blood. The same effect has been observed in female talapoin monkeys being attacked by more dominant females—their prolactin level goes up, and they don't ovulate."

Wasser says that if we want to understand fertility, we must first realize that a woman's body basically knows what it's doing. Ultimately, the conditions she experiences as stressful are the kind that have been less than ideal for child rearing ever since our ancestors evolved as hunter-gatherers.

"The question is, 'Should I make a baby now or not?'" says Wasser. "It's very important that she get the right answer—if the kid dies or isn't healthy, she's wasted a tremendous amount of

CERTAIN HUMAN INTERACTIONS ARE DESIGNED
to damage another's social support network.
Women might try to accomplish with gossip and insult
what baboon females do with bites and blows.

time. If conditions are bad now, it's better to shut down and wait for a better time. A lot of healthy women have trouble conceiving and keeping a pregnancy when things in their environment aren't really right."

In Wasser and Pagel's study, the Family Medicine Clinic patients and members of prenatal classes were asked about any nearby family and friends. On the savannah in Tanzania, Wasser was able to measure the strength of the "support network" of each of his subjects more precisely—by observing how many other females dared to pick on her. In each case, those with strong social support suffered significantly fewer reproductive problems than the others.

Do human females have the means or the desire to interfere with each other's fertility?

BECAUSE a woman's body may respond to a bad social environment by suppressing her fertility, human beings may have evolved a strategy to take advantage of that fact. It is interesting to speculate that one woman may try to make the social environment of another as bad as possible. Human females might be trying to accomplish with words what female baboons do by bites and blows.

It seems likely that words have always been important weapons in the human arsenal, according to anthropologist Richard Lee. When women of the Kalahari Bushmen of south-central Africa (who lived as hunter-gatherers until a few years ago) are truly furious at each other, they use a form of sexual insult called *za*. Popular *za* expressions include "*Du a !gum*" (Death on your vagina!) and "*gum/twisi=dinyazho*" (Long, black labia!). The response to these insults is most often suicide, assault, or a tribal split. *Za* is a serious matter.

The business of science is constructing theories, or stories, to explain things. Like anyone else, scientists talk about what is on their minds, so the stories of our scientists may tell us something about our culture's preoccupations.

In human reproductive terms, these are unusual times. If current trends continue in the United States, the divorce rate will be one in two; half of women use contraceptives; each year, about 1.5 million abortions are performed; the birth rate is so low (at 1.8 births per woman in her lifetime) that for the first time since such records were kept, we are not even replacing ourselves.

Anthropologist William Irons of Northwestern University, widely known for his work on human reproductive strategies, says that effective, voluntary birth control is used for the same reasons that prompt miscarriages and infertility. Consciously and unconsciously, we have always been reproductive strategists. "Most living things have an optimal number of offspring," says Irons. "Animals adjust their fertility downward as the environment toughens."

Some conscious strategies are not high-tech: women of the nomadic Ayoreo Indians in South America were lately reported by anthropologist Paul Bugos to be committing infanticide. It was especially high during times of warfare. It was highest among unmarried women, who did not think their infants would survive such dangerous times without a father.

Irons suggests that competition is so intense in technological society that people delay having children for fear of being economically left behind. "As you go back in human history a few thousand years," says Irons, "you get to a point when nobody can build up much in the way of property or special education. The only advantage one person has over another, besides some personal qualities, is how many kin he has, who'll back him up in a dispute or take him in when he's down and out. One reason nontechnological people like big families is that it's a kind of wealth.

"But we've gone through a radical change; now we've got all kinds of alternative things that didn't exist before that we can use to stimulate our pleasure centers and get status—travel, VCRs, fancy cars, swimming pools.

"One thing that happens is your idea of what's an adequate situation for rearing a family starts creeping up, just because people have always tried to keep a little ahead of their neighbors. Nowadays, a woman used to a very high standard may be saying to herself, 'Until I can secure a life-style that fifty thou a year supports, I don't want kids.' "

In any month, screaming from the covers of women's magazines in the supermarket are 10-step solutions to the great dilemma: how to start a family, which has one sort of value, without losing one's value in the world of careers and status.

Irons says this is a new situation: as machines and high-tech toys have grown more potent, they have dwarfed the value of families and offspring to each other. "There just isn't as much to be gained here from having relatives," Irons says. "It's pretty unusual to get a big loan from a sibling, or a job. In our environment, we know that extended-kin networks aren't that valuable, and that's part of our attitude about having children. They're not of *no* value, but on balance, they're nothing to get terribly impressed about."

Looked at in this light, it seems understandable that modern social relations are tenuous and that many modern women feel cosmically underappreciated. The wealth of kin, which only women can bring forth, is no longer respected the way it once was. Exotic substances such as petroleum have replaced mother's milk as the source of power and status and are obliterating the social substance of our lives, severing our links with past and future.

THE PIONEER RESEARCHERS of female competition took a world conventionally assumed to be relatively stable, friendly, even cozy—that of females and their babies—and revealed it to be of a piece with the rest of nature, a harsh, rigorous, often dangerous environment, where raising offspring is sometimes not worth the effort.

If Darwin's view describes us accurately, we were not bred to await salvation passively, collecting shiny pebbles and renouncing the future. The idea is to sometimes lie in wait—and to appear, when our moment arrives, and make good use of time and imperfect fortune. ∎

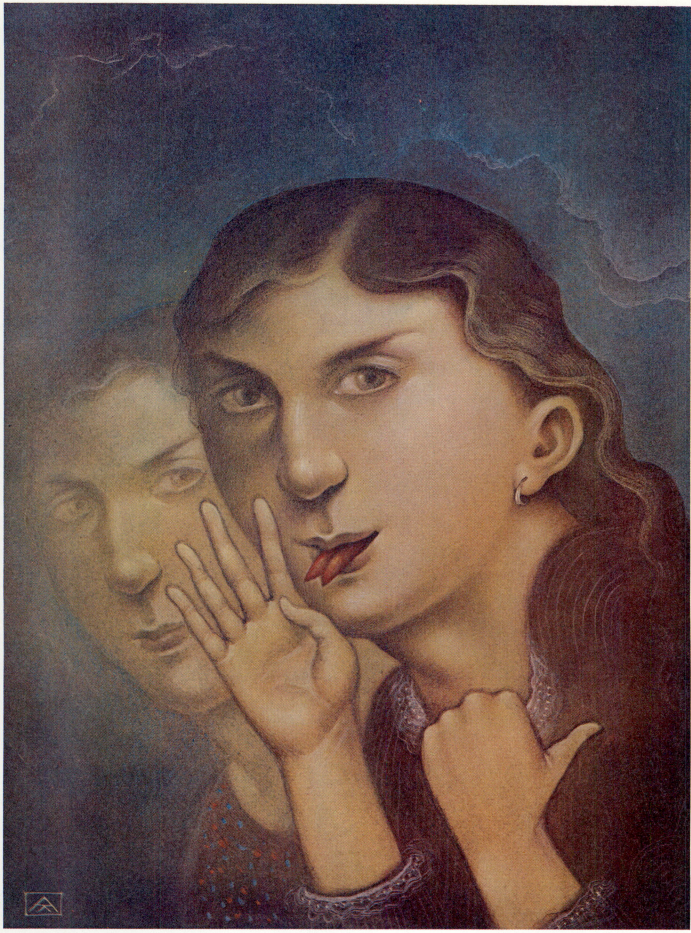

OUR DUAL MEMORY

It turns out the brain stores skills and facts differently.

BY JOSEPH ALPER

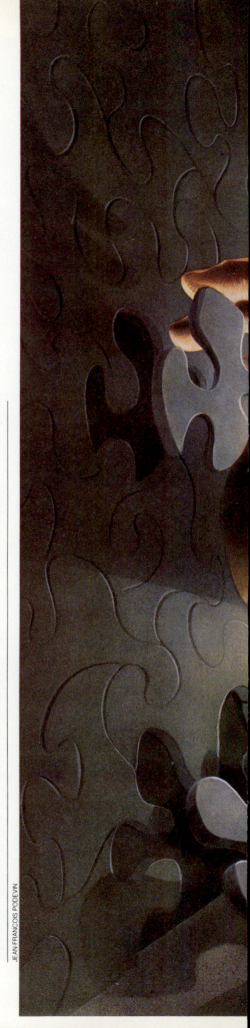

REMEMBER MICKEY MANTLE, the Baseball Hall of Famer? I recently read his autobiography, and it brought back vivid memories of the day I tried out for the Little League. It was April 27, 1963; I was almost nine years old, and my grandpa took me to the trials. I had my Nellie Fox glove that I had gotten for several books of S&H stamps, a Chicago White Sox cap, and some used baseball cleats my dad had bought me the day before.

I registered at a long table, and when they called my name I went over to the diamond, where a fellow with a stopwatch—I remember he had a moustache and wore a Cubs cap—recorded how fast I ran around the bases. Next I played catch with one of the coaches and then hit a few pitched by another coach. He said I did real well, and I must have, for a few minutes later a woman came over to where my grandpa and I were sitting and handed me my first baseball uniform—a gray wool shirt and pants, blue leggings, and a cap with the Little League emblem on it.

I hadn't thought about that day for probably 20 years, yet as soon as I started reading about Mickey Mantle's earliest baseball experiences in rural Oklahoma, mine in suburban Chicago popped into my mind. If those Little League days were still in my head somewhere after all these years, I wonder what other distant memories are hidden there, wherever "there" might be.

Philosophers and psychologists have long made their livings wondering what memories are and where they are stored. Memory, after all, is the very foundation of our humanity, the basis of our intellect, our ideas, our discoveries. We have the remarkable ability to call up a memory, associate it with other facts or feelings, and use it to create the fantasy world of fiction or explore the invisible world of science.

"We've come to realize that memory is a large word, an umbrella term, for a whole range of processes that the brain uses to translate experience into ability," says Neal Cohen, assistant professor of psychology at Johns Hopkins University in Baltimore.

"This is a golden time in memory and behavior research," says Larry Squire, professor of psychiatry at the University of California at San Diego and research scientist at the Veterans Administration Medical Center, who studies memory deficits in patients with brain injury or disease. "Studies at the molecular level have given us some reasonable ideas about how one nerve can induce permanent, long-lasting changes in another nerve, which tells us about the physical nature of memory.

"At the more global level," Squire says, "we know where certain kinds of sensory information are processed and

Joseph Alper is a contributing editor of Science 86.

116

stored to extract different memories. We're starting to make sense of the black box called the brain."

One of the biggest theoretical breakthroughs was the demonstration that there are at least two types of memory, perhaps stored by distinct biochemical mechanisms in different parts of the brain. This idea first surfaced in the 1950s when psychologists started systematically testing the memory deficits of amnesia patients. The first and most famous case was that of a man known as H.M. who had a particularly severe form of epilepsy. Medication had little effect on his seizures, so in 1953, when H.M. was 27, his doctors decided on a drastic treatment—removing a small section of the brain that included most of the hippocampus, the amygdala, and some surrounding cortex.

H.M.'s surgery had the hoped-for result—the epileptic seizures became less severe—but there was one unexpected problem: H.M. could no longer learn new facts, and still cannot to this day. Introduced to his doctors, he forgets their names within minutes regardless of how many times the introductions have been performed before. He can't remember that one of his favorite uncles has died, so he experiences shock and grief each time he hears of the death. He can solve mechanical puzzles—he has even gotten better at solving them—but he never remembers having done so.

H.M.'s form of amnesia demonstrated that there are different forms of memory connected with different parts of the brain. One form, declarative memory, represents memories of facts: names, places, dates, baseball scores. This is the type of memory that can be brought to mind and declared: "I know how to solve this puzzle." It is this type of memory that H.M. is no longer able to acquire.

The other form of memory, which is not affected by damage to the hippocampus and amygdala, is called procedural memory. It is the type of memory acquired by repetitive practice or conditioning and includes skills, such as riding a bicycle. H.M. used procedural memory to solve puzzles. But he didn't know he had learned those skills because he lacked declarative memory.

"H.M. gave us the insight we needed to start a detailed search for those parts of the brain that are important in processing different types of memories," says Mortimer Mishkin, chief of neuropsychology at the National Institute of Mental Health in Bethesda, Maryland. Mishkin himself had already begun the elegant experiments that would give the first glimpse of how the brain processes sensory information into declarative memories.

Mishkin focused on how rhesus monkeys process visual information. To test visual memory, he used a game that takes advantage of a monkey's natural curiosity. Given a board on which a block covers a well containing a peanut or food pellet, a monkey picks up the object to find its reward. After a brief delay, the monkey gets another look at the board with the original block plus a second that differs in size, shape, and color; both objects cover wells but only the new one covers a treat. The monkey quickly learns that it must pick up the new item, thus demonstrating that it can remember what the first one looks like and avoid it.

After the monkeys learned how to play the game, Mishkin carefully removed selected pieces of tissue or severed connections in the brain thought to be involved in the processing and storage of visual information. After a two-week recovery, the animals were tested again to see if their visual memory had been affected. From experiments such as these, Mishkin has developed a detailed map of how visual signals pass through the brain and wind up as memory.

What he has learned is that the most important parts of the visual memory system are the hippocampus and amygdala, which together with other structures make up the limbic system. "One structure is able to pretty much compensate for the other in recognizing things," says Mishkin. On closer examination, he found that each performs a unique function as well. Removing the hippocampus destroys an animal's ability to remember how two objects are related to each other spatially. "If you lost the function of your hippocampus, you could remember what the houses on your block looked like, but you might not remember which houses were next to one another," Mishkin says.

The amygdala, on the other hand, stores information with emotional overtones. Removing the amygdalae did not alter the animals' performance on tests of spatial relationships, but other researchers showed that monkeys could no longer remember their position in the social hierarchy of their colony, nor did they remember socially correct grooming and fear responses. "Without your amygdala you could remember what your hometown looked like," Mishkin says, "but seeing the town might not evoke the fond remembrances connected with living there."

Like others who have pondered the seeming coincidence that the limbic system is a seat of both emotion and memory, Mishkin believes that emotion serves as a gate for what is stored. "We can't store everything, so the brain must discriminate somehow, and if you think about it, your strongest memories are those connected with very emotional events."

Our moods, in fact, appear to exert an extremely powerful influence over what we remember. Psychologist Gordon Bower at Stanford, for example, has reported that a person who learns material in one mood, say a sad one, will recall more of that information later on if he is sad then, too.

It turns out that the amygdala plays a role in other aspects of declarative memory as well. Mishkin and colleague Elizabeth Murray showed monkeys a variety of objects. Then, using a variation of the previous test, they assessed the monkeys' ability to identify the new object by sight alone when they had only felt the first object in the dark. After operating on the animals as before, they found that animals without hippocampi could still make the right visual choice, but the performance of monkeys without amygdalae was only slightly better than chance. Clearly, the amygdala was required for integrating visual and tactile memories.

Other studies have shown, in fact, that each of the five senses has neural connections leading to the amygdala. "We think that when the amygdala is presented with a tactile stimulus, for example, it

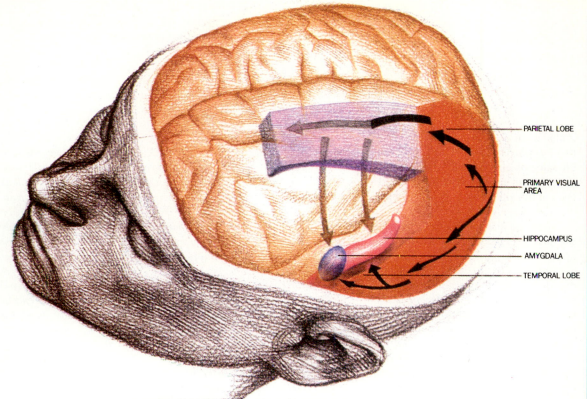

PARIETAL LOBE

PRIMARY VISUAL AREA

HIPPOCAMPUS

AMYGDALA

TEMPORAL LOBE

WHERE MEMORIES ARE PROCESSED

*Visual information travels from the eye to the primary visual area at the
back of the brain. From there, the input simultaneously travels along two separate pathways for processing.
As the information travels down toward the temporal lobe, the physical qualities—size,
shape, and color—are identified. Spatial qualities—location with respect to other objects—are processed
along the second pathway, which leads upward to the parietal lobe. From the temporal and parietal lobes,
the information travels through the brain to the hippocampus and amygdala,
where scientists think memories may be stored. Without these structures,
a scene can be perceived but not remembered.*

HOW MEMORIES ARE FORMED

*A nerve spine in the hippocampus changes shape after receiving the type of stimulation that occurs
during a learning experience. Below left, the first of several bursts of electricity causes a chemical
neurotransmitter to be released from a neighboring neuron onto the receptors of the
nerve spine shown here. Calcium enters the cell. The calcium activates calpain (orange), an otherwise
dormant enzyme, which begins to degrade fodrin, the structural material of the
spine. With additional bursts of electricity, the fodrin continues to break down, and more receptors appear, below right.
More receptors result in a greater influx of calcium, and therefore more calpain activation and even greater
fodrin degradation. With significant loss of structural material, the spine changes shape.
A new spine may also begin to extend through the membrane. These permanent changes result in new
connections between neurons in the brain, a plausible explanation for memory.*

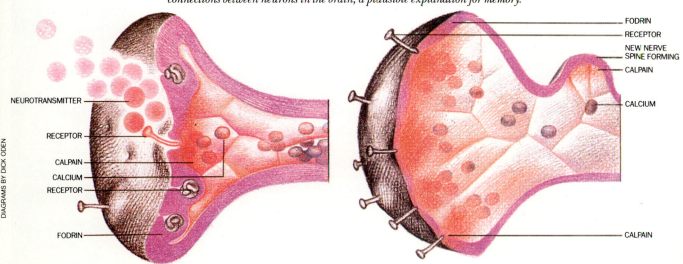

NEUROTRANSMITTER

RECEPTOR

CALPAIN

CALCIUM

RECEPTOR

FODRIN

FODRIN

RECEPTOR

NEW NERVE SPINE FORMING

CALPAIN

CALCIUM

CALPAIN

is able to tickle some area in the cortex that has stored a visual representation of the same object," Mishkin explains. The ability of our memories to make associations of this kind is what gives the human brain its enormous power.

Equally exciting work to determine the site of procedural memory is being done by psychobiologist Richard F. Thompson at Stanford. Working with rabbits, he has determined that procedural memory seems to be stored in a different part of the brain than is declarative memory—in the cerebellum, a structure at the back of the head under the cortex.

Thompson implanted many tiny electrodes in select locations of the brains of laboratory rabbits and recorded the electrical activity as the animals learned to associate a certain tone with an unpleasant stimulus. This type of learning, called classical or Pavlovian conditioning, is considered a prime example of procedural knowledge.

When a tiny puff of air is blown into a rabbit's eye, the animal blinks automatically. On the next trial, a tone sounds just before the rabbit gets a puff. If the tone is paired with the puff enough times, the rabbit comes to associate the two events and will blink its eye at the tone alone. The animal has learned.

Thompson found that a rabbit has much higher electrical activity in several specific areas of its cerebellum when it is learning this procedural task. When he removed those parts of the cerebellum, animals that had learned the task immediately forgot it, although they still blinked their eyes when air was blown into them. But when the animals' hippocampi were removed, their ability to undergo classical conditioning was not impaired in the least. This, according to Thompson, is another demonstration that different types of memory are stored in different parts of the brain.

Studies such as Mishkin's and Thompson's are particularly exciting to neuroscientists because they provide a basis for investigating the physical nature of memory—what changes take place in the brain when a memory is formed. Once researchers know where memories are stored, they can look at neurons in those regions to see if they have been changed

"Characterizing the nature of memory is probably going to be more difficult than determining where the information contained in a memory is stored in the brain," says Neal Cohen, assistant professor of psychology at Johns Hopkins University in Baltimore. "That's because when we look at even one specific memory we're talking about a whole group of psychological processes that takes place all at once to form what we perceive as a memory."

Some believe, in fact, that it may be impossible to define the borders of a single memory. As an example of how complex the problem is, take the word apple. *How many pieces of information, how many concepts, might the brain extract from this simple word?*

The first time your brain formed the memory apple, *it was probably as a red, crunchy thing that was good to eat. But, more than likely, you store the categories* apple=red, apple=crunchy, *and* apple=food *separately, for if you are asked to list things that are red or things that are crunchy or things to eat, you would be likely to include* apple *in all three groups.*

The idea that each of these concepts is stored as its own memory is supported by studies on patients with language disturbances, or aphasias. One unusual case involves M.D., a 35-year-old man who suffered a stroke in the left side of his brain. At first, M.D. had severe aphasia, but most of his language abilities returned within a month— all except for his ability to identify fruits and vegetables.

When asked to name various objects, either from photographs or when handed the real thing, he could do so easily for toys, tools, animals, body parts, kitchen items, colors, and clothing. But when it came to identifying fruits and vegetables he was at a loss. "Other foods he could name perfectly, but when we gave him an apple or showed him a picture of lettuce he couldn't tell us what they were," says Alfonso Caramazza, professor of psychology at Johns Hopkins.

Caramazza says, however, that M.D.'s memory loss was not a matter of having no knowledge whatsoever about fruits and vegetables. When given a group of objects and asked, "Which one is an apple?" he could point to the apple with no problem. Moreover, M.D. could respond eloquently and correctly when Caramazza asked him to describe an apple. Thus, M.D. still retains the many memories that together represent apple. *It was the general question "What is this?" that he could not answer correctly. His problem must lie in accessing these memories to select the proper name.*

All this suggests that the brain not only stores memories as discrete pieces of information but also somehow organizes this information along a framework that guides its retrieval. Since memory is an active process, this organization must be flexible, as must the framework, for we are continuously exposed to new information, storing some of it as memory and assimilating it into our view of the world. —J.A.

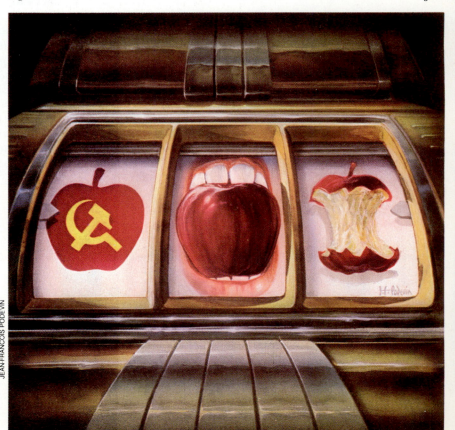

JEAN-FRANCOIS PODEVIN

TAKE THE WORD *APPLE*.
**HOW MANY PIECES OF
INFORMATION, HOW MANY
CONCEPTS, MIGHT
THE BRAIN EXTRACT FROM
THIS SIMPLE WORD?**

in a way that might account for the ability of the brain to make permanent records.

Some of the first evidence that there is a physical memory trace came from researchers like Eric Kandel of Columbia University and Daniel Alkon of the National Institutes of Health, who found lasting changes in specific neurons of sea snails that had undergone different kinds of learning trials. Other researchers found that a certain pattern of electrical stimulation could make hippocampal neurons more sensitive to further stimulation for weeks at a time; that is, the cells would respond more intensely to a given stimulus. This effect, called long-term potentiation, was the first demonstration of a possible mechanism for long-term memory formation.

Intrigued by this effect, neuroscientist Gary Lynch at the University of California at Irvine performed similar experiments using rat brain tissue. "Sure enough, we got long-term potentiation," says Lynch. Much to his surprise, he also found structural changes in nerve cells: the number of connections between neurons increased, and certain parts of the neuron actually changed shape, something no scientist had ever seen before. "This was simply the most unusual event I've ever seen. This observation removed the mystery that is memory because it showed that neurons could change in a permanent way in response to physical stimuli," says Lynch.

Lynch and colleague Michel Baudry focused on the hippocampal neurons, and how nerve impulses cross synapses, or gaps, to reach the next neuron. To pass along the electrical impulse, the neuron sending the signal releases a chemical known as a neurotransmitter. Diffusing across the synapse, the neurotransmitter binds to receptors on a spine of the next neuron. This activates those receptors, causing charged particles to flow through the membrane of the second, or postsynaptic, neuron, setting off another nerve impulse.

When Lynch and Baudry zapped the hippocampal neurons with electrical pulses to induce long-term potentiation, they discovered an amazing sequence of events. The postsynaptic cells became flooded with unusually large amounts of calcium, which in turn activated a dormant enzyme, called calpain. The primary role of this enzyme seems to be to break down certain proteins.

One of these proteins, named fodrin, is the major structural component of the spines of neurons. When calpain begins to break down fodrin, Lynch believes that extra receptors for the neurotransmitter glutamate are exposed. Since glutamate is the neurotransmitter that hippocampal neurons need to communicate with one another, the uncovering of additional glutamate receptors makes the postsynaptic neuron more responsive to glutamate released by its neighbor.

When this postsynaptic neuron is stimulated again, more calcium enters the cell, causing calpain to break down more fodrin. At that point, says Lynch, "the whole system is free to change its shape because the protein skeleton has been broken down." The shape of the neuron can change, or new nerve connections can form. "This chain of events is a plausible candidate for a memory mechanism," says Lynch, "because it occurs at the synapses in response to a physiological event, changes the responsiveness of the synapse, and is permanent." Furthermore, this mechanism appears to function best in those regions of the brain that are involved in declarative memory.

Long-term potentiation may be a good model for studying what takes place in the hippocampus when declarative memories are processed there. But Lynch felt that until he could show that calpain is involved in forming memories in a live animal, the calcium-calpain-fodrin cascade would be little more than an interesting biochemical process that just happened to take place in hippocampal neurons.

To nail down calpain's role in declarative memory, Lynch used the chemical leupeptin, which inhibits calpain's ability to degrade fodrin. Lynch fitted rats with tiny pumps that released a steady flow of the chemical into all areas of the animals' brains.

None of the rats showed any difference in eating, drinking, or sleeping behavior. However, rats that could remember where to look for rewards in complex mazes could no longer perform the task after getting leupeptin; the same effect is seen in rats whose hippocampi and amygdalae have been removed. "Rats clearly evolved for running mazes, for they normally do so with great enthusiasm and learn quickly," says Lynch, "but the leupeptin-treated animals were real dunces. I think we can infer from this that calpain and the synaptic changes it produces are important for declarative knowledge acquisition."

But what about procedural knowledge? Some investigators have proposed that when this kind of memory forms, neurons must make new proteins. So Lynch gave one group of rats anisomyocin, which blocks protein synthesis, and gave another group leupeptin. When he tested the rats for their ability to learn shock avoidance, a procedural-type task, the results were reversed—the leupeptin-treated rats did as well as the controls, while those receiving anisomyocin did poorly at this task.

The enzyme calpain seems to play a prominent role in declarative memory, while an undetermined chain of events requiring protein synthesis may be involved in procedural memory. The properties of the two chemical systems fit those of the two behavioral systems. "We think of procedural memory as a kind of memory that takes a lot of time to form, and protein synthesis is a slow process as far as biochemical events are concerned," says Lynch. "On the other hand, declarative memories form much faster, and on a biochemical time scale the calpain-fodrin reaction is pretty fast."

Lynch says that while it is satisfying to have developed a reasonable candidate for the molecular basis of one type of memory, his model does not say much about how we learn and think. "We're witnessing the very beginnings of a concerted, coordinated, intelligent attack on human intellectual thinking," he says. "I really believe that in the next two to three years, theorizing about the nature of memory is going to become the philosophical playground of the Western intellectual world. It will replace evolution as the arena in which anyone interested in philosophy will put their intellectual energies." **S**

When depression starts in childhood or adolescence, it is likely to have a genetic link.

they just had 'adolescent adjustment problems,' so most psychiatrists didn't and still don't think to look for it in kids. Now, however, we know that idea is dead wrong. Adolescents, even children, suffer from major depression as much as adults do."

Research is only just beginning, so estimates vary of how many young people suffer from major affective disorders, which include depression and manic-depression, an illness characterized by elation, hyperactivity, or irritability, alternating with depression. Depending on the age of the youngster and how his illness is defined, the estimates can range from one to six percent. There is no question, however, that the problem is serious and that it is growing. One study indicates that the percentage of older teenagers with major affective disorders has increased more than fivefold over the past 40 years.

"The chilling fact is that we may be on the verge of an epidemiclike increase of mania, depression, and suicide," says Elliot S. Gershon, chief of the clinical psychogenetics branch at NIMH. "The trend is rising almost exponentially and shows no signs of letting up. I would go so far as to say this is going to be *the* public health problem of the 1990s and beyond if the trend continues."

Buttressing Gershon's concern are studies revealing that many adults with affective disorders showed the first signs of their illness when they were teenagers or children and that the earlier the onset, the more severe the disease. "So if we are seeing more depression in kids today," he says, "we could be in for real trouble when these kids hit their 30s," the prime time for showing the classic swings of depression.

Not everyone agrees with Gershon's gloomy outlook. Some claim the dramatic rise is due to better reporting and diagnosis, not to rising incidence of disease. But they don't disagree with the trend.

"Depression is a crucial problem," says G. Robert DeLong, a pediatric neurologist at Massachusetts General Hospital, "because this illness clouds a child's or adolescent's perceptions at such a critical time in his social and psychological development. As a result, young peo-

ple often develop long-lasting problems aside from the original depression or mania. So the earlier we diagnose these kids and treat them, the better chance they have of developing into adults who can enjoy a more normal life."

These findings have important clinical implications. Some psychiatrists believe that if young people can control their affective disorders with drugs during the particularly stressful adolescent years, their biochemistry may stabilize so they need not continue taking drugs for a lifetime as many adults now must.

Furthermore, there is mounting evidence that a constellation of harmful behaviors that accompany depression—suicide attempts, drug abuse, anorexia, bulimia, and juvenile delinquency—may be methods that young people use to try to cope with the anguish they feel. So if depression can be curbed, many of these disorders might disappear as well.

"We're talking about a whole spectrum of problems to which affective disorders seem to be linked," says Joseph T. Coyle, head of child psychiatry at Johns Hopkins. "This is not to say that every kid with these problems has a major affective disorder. But the odds are good he has."

Ben, for example, was eight when his parents brought him to Robert DeLong in 1974. Ben was smart, with an IQ of 128, a nice kid who had become aggressive and nasty. His teachers complained that the boy was extremely disruptive, and neighbors kept calling his folks to report that he had broken a window or beaten up their kid.

DeLong, one of the few nonpsychiatrist physicians to take an interest in childhood mental illness, talked extensively with Ben, who reported feeling very sad and confused at times. "He was a classic manic-depressive—wild, aggressive, manic behavior followed by profound sadness," DeLong says. He put the boy on lithium, which is often used to treat manic-depression in adults but rarely in children. "Everyone who knew the child was stunned by his change for the better." Today, thanks to early diagnosis, lithium, and supportive psychotherapy, Ben is a well-adjusted college student who no longer needs lithium.

Ben was fortunate that he was sent to a physician who hadn't swallowed the orthodox view that children can't be manic-depressive. Grace, who is now in her mid-20s, was not as lucky. When she was about 13, she began feeling a bit down in the dumps. Then, at 15, though a promising musician, she started doing poorly in her musical studies, and she began vomiting after meals. It improved her mood, she said.

When her parents started finding jars of vomit hidden around the house, they took her to a psychiatrist, who made a diagnosis of borderline personality disorder, a serious illness involving self-destructive, impulsive behavior that usually does not respond to medication and has a poor prognosis. Grace had a lot of trouble over the next nine months, but then she spontaneously got better. That lasted until she was 18, when she again became depressed. This time she started cutting her wrists, explaining that it made her feel better. She was hospitalized. Again she recovered nine months later. She went to a prestigious college on a music scholarship and did well for another two years but once again became depressed and wound up at the Johns Hopkins Hospital. This time, Raymond DePaulo Jr., director of the affective disorders clinic, diagnosed Grace as manic-depressive and treated her with an antidepressant and lithium. Within a month she was feeling good.

But Grace can't cope with the idea of being seriously ill, so she has stopped taking her medicine, believing that she can control her moods with vomiting and wrist slitting. The years of turmoil have torn her family apart and seriously damaged her musical career. "This is a good example of how early diagnosis and treatment of an affective disorder would have probably alleviated many of the psychosocial problems this girl and her family now have," DePaulo says. "The odds are she'd be in much better shape today if she'd been diagnosed correctly at 15."

But diagnosing affective disorders is not easy, especially since young people show a more diverse set of symptoms than do adults. And it can be hard to tell which kids are showing typical signs of rebellion and which are depressed. Be-

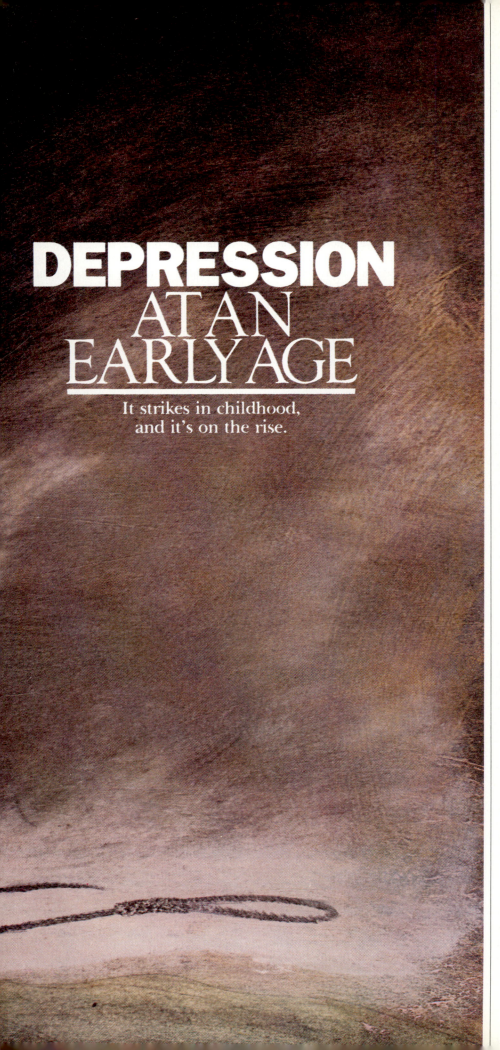

DEPRESSION
AT AN EARLY AGE

It strikes in childhood,
and it's on the rise.

BY JOSEPH ALPER

ILLUSTRATIONS BY GREG SPALENKA

JANET WAS A BRIGHT GIRL, well liked by her teachers and friends. When she entered junior high and started having trouble paying attention in class, no one made much of it. After all, kids can get pretty restless at that age. In high school she did rather poorly, but since she was quiet and didn't make trouble, her teachers left her alone and assumed she just wasn't much interested in school. Her parents were a bit worried, but there didn't seem to be anything they could do. And the school counselor reassured them that Janet's attitude was just a normal part of adolescence, that she would eventually outgrow her problems.

Instead they got worse. The summer before her senior year, Janet started having trouble getting up in the morning, and when she did make it out of bed, she couldn't get motivated to do anything; it was as if she were stuck in low gear. She lost her appetite, slept poorly, and couldn't stop crying. Her parents decided this was no longer just part of growing up and took her to their family physician. He referred them to the affective disorders clinic of their local hospital, where a psychiatrist who had treated dozens of kids like Janet talked to her and her parents. He told them that Janet's lack of energy, motivation, and appetite were signs of depression and prescribed amitriptyline, an antidepressant.

Within a month, Janet was feeling better than she had for as long as she could remember. She started making new friends, and her schoolwork improved dramatically. The following year she made the dean's list at college. And today, several years later, she continues taking her medication, does well in school, and has a good outlook on life.

"Until maybe 10 years ago, we believed that severe depression was solely an illness of adults," says psychiatrist Frederick K. Goodwin, scientific director of the National Institute of Mental Health in Bethesda, Maryland. "Adolescents didn't develop 'real' depression—